ADVANCES IN CONTEMPORARY EDUCATIONAL THOUGHT SERIES
Jonas F. Soltis, EDITOR

THE CHALLENGE TO CARE IN SCHOOLS

An Alternative Approach to Education

SECOND EDITION

Nel Noddings

TEACHERS COLLEGE PRESS

TEACHERS COLLEGE | COLUMBIA UNIVERSITY

NEW YORK AND LONDON

Published by Teachers College Press, 1234 Amsterdam Avenue, New York, NY
10027

Copyright © 2005 by Teachers College, Columbia University

All rights reserved. No part of this publication may be reproduced or transmitted
in any form or by any means, electronic or mechanical, including photocopy, or
any information storage and retrieval system, without permission from the pub-
lisher.

Library of Congress Cataloging-in-Publication Data

Noddings, Nel.
   The challenge to care in schools : an alternative approach to education / Nel
Noddings.—2nd ed.
     p. cm. — (Advances in contemporary educational thought series)
   Includes bibliographical references and index.
   ISBN 0-8077-4609-6 (pbk. : alk. paper)
    1. Moral education—United States. 2. Teacher–student relationships—United
States. 3. Parent and child—United States. I. Title. II. Series.
LC311.N57 2005
370.11′4—dc22   2005043072

ISBN 0-8077-4609-6 (paper)

Printed on acid-free paper
Manufactured in the United States of America

To all the teachers
from elementary school through graduate school
who made a difference in my life.

Contents

Foreword

In this masterful extension of her work on caring, Nel Noddings asks us to seriously question some of our most deeply entrenched ways of thinking about education. She argues that a general curriculum based on the liberal arts is not the best education for all; that our focus in schools on verbal and mathematical achievement cripples many whose talents and abilities lie elsewhere; and that we need a radical change in both curriculum and teaching to reach all children, not just the few who fit our conception of the academically able.

Writing in a most engaging style—a blend of careful, scholarly argument and intimate, personal voice—she is unafraid to speak her mind as a philosopher, as a former math teacher, as a mother, and as a compassionate and caring person. She insists that the main aim of education should be a moral one, that of nurturing the growth of competent, caring, loving, and lovable persons. To that end she describes in great detail a curriculum organized around centers of care: care for one's self; for intimate others as well as strangers and distant others; for animals, plants, the earth; and for human instruments and ideas. She gives concrete examples of both math and arts teaching from this perspective.

Basic to this design of the curriculum is the assumption of multiple intelligences and the great variety and variability of children. Each child has unique talents, abilities, and interests in need of engagement and development by caring teachers and others in schools. Noddings uses the image of a very large family to convey the caring way to think about the task of schooling a diverse group of students. Imagine them as your own children, she urges, and you will see them each as unique individuals that you care about and want to help become confident and competent persons. She puts the human dimension back into an educational system that has become dehumanized.

The Challenge to Care in Schools first appeared in 1992. Now, with the publication of this new edition, Noddings has written a new Introduction that recognizes that the 21st century has brought an even heavier emphasis on academic achievement, accountability, standards, and testing that will probably make her pleas for a central place for caring in our schools fall on deaf ears. So, in her new Introduction, she recasts her argument in a traditional versus progressive education framework—one that sees the pendulum of policy and educational philosophy currently swinging heavily toward the traditional side. But she wonders if the pendulum must always swing back and forth and whether it might be possible for caring to have a central place in our schools even in the current traditionalist environment. She argues, contra an either/or view of education, that both traditionalists and progressives could embrace caring as a central aim of educating without needing to give up their basic principles and philosophies. Her new Introduction sketches a way to do this and truly represents an advance in contemporary educational thought. Anyone who reads this book will come away with a feeling that the kind of change in schooling that Noddings advocates is both desirable and possible.

Jonas F. Soltis
Series Editor

Acknowledgments

Every writer owes a great debt to other writers—often uncited—who have influenced his or her thinking. That is certainly true for me, and I gratefully acknowledge many insightful predecessors and colleagues.

Special thanks go to Denis Phillips, Jonas Soltis, and two anonymous reviewers who made helpful comments on various drafts. I also thank the Lilly Endowment for a grant that enabled me to spend the necessary time in research and writing. The Endowment deserves widespread public thanks for its active interest in caring and its support of research on caring. Thanks also to Osmund Stromnes of the *Scandinavian Journal for Educational Research,* who published an earlier version of chapter 5 on caring and continuity.

Several colleagues lightened the load for me on projects I shared with them so that I could put more time to this book. For their generosity, I thank Carolyn Maher and Robert Davis of Rutgers and Carol Witherell of Lewis and Clark.

My husband, Jim, deserves thanks for doing so many things to make my writing possible. As usual, my secretary, Jane Wassam, has cheerily encouraged me through drafts and revisions even though every change has meant more work for her. Many thanks.

In preparing this second edition, I want to also thank the many students and instructors who have contacted me with questions and comments on the first edition. The many responses from readers have been very helpful.

Finally, I thank Carole Saltz, Brian Ellerbeck, and Karl Nyberg at Teachers College Press for their support and friendship.

Introduction

In the 1992 Introduction to this book, I argued against an education system that puts too much emphasis on academic achievement defined in terms of test scores and the acquisition of information. Today the case could be made even more strongly. Students spend weeks— even months—preparing for and taking tests. Many of us believe that these are weeks that should be spent exploring new ideas, discovering new interests, extending established ones, and expressing thoughts in art, drama, music, and writing. In particular, we believe that students should be given opportunities to learn how to care for themselves, for other human beings, for the natural and human-made worlds, and for the world of ideas. This learning to care requires significant knowledge; it defines genuine education.

Not everyone feels this way. Many people believe that children should be encouraged, even forced, to learn a prescribed body of material, and that they and their teachers should be held strictly accountable—through standardized tests—for the acquisition of this material. However, this heavy emphasis on testing should not be confused with traditional or classical education. There are many thoughtful, traditional educators who share my disgust with the current trivialization of education. They may not agree with everything in this book, but they do agree that schools should be more responsive to the expressed needs of parents and students (see, for example, Sizer, 2004; Troen & Boles, 2003). For now, I'll use the word "traditional" to refer to both the advocates of classical (or disciplinary) education and to the current proponents of test-based accountability. Thus defined, traditional educators are in opposition to the progressive educators whose objections and vision I alluded to above.

Is there a way that both traditional and progressive preferences can be accommodated in one school system? I suggest here a way we might try—by making the responsiveness characteristic of caring more basic than accountability. I argue that we really must do something along these lines if we want to preserve our public schools and avoid privatization. Finally, I suggest how the themes of care described in this book can enhance either a progressive or a traditional approach to schooling.

CARING AND RESPONSIVENESS

Schools, we are told, must be held accountable for the results they produce. I agree. Indeed, I have never encountered an educator who does not agree that schools and teachers should be held accountable. But for *what* should schools be held accountable? Surely they should be accountable for more than test scores in basic reading, mathematics, and science.

In the years since the original publication of this book, I have thought more and more about the obligation of schools to be *responsive*. To listen attentively and to respond as positively as possible are the very hallmarks of caring as I have described it (Noddings, 2003). But I have also learned in the past 10 years that people differ on what they mean by *caring*. From a perspective quite different from mine, some policymakers and educators believe that caring is a pedagogical virtue demonstrated by forcing students to achieve the skills and acquire the knowledge that has been prescribed for them. From this view, a teacher exercises the virtue of caring by making students do what is thought to be good for them. The two points of view are dramatically different, and it may be impossible to satisfy both under one description of schooling. Indeed, many people are beginning to think this way—that some form of pluralism must become available in schools—but, whereas some see privatization as a solution, I will argue that public schools are necessary to our American democracy. *Responsiveness* captures the ideal that may provide a solution, and our public schools can be and should be more responsive.

To launch my argument, I ask readers to consider the phenomena we refer to as "swings of the pendulum." When things are too discipline-centered, traditional, and teacher-centered, progressives hope and work for a swing of the pendulum toward more flexible, present-oriented, and child-centered ways. When that has been accomplished (or threatens to be accomplished), traditional thinkers hope and work for a swing that will return schools to the discipline-centered ways they prefer. Swings of the pendulum have rarely represented changes in minds and hearts, except in the case of a few students in teacher education; the changes have been and can only be shifts in power. Those who prefer traditional education will be unhappy in progressive eras, and vice-versa.

If I am right on this, those of us who espouse progressive forms of education and, especially, an ethic of care, are in a tough spot. We are committed to responsiveness; that is, we must listen to others and try to address their legitimate expressed needs (Noddings, 2002). We can't simply dismiss the expressed preferences of traditional educators. But traditional educators (those who hold a different view of caring) claim to know the best form of education for everyone and are quite willing to impose it on us—for our own good. (I'm leaving aside temporarily those who would establish privatization as a solution that would allow all of us to go our own way.)

To continue the analysis, it is necessary to say more about the two different views of caring. An ethic of care embodies a relational view of caring; that is, when I speak of caring, my emphasis is on the relation containing carer and cared-for (see chapter 2). Both carer and cared-for contribute to this relation. If, for whatever reason, the cared-for denies that she or he is cared for, there is no caring relation. When that happens, it is not necessarily the fault of the carer; it may be that the cared-for is stubborn, insensitive, or just plain difficult. Then again, it may not be the fault of either the carer or the cared-for. The situation in which carer and cared-for meet may make it difficult to establish caring relations. In many of our schools today, we find teachers who are trying to care and students who want to be cared for, and yet many of those students claim, "Nobody cares!" One purpose of this book is to suggest changes in the structure of schooling and, especially, of curriculum that will provide a climate in which caring relationships might flourish.

Does emphasis on the caring relation ignore caring as a virtue? No, but it defines the virtue in terms of a carer's proven capacity to establish caring relations. It is not enough for someone to say, "I care," and to work hard imposing her educational ideas on students. At best, it may be acknowledged that such people are trying to care. To be credited properly with the virtue of caring, one must regularly succeed in establishing caring relations.

The second (opposing) view of caring starts not with the relation but with caring as a virtue belonging to carers (see Noddings, 2005). From this perspective, carers, in what they see as the best interests of those for whom they care, may decide what those best interests are without listening to the expressed needs of the cared-for. Most of us have known a parent or teacher who cared in this fashion, and we often heard, when forced to do something we preferred to avoid, "Some day you'll thank me for this!" And sometimes that turns out to be true; we do appreciate the stern teacher who made us do the "right thing." But sometimes we misunderstand our own needs and thank the parent or teacher for forcing us to do something that was really not best for us; it was not the "right thing." Unwittingly, we often evaluate such coercion as a good thing and energetically impose it on the next generation. This, in my view, is one of the great tragedies of traditional education. Biography, fiction, and history are filled with stories of well-intentioned carers whose efforts turned out for the best in the long run, of others who so alienated the cared-for that an objective outsider would have to say there was a complete failure of caring, and of still others whose effects were accepted to the unacknowledged detriment of the particular cared-for and future generations. (For stories in this last category, see Noddings, 2002).

With an understanding of these two quite different concepts of caring, we can analyze more effectively the current debate over accountability in education. If we suppose that we know exactly what schools should accomplish, we can lay out our plan clearly and hold schools accountable for achieving it. However, advocates of accountability may disagree substantially on what it is that schools should accomplish. At present, the single-minded emphasis on raising test scores in reading, math, and science has defined what schools are to accomplish and, therefore, the results for which they should be held accountable. Many critics object to the narrow emphasis on test scores, and a few even suggest that schools should now be held accountable for widespread fear among students, a possible drop in graduation rates, the demoralization of teachers, and the growing corruption of administrators who are using questionable strategies to keep their schools off the failing list (Kohn, 2000; Troen & Boles, 2003). It does seem reasonable to hold schools responsible for the direct effects of enacted policies, whether those effects are intended or not.

I suggest we would do better to start with responsiveness and then construct a defensible structure for accountability. One great fault of the present system (under the No Child Left Behind Act) is that it forces on all of us a form of schooling that many of us find not just unsound but deeply offensive. The temptation, then, is to fight back and try to change the system into one more congenial to our way of thinking. We work, that is, for a swing of the pendulum. Let the other folks come around to our view! Or . . . well, let them be as unhappy as we are now. An alternative is to provide a system that will let both traditional and progressive ways flourish. Such a system would be, first of all, responsive. Then school people in each model could think reasonably about accountability.

Those of us who espouse a relational ethic of care should be attracted to this alternative. To be faithful to our view of caring, we must respond sensitively, if not always positively, to expressed needs that are morally and educationally defensible. If people express a need for schools that emphasize strict discipline, standardized testing, published comparisons of schools on the basis of test scores, and severe sanctions for schools that do not meet the established criteria, they should have the option of sending their children to public schools that satisfy this need. But such a system should not be forced on those who hold a very different view. A responsive system would provide within it for the two substantial views that have been, historically and popularly, associated with swings of the pendulum.

The practice of providing a choice between progressive and traditional schools is not entirely unknown in public schooling. There are school districts that already provide such options—for example, a structured, traditional middle school and a more open, progressive one. Policymakers and educators may point out that it is not always easy to offer this choice. Suppose, for example, that a district has only one middle school. It may still be possible to offer options within one school building. If the school itself cannot be divided into two schools within one building, it may be possible to place students with teachers who practice the favored philosophy. This is where the continuity discussed in chapter 5 becomes of major importance. Elementary school children can be placed with a teacher (whose philosophy is compatible) for 3 years instead of the typical 1 year. Middle school students might work with the same philosophically compatible team of teachers for 3 years, and high school students might work with, say, the same math teacher for 3 or 4 years. All but the smallest schools should be able to accommodate this alternative.

In keeping with the theme of responsiveness, teachers and students should stay together by mutual consent, and no student should be forced to stay with a teacher he or she hates or fears. I am arguing that it is important for families to have a choice between broadly different approaches to education, but if a child is miserable with a teacher whose approach seemed at first theoretically compatible, a change should be made. A child from a progressively oriented family might, under some conditions, be happier with a traditional teacher than with a progressive one who is actively disliked. This kind of flexibility is part of what it means to be responsive.

Schools should be responsive to teachers, too. Some years ago, when I was a curriculum supervisor, I was asked to work as a "change agent" to convert a whole school system to one modeled on progressive principles. This was the model that I, as a teacher and parent, preferred. But I was very uncomfortable in imposing my preference on all of the teachers. Some agreed enthusiastically, and we got along beautifully. Others were obviously unhappy, and I reported this to the superintendent. "Let them leave!" he responded. He wanted a philosophically homogeneous staff—everyone on "the same page"—so that the progressive system he envisioned could be implemented effectively. We were to be a model progressive system.

Many, perhaps most, school systems operate this way. Because they do, we continue to experience swings of the pendulum. I preferred, even then, a mode of supervision that would help all teachers to do their best work according to their own legitimate philosophy. I emphasize *legitimate* philosophy to acknowledge the fact that reasonable people can differ on important elements of educational philosophy but that any *legitimate* philosophy is well-considered, guided by a justifiable conception of the good, educationally defensible, and compatible with the principles of liberal democracy. Today, I feel even more strongly that this way of organizing our schools is a healthier, more practical way of working.

But if I really believe in a progressive approach, one that offers many choices for students on topics of study, ways of learning, and forms of assessing what has been learned, how can I abandon hosts of students to traditional methods? The most basic idea of relational caring is to respond to each individual in such a way that we establish and maintain caring relations. My particular philosophy of education is important to me, and I am committed to it for my own practice. *But the living other is more important than any theory*, and my theory must be subordinate to the caring relationship. This does not mean, of course, that I will stand aside quietly while others do highly questionable things to children. That would be a travesty of caring. Carers will not permit cruelty, sarcasm, ridicule, brainwashing, or gross incompetence of any sort. But traditional education at its best is not guilty of such malpractice. I will, of course, try to persuade uncommitted educators and, especially, new generations of teachers that the alternative presented in this book is worthy of serious consideration, but I do not want to perpetuate educational warfare and swings of the pendulum.

The living other is more important than any theory. This is a central idea in an ethic of care. It is pre-theoretical, rooted in natural caring. It is, however, often very hard for teachers to accept, because teacher education and educational research inculcate certain theories and modes of practice as the scientifically approved ways of doing things. In the past few decades, for example, an idea called "constructivism" (which, for the most part, I endorse) has been influential in teaching. I have listened to teachers insist that they would *never* use drill and practice methods in their classrooms because children "learn best" when they "construct" their own knowledge, and drill is clearly proscribed by constructivism. What if children clearly need some drill? What if some children might even enjoy some routine practice? What if such a practice might move a class more quickly (through routinization) to a level of facility that would make deeper investigation more fruitful? The answer I frequently get to these questions is that these contrary practices could not possibly be either attractive to or useful for students. Children never *need* drill. No child enjoys routine practice. Routinization cannot possibly facilitate deeper investigation. "Constructivism says . . ." and so the child is sacrificed to the theory. This happens repeatedly with fashionable ideas in education—the most pernicious of which are products of dramatic swings of the pendulum. Too frequently we give up the good along with the worst of old practices.

The responsiveness that I am suggesting recognizes two great lines of educational thought. It cannot accommodate every innovative (or flaky!) idea that comes along. Indeed, compared to some other calls for increased responsiveness, my suggestion is modest. Within each of the two recognized movements, there will be disagreements and a need for further refinements. I can imagine, for example, several competing models of traditional schools and, certainly, of progressive schools. That is as it should be. Not only will each group be encouraged to improve itself, but the very existence of a vigorous alternative will be a constant goad to better practice. Traditional schools may become more humane and less authoritarian. Progressive schools may be reminded to avoid the mistakenly permissive practices that so worried John Dewey in his critique of the "new education" (Dewey, 1963). The two will not become identical; indeed, they may become more different, but they will learn from one another.

Everyone stands to gain in such an arrangement. No longer in fear of the others who may take over the whole enterprise, we can look, perhaps even a bit jealously, at their successes. Are they doing things that, adapted to our philosophy, might improve our practice? My guess is that parents who freely choose a traditional, structured education for their children will quickly demand an end to the present emphasis on tests and standardization when they see that children in less structured environments are progressing well and happily. Similarly, progressive teachers and parents will learn to ask appreciative questions about the inclusion of classic material in the progressive curriculum. Both should develop more powerful and varied methods of evaluation.

We can return now in a more intelligent way to the concept of accountability. Schools should be accountable for the achievement of their stated purposes. Those of us who place ourselves (at least roughly) in the progressive camp, ask much more of our schools than acceptable test scores on basic subjects. We look for the development of democratic character, critical thinking, and caring. We will hold our schools responsible not just for outcomes (we know these will vary), but for the opportunities and choices they offer. But we must demand the right to be served by public schools that espouse the educational purposes we cherish. At present, we live in a tyranny of opposing purposes; it serves none of us well.

SHOULD PRIVATIZATION BE AN OPTION?

If I advocate responsiveness and the provision of alternatives within the public school system, why not embrace partial privatization—through a voucher system—and try to satisfy all parental interests? I will offer here four important reasons why privatization should be rejected. Before discussing those, however, I would remind readers that privatization is not necessary; the public schools can, if they commit themselves to doing so, respond effectively to two quite different philosophies of education, and within those, many interesting variants might appear. But notice that I am talking about *educational* differences—not differences based on political, racial, gender, religious, or economic ideologies.

The first objection to privatization is economic. It would almost certainly exacerbate economic inequalities in the population. It is not entirely honest for advocates of vouchers to claim that, under their plan, all families would enjoy the privilege now held by only a few (Chubb & Moe, 1990). The basic voucher would severely constrain the choice that poor families could make, and the difference between that choice and what is now spent by wealthy parents on private education is dramatic. Can it reasonably be said that a family with a $5,000 voucher has a choice equal, or even similar, to that of a family that can spend $30,000 or more?

But we may be headed toward privatization heedlessly. Some critics of the No Child Left Behind Act believe that its aim is to destroy public education (Kohn, 2004). What better way to accomplish this destruction than to demand the impossible of public schools? To insist that all schools bring 100% of their students to "proficiency" by 2014—when virtually no school with an intellectually heterogeneous population has ever done this—is surely unreasonable (Linn, 2003). It seems to be only a means to a frightening end—privatization.

Even before raising objections to privatization, we should raise serious objections to NCLB from the perspective of caring. When we care for others, we do not try to motivate them by threats, sanctions, invidious comparisons, and harsh penalties. We do not ignore the expressed needs and varied talents of students and insist on a deadly standardization. And we would never create and enforce a law that corrupts instead of correcting—one that encourages students to cheat, teachers to put aside their most serious educational duties, and administrators to design ethically questionable strategies to subvert the law (Troen & Boles, 2003). Thus, even if the end—privatization—could be justified, the means should be condemned.

What is so frightening about privatization? I have already mentioned the exacerbation of economic differences as one important objection. A second is that the very promise of privatization—its emphasis on the benefits of competition—is very frightening. The promise of voucher advocates is that the market will work to drive out unsuccessful schools, as it drives out other unsuccessful businesses. But schools are not businesses, even if they can profitably use some business management techniques. Schools, like homes, are special places in the lives of children. They should be centers of stability and community. When the corner drug store closes, its customers are inconvenienced, but they will find another drug store. When a child's school closes, a substantial part of her life has been foreclosed. Where will she go? Will her friends be there? Who will be her teachers? How will she get there? Will it, too, close before she finishes her studies? To treat schools like businesses is a category mistake of significant proportions. The very success promised by privatization schemes should be cause for great alarm. Consider, too, that it is the economically poorest schools—not necessarily the educationally poorest—that would be driven out. The wealthiest private schools would have little to fear.

Privatization, by its own rationale, would convert education from a public good to a consumer good (Anton, Fisk, & Holstrum, 2000; House, 1998). When we buy a refrigerator or car, we are concerned primarily with getting the product we want at a price we can afford. Refrigerators and cars are consumer goods. But when we think of education as a public good, we should be concerned with the quality of education for all children. Disparities in what families will have to spend and the likelihood that poorer schools will close make privatization, despite the claims of its advocates, anti-democratic. As a public good, the proper education of every child contributes to the well-being of all and to the health of our democracy (Goodlad & McMannon, 1997; Norton, 1991; Soder, Goodlad, & McMannon, 2001).

An important objection to my insistence on the relation between public education and democracy is the observation that our present system of education can hardly be defended on democratic grounds. Many children, especially minority children in urban schools, have been badly served. Change is necessary. The responsiveness that I recommend would allow some significant choice and would have the salutary effect of involving parents in making that choice. A choice between poor and unreliable alternatives is not the best answer, and the current "alternative"—NCLB—seems to be making things even worse for many minority children (Darling-Hammond, 2004).

The responsive public school is a much better answer, but it cannot stand alone in caring for our children. We should launch a campaign to recruit as many citizens as possible to a movement that will care for our children on all fronts. That campaign must address basic social problems in the whole society (Noddings, 2002). It must press for adequate housing (lead-free, mold-free, rat-free interiors), universal medical insurance, a living wage, a reduction in urban air pollution and accessible means of transportation. To care means to respond to needs, and needs do not stop (or start) at the schoolroom door.

Still another reason to reject privatization is to avoid conflicts that will surely arise if sectarian groups apply to use voucher monies for their schools. In interesting recent work, Theodore Sizer (2004) has made a plea for responsiveness that is in many ways attractive. But he would broaden the field of choice in a way that might be dangerous to our democracy. Public funding in a liberal democracy should not be used to support schools that, because of their religious or ideological beliefs, undermine the democracy's social agenda. Groups that deny, or strongly discourage, the full participation of women in public and professional life, should not be supported by a government that places such full participation high on its social agenda. We could insist, of course, that schools commit to teaching the fundamentals of democracy as a condition of licensing, but it would be very difficult to monitor their compliance, and nominal compliance could easily mask a whole way of life that promotes a different story. In her discussion of independent schools, Amy Gutmann (1987) looked at some of these problems and decided, somewhat reluctantly, that it is more democratic to allow such schools than to prohibit them. But allowing them to exist does not suggest supporting them with public funds. Today the arguments for a wall of separation between church and state are more urgent than at any time in our recent history (Jacoby, 2004).

There are those who argue that the "money should follow the child"; that is, government should supply the funds, and families should decide where that money will be spent. Sizer (2004) seems to be making this argument. However, government also has some responsibility to ensure that children be at least exposed to the opportunities that a liberal democracy holds open to them. We cannot forbid parents to raise their children in anti-democratic religions and ideologies, and we would be unfaithful to our own democratic commitments if we were to do this. But we can insist that the public schools and any money provided by public funds be used to make all children aware of their opportunities and of their country's commitment to the full participation of all its citizens. The basic test of publicly funded choice must be *educational*, not religious or ideological.

THEMES OF CARE

Both traditional and progressive schools can teach themes of care, but they are likely to approach them in very different ways. Traditional educators organize the curriculum around the disciplines, and themes of care would have to arise within a discipline and be treated as an integral part of disciplinary study. Some vigorous defenders of the disciplines put great emphasis on existential questions of the sort treated in this book: Who am I? What sort of person should I be? What is my place in the universe? How should I meet and treat other human beings? Traditional educators often rely almost entirely on philosophy and the great books to answer these questions. In doing so, they claim to be responding to student needs. Allan Bloom, for example, writes: "For there is no real education that does not respond to felt need" (1987, p. 19). Where he differs dramatically from the alternative offered in this book is in his way of identifying those needs; he insists that they must be "the permanent concerns of mankind" (p. 19). He claims to know what the needs are before he meets his students, because he knows the unchanging quality of human nature.

Progressive educators are interested in the eternal questions, but we also want to respond to personal and current questions: How shall I make a living? What do I owe to nonhuman animals? Are there objects I should cherish? What does it mean to be a parent, friend, or citizen in today's world?

Progressives differ with traditionalists not only on the range of felt needs to which we respond, but also on the sources to which we turn for answers. Although we have respect for disciplinary knowledge and the classics, we are willing to use current sources and, even, to help students seek guidance in places familiar to them and, perhaps, unknown to us. It is the inquiry, dialogue, reflection, and response—not a particular set of books—that guide our exploration of themes of care.

I argue in chapter 3 that the standard liberal arts are no longer adequate as a framework for universal education. (That is a major difference between traditional education and the alternative I propose.) Most of today's students find the learning of discrete, unconnected subjects difficult, boring, and irrelevant to their lives, and much of what is laboriously learned is promptly forgotten when there are no more tests to be passed. It would be far more defensible to organize school learning around themes of care and encourage students to seek far and wide for possible answers to their questions. In the process, we would suggest many of the classics treasured by traditionalists and invite (not require) students to read them, but we would not suppose—as Robert Maynard Hutchins (1964) did—that students need to have mastered these classics before even beginning their personal/existential quests. Both Hutchins and Bloom invested the humanities with the entire task of teaching the great existential questions. They failed to see that the questions central to a full human life can be pursued in almost any subject that intrigues the human mind.

I believe that these important questions *must* be addressed in every subject the school offers. Although I would prefer a complete reorganization of the curriculum, I know that such a change is unlikely to happen. However, we can reasonably insist that each of the disciplines be stretched from within. As a former mathematics teacher, I have given examples of how we might treat themes of care in math classes. Instead of depending solely on the humanities to teach the great themes—and today often denying them opportunities to do so, emphasizing instead factual details from the readings—we must include the themes in all of our courses.

Moreover, themes of care are accessible, in a variety of forms, to all students, not only to the academically talented. Young children can learn something about the meaning of friendship from reading books by Dr. Seuss, older children from the Harry Potter series, and late adolescents from books such as John Knowles' *A Separate Peace*. Of course, teenagers who are interested may profit from reading Aristotle on friendship, and teachers should be able to convey the central ideas from his work on the topic, but we may do more harm than good when we *require* students to read and pass tests on classic texts. Indeed, we might better encourage lifelong reading by suggesting, inviting, sharing with delight, and mentioning with appreciation those books we think contain great wisdom.

Responsiveness is at the heart of caring and also at the heart of teaching themes of care. It is obvious that caring demands a response from us. When we care for others, we attend and respond as nearly as we can to expressed needs. When we have to refuse a request—because we lack the necessary resources, find the request unwise, or even evaluate it as morally wrong—we still try to support a caring relation. It can be very difficult, but our purpose is to connect with the other, to make both our lives ethically better—not to overcome, defeat, ostracize, or eliminate him.

I extend the idea of caring beyond the circle of moral agents. When we care for nonhuman animals and plants (chapter 9), for example, we do not expect them to respond by caring for us. They are not capable of the full reciprocity of moral agents. However, many animals respond to affection with affection, and the vast majority are capable of suffering and, thus, of responding to the alleviation of pain. Plants do not feel pain as animals do, but anyone who has worked with them knows that they, too, respond to adequate care and show signs of debility (suffering?) when that care is not given.

It is perhaps harder for students to interpret the concept of care with respect to the human-made world and to ideas (chapters 10 and 11). Yet caring for buildings, furniture, highways, mechanical contrivances, household objects, and art works is important for students to consider. How can we preserve our tools and furnishings? Can we reverse the trend toward a throw-away society? Are there objects we should cherish? Is there a sense in which objects respond to our care? What does this response look like?

Few students really believe that ideas—the material of the disciplines they are forced to learn—have any capacity whatever to respond. Yet great artists, mathematicians, composers, writers, and scientists have spoken eloquently about the ways in which subject matter "responds." I have sometimes advised students to stop thinking for a bit, stop forcing a strategy on a recalcitrant problem. Instead, look at it, listen to it. Invite it to come along with you and watch over your shoulder. It may speak in some way and reveal itself. Is this romantic nonsense? There are many, many biographical accounts that can be used to convince students that the world of ideas is capable of response (Noddings & Shore, 1998).

But we are primarily concerned here with caring and responsiveness in schools. In the first edition of this book, I noted that we had been neglecting our non-college-bound students. I quoted William Brock, former secretary of labor, who warned us that we would lose more and more of our students by forcing them into a single academic curriculum: "No wonder they drop out, because the market signal says to them, We don't care about you . . ." (1990, p. 14). Today the case is even more critical. We seem to have decided that there should be no "non-college-bound" students. Thus youngsters who are not attracted by academic studies are doubly cheated: They are made to feel like failures in the standard academic program, and they are deprived of the courses in which they might do well. We must put more resources into fine vocational programs, and those programs can easily include themes of care.

I invite readers to join me in an extensive thought experiment. We will pretend that we have a large heterogeneous family to raise and educate. Our children have different ethnic heritages, widely different intellectual capacities, different physical strengths, and different interests. We want to respect their legitimate differences. At the same time, we think there are some things they all should learn and some other things to which they should all be exposed so that they can make well-informed choices. Our general aim is to encourage the growth of competent, caring, loving, and lovable people. How shall we educate them?

THE CHALLENGE TO CARE IN SCHOOLS

An Alternative Approach to Education

SECOND EDITION

CHAPTER 1

Shallow Educational Response to Deep Social Change

Social changes in the years since World War II have been enormous. We have seen changes in work patterns, in residential stability, style of housing, sexual habits, dress, manners, language, music, entertainment, and perhaps most important of all in family arrangements. Schools have not responded in an effective way to these changes. Indeed, schools have responded, albeit sluggishly, to technological changes with various additions to curriculum and narrowly prescribed methods of instruction, but they have largely ignored massive social change. When response has occurred, it has been piecemeal, designed to address isolated bits of the problem. In this chapter, I will describe some of the changes that have appeared in social structures and the kinds of things schools have done in trying to cope with these changes.

In today's typical classroom there are many children from homes in which both parents do paid work, other children who have single parents, many who have half-siblings or temporary siblings unrelated by blood, some who have foster parents, and some who really have no parents at all. In a survey sponsored by the Girl Scouts of America (1989), one child in 100 claimed that no adults really cared for him or her. (Seven percent of the poorest children said this.) Although one percent sounds small, think how many children this means nationwide. Think also how desperately children want to believe someone cares, and therefore how proud and generous many would be in responding.

Many children arrive at school by bus, and their teachers have at best a vague notion of where they live. Only one third of the students in the Girl Scout survey said that their teachers care for them, and the proportion decreases as students get older. Only seven percent say that they would go to teachers for advice! Not only do students lack trust in their teachers, but many lack even the most basic human respect. In a newspaper account, a journalist who sat in on local high school classes reported the result of a teacher's reprimanding a student for cheating. The student responded, "What crawled up your ass and died?" (Simon, 1990).

On a given day, most students in any class have watched murder, assault, love-making, war-making, and/or competitive sports on television the previous night. For many—especially at the secondary level—their classrooms are located in large schools, 1,200–2,000 students, sometimes more. Teachers in these schools often cannot distinguish students from strangers on campus. In some such schools there are security guards and rigid rules about entering and leaving the campus. Students need passes to use restrooms and, once inside, they may be accosted physically or verbally, while outside someone may be timing their stay to prevent loitering.

It is not surprising that the single greatest complaint of students in these schools is, "They don't care!" (Comer, 1988). They feel alienated from their schoolwork, separated from the adults who try to teach them, and adrift in a world perceived as baffling and hostile. At the same time, most teachers work very hard and express deep concern for their students. In an important sense, teachers do care, but they are unable to make the connections that would complete caring relations with their students.

Schools were not always like this. When my husband and I were in high school, we knew our teachers cared, and we felt their all-too-watchful eyes on us constantly. I had the same teachers for four years of math, Latin, and physical education, for three of my four years of history, for three years of public speaking. I had different teachers each year for science and English, but I had four years of each subject. Some readers may react by exclaiming, "Ali, that's the way schooling should be—four years of English, Latin, math, science, and history! Even three years of public speaking! Wonderful!" Actually, it was not all that wonderful intellectually. Most of our teachers were not very good at the subjects they taught, but they knew us, talked with us, encouraged us. They worked us moderately hard, and I was always tired but sorry when summer came. School was a second home for me.

It is natural to feel nostalgic about our own school days if they were happy ones. But we cannot build our children's future on nostalgic dreams. We probably cannot reconstruct the small communities that supported rich personal interactions in the past. What is important is to recognize and admit that curriculum content—in the form of traditional subjects-was not a big contributor to satisfaction with schooling. Periodically, curriculum is touted as the key to educational reform and huge amounts of money are spent on its revision, but astute observers have commented more than once that a focus on curriculum revision is "not the answer" (Bruner, 1971).

A word of caution is needed here. I agree with Bruner's observation that curriculum revision cannot be an adequate response to the social problems that face schools—problems that are more serious today than when Bruner made his comments. But this is not to say that curriculum change has no part at all in grappling with these problems. Tinkering with the standard curriculum, I will argue, is futile, but drastic change may contribute to a new environment in schools.

The emphasis on revision of the standard curriculum, far from contributing to school reform, may actually have induced greater alienation and unhappiness in students. In the late fifties and sixties, in response to a perceived national need for technical excellence, we saw a movement called the "structure of the disciplines movement." Scholars and educators associated with this movement put tremendous emphasis on an understanding of the fundamental structure, principles, and methods of the disciplines with which they were involved (Bruner, 1960). Mathematicians, scientists, and linguists gave advice and sometimes participated actively in curriculum construction. Psychologists and philosophers described and debated what it meant to teach the structure of a discipline. The federal government, fearing the possible superiority of Russian technology, supported curriculum development projects and teacher training. It was a heady time for educational theorists who saw almost no bounds to what could be taught if we just found the right way.

The movement brought with it a prescription for bigger schools (Conant, 1959, 1967). How else could we offer physics, advanced math, and several foreign languages and still be financially and intellectually responsible? Further, an expanding population required new and larger facilities. So began the drive to phase out small high schools and offer intellectually challenging courses in large, "efficient" school plants. Where there had been one hundred in my high school graduation class, there would be four or five hundred or more in my children's classes.

Those of us in education at the time were swept along in an intellectual frenzy. As a high school mathematics department chairperson, I had responsibility for converting an entire district to the new math. It was not entirely a wrongheaded movement; the old math curriculum was badly out of date. And it was such a joy to learn new material instead of teaching the same old routines. I had great fun with rings and fields, with concepts such as commutativity, identity, transitivity, and multiplicative inverse. Many of my students had fun, too, and graduated from high school with a fair knowledge of calculus, probability, abstract algebra, and modern geometry. But it was not fun for everyone. Lots of students could not see what multiplicative inverses had to do with everyday life, and many students persisted in spelling commutative "communitive" no matter how often I corrected them. To them, it was a word and not much more. We finally awoke from our intellectual dream, but headachy—with a desire to forget the whole thing. In a misguided attempt at fairness, we gave up our curricula aimed at the intellectually elite and went overboard for "the basics."

We decided that curriculum could be reduced to an elaborate set of behavioral objectives. Teachers were urged to state exactly what students would do, under what conditions, and to what standard. A typical behavioral objective for fifth grade mathematics might read:

> Presented with 10 exercises of the sort $\frac{2}{5} + \frac{1}{3} =$, students will add fractions with different denominators up to 24, give the answer in lowest terms, and get at least eight of the ten correct.

Experts roved the country teaching administrators and teachers how to write precisely stated objectives. One had to say exactly what students would do; one was not allowed to say, "The students *will be able* to . . ." because such latent competence is not observable. Further teachers had to specify how the students would prove themselves: by test (paper and pencil? how long? with what constraints on words, numbers, variables, etc.?); by essay (how long? what kinds of sentences? content? form?); by speech; by project; and so on. Finally teachers had to specify the standard. What would count as competent performance? (Mager, 1962).

All over the country, states and districts buckled down to write every course of study in this form. Many educators compromised and concentrated on what the students would do—de-emphasizing the conditions and the standard—and, even so, long lists accumulated. Volumes accumulated. One can find these volumes in almost any school district, neatly arranged on shelves in curriculum offices or, sometimes, packed away in storerooms. I have often wondered how many person-hours went into that monumental task and, by implication, what the whole enterprise cost.

Many of us opposed the behavioral objectives movement (Eisner, 1969). I remember vividly my first encounter with this way of thinking. I was listening to students in my homeroom study for a history test. They had all the questions and were coaching each other on the answers. Oh, dear, I thought, these kids—good kids, some of my best math students—had got hold of the test; they were cheating. But, happily, that was not so. Their teacher had bought into the behavioral-objectives/criterion-referenced testing idea and had said, "Here's what you'll be tested on; learn it."

Was this an enlightened new way of teaching? On one level it sounded sensible. If you want kids to learn, for goodness' sake tell them what you expect them to do. First, make sure you know what they are to do; then tell them. It seemed a lot fairer and easier than the method my own teachers had used. When we asked what would be on an upcoming test, the answer was usually, "Everything!"

But is it a sensible way to start teaching? Consider the number of things we learn for specific purposes and how quickly we forget them. We learn a telephone number, cross the room, dial, talk, and promptly forget the number. We park our car for three days at the airport and carefully remember that it is at K-14 when we return, but then we forget that bit of information. If kids learn things for a specific test, might not the same thing happen? If the item or skill learned is one that will be practiced over and over again in future learning, the problem of forgetting may not be so great, but teachers and curriculum makers would have to engage in some analysis to ensure that skills learned for an immediate purpose (the test) are actually embedded in future lessons. This has rarely been done.

In many districts, the use of behavioral objectives—often poorly or vaguely written as "competencies"—became the heart of tests for graduation. To assist students who were struggling to pass these tests, educators often broke major topics into tiny subtopics and allowed students to pass the tests in segments. Indeed, educators in a number of schools told me (in my new role as professor) how proud they were of their passing rates. Many of us had worried that students would be unable to pass the new competency tests, but here they were passing. By breaking learning into manageable segments and telling students exactly what they would have to do, educators found they were learning and passing. I was impressed. Surely this new burst of learning must have caused a considerable increase in standardized achievement scores, I said. Well, no, I was told, those had not changed. Kids could add $\frac{2}{5}$ and $\frac{1}{3}$ at time x, when that is all they had to do, but by the end of the year when they faced $\frac{2}{5}$ + $\frac{1}{3}$ along with $\frac{7}{8} \div \frac{4}{5}$ they did not do so well. This pathetic result confirmed the earlier intuitive concern I had as a teacher.

Many readers will react to the account I have just given as proof that educational researchers and professors of education are not very bright. But actually, the method I have just castigated has its proper uses. Suppose I am a geometry teacher, and my class will soon study the Pythagorean Theorem and its applications. This is an important theorem that appears again and again in both theoretical and practical mathematical problems. Many of its applications and corollaries require facility with square roots and radicals. Knowing this—having analyzed the major concepts so that I am aware of the skills required to handle them with ease—I may well guide three or four days' instruction with behaviorally stated objectives. I may even test them piecemeal, but not to show that the students have mastered something important. Rather, I test to find out whether my instruction has been adequate, and I tell my students that the purpose of this skill-honing is to prepare them for interesting proofs and challenging problems. I do not want my students to be distracted from central mathematical issues by uncertainty with algorithmic skills. They are not learning how to simplify the square root of 12 and to memorize the squares of integers from 1 to 25 in order to pass a test (and then forget). They are learning these skills, which are embedded in the coming work, to free their thinking for important concepts and problems.

The people who advocated, and still advocate, instructional objectives stated clearly in terms of student performance made a contribution to educational thought. It is important that our efforts at teaching result in something observable in students. But they went too far. Many of them would still insist that the vital conceptual work I mentioned above could itself be approached by stating precise objectives. This is an error so huge that it almost destroys the contribution. To think—to identify problems, define them, solve them, generalize from them—requires freedom from narrow constraints. It is a different sort of learning entirely, and wise teachers know this.

Teachers had additional complaints about the behavioral objectives movement. In working with a large school district where this method was mandated, I was told by elementary school mathematics teachers that they needed help with instruction. What good is it to state exactly what you want the kids to do, they asked, if you don't know how to get them to do it? These teachers protested that they had always known that fifth graders should add ⅖ and ⅓ successfully. How should they teach addition of fractions so that their students would succeed? The behavioral objectives movement was mute on modes of instruction.

Teachers also had ethical concerns. In the district mentioned above, the superintendent had told teachers he "didn't care" how they got the kids to perform—"You can stand them on their heads in the back of the room for all I care"—but perform they must. His teachers knew the superintendent was not totally serious in his neglect of means, but he seemed too serious for his conscientious teachers. They saw teaching as a moral enterprise, not one in which the end justifies the means. Ostensibly they were free to use their professional judgment in choosing instructional means, but they were forbidden to tamper with the ends. Such constraint is not the mark of a professional, and these teachers resented it. Theorists who wanted to get teaching onto a firm scientific footing failed to consider that students might not want to do the things so carefully stated by their teachers. They ignored the possibility that students might have pressing cares and interests not addressed by the subject matter presented in schools. These theorists insisted that it was up to teachers to motivate students to do what teachers wanted them to do. Yet, even as these recommendations were being made, teachers and students were drifting farther and farther apart as persons. They were becoming "treatments" and "subjects"—part of a concerted drive to find one best way of getting people to learn.

The desire to reduce all teaching and learning to one well-defined method is part of a larger pattern in science, epistemology, and ethics. It has been criticized by many contemporary theorists. Feminist theologian Mary Daly (1973) has called the pursuit "methodolatry," the worship of method. Philosophers, scientists, ethicists, and many other thinkers have tried since the time of Descartes to substitute foolproof method for the situated, living human being who must think and decide. Method became all-important. Naomi Scheman (1989) comments:

> Anyone—so the rationalists and empiricists equally proclaimed—who followed whatever method was recommended would be in a position to know, and what they knew would be the same as what was known by anyone else who followed that method. Thus, replicability became the hallmark of reputable experimentation, as universalizability became the hallmark of reputable moral thought: who you were in particular, to whom you were particularly connected, where you were particularly placed, was supposed to make no difference to how things seemed to you—provided, of course, that you were following the prescribed method, the main features of which were designed precisely to insulate your judgment from all those particularities. (p. 41)

Epistemologists have begun to question whether such single-minded emphasis on method yields the objectivity ascribed to it. Ethicists have challenged universalizability as a methodological error that undermines moral sensitivity. And some educational theorists argue that teachers should not be regarded as interchangeable "instructional treatments." Who the teacher is, who the students are, what they are trying to accomplish separately and together all matter in designing instruction.

Educational research, like behavioral science in general, has made the error of supposing that method can be substituted for individuals, and this attempt may well have increased the alienation of students. Often when researchers are trying to determine whether A or B is a better method of instruction ("treatment"), they try to strip away the special qualities of teachers and students so that the various settings in which A and B are being tried can be regarded as comparable. As many variables as possible are controlled. But teachers are not interchangeable; they cannot be regarded as delivery systems or treatments. Nor are children interchangeable. One impish grin in the middle of a lesson can change what follows.

It is not just educators who are infected by the mad desire for method. Parents, too, seek a way to raise their children without spending a lot of time with them. We search for—invent—quality time. School principals look for workshops that will make all of their teachers good managers, although some already are, some have no wish to be, and others need patient and persistent help. Administrators assume that there must be a method that will allow teachers to meet 150–200 new students every year and yet establish the atmosphere of caring that teachers such as mine did years ago. A main message of this book is that there is no such method. People are not reducible to methods except, perhaps, in their work with objects. This form of reduction is called automation, and it simply does not apply to interpersonal activities.

The search for a universal method in curriculum was soon accompanied by one in the area of instruction. Given the premises of educational researchers, such a move was inevitable. They did not consider the possibility that students simply did not want to achieve the objectives so carefully laid out. Failure to meet the objectives must be, it was held, instructional failure. Teachers were advised to use a five- or seven-step standard lesson: Briefly review the previous day's work; state the objectives of today's lesson; present new material (in small, manageable steps); check on understanding; provide guided practice; check again on understanding; give independent practice (see Rosenshine & Stevens, 1986). This is almost exactly what I did as a math teacher when I decided on three or four days of skill development before tackling the Pythagorean Theorem and its corollaries. Such a procedure has long been the backbone of every math teacher's instructional repertoire. It is not at all clear that it should be, but it has been.

The problem is that the standard lesson is almost useless for teaching major concepts and engaging students in problem solving, reflection, creative expression, cooperative interaction, or intellectual discernment. Even for some ordinary skill development lessons, it is better to vary the steps. For example, there are times when it makes sense to find out first how students approach a task and then to present, or have *them* present, two or three ways of performing it. In teaching division of algebraic fractions, a teacher might present a problem and ask, How would you do this? Independent (or cooperative) investigation would precede teacher presentation, and the eventual teacher summary or presentation would draw heavily on student contributions. Thus the standard lesson is not only useless for higher-order thinking tasks; it is also unnecessarily limiting as a universal approach to skill development. Finally, if we accept it for skill development and reject it for other intellectual tasks, we fall into the error of supposing that skills and conceptual development are easily separable, and they are not.

Just as workshops blossomed all over the country to teach the writing of behavioral objectives, workshops were next conducted on the standard lesson. In many districts, teachers are still evaluated on their adherence to the standard form. Three questions drive a large part of teacher evaluation: Does the teacher have a clearly stated instructional objective? Does the teacher use the standard five- (or seven-) step lesson? Does the teacher have a well-managed classroom? Now the demand is that every lesson be driven by a "standard" and evaluated on the basis of whether students meet it. The pervasive goal is control: control of teachers, of students, of content.

It is not surprising that the combination of narrowly stated learning objectives and pat, routine lessons induces boredom. And boredom leads to something educators call "random behavior." This is behavior that is not directed to the task at hand. Educators are also fond of talking about "off-task" behavior. Both ways of talking assume that students who are not tuned in to the teacher's goals and tasks have no goals or tasks of their own. When I was a public school student, such behavior was simply misbehavior, disruptive behavior, or—most revealing of all—disobedience. This last said clearly that the student's purposes were at odds with those of the teacher, and the usual remedy was a "good talking-to" either in class or after class. As a teenager who had lots of goals at cross-purposes with my teachers, I received my share of these "talking-tos."

Once again, the search for a method has tried to eliminate both the undesirable behaviors and the need for teachers to talk to their students about the behavior. Workshops on "assertive discipline" proliferated. The idea here is that teachers should not interrupt their standard pursuit of well-stated learning objectives to talk to their students about random or off-task behavior. They should, instead, simply put a stop to the behavior. If Jimmy talks to Barb when he should be listening to Ms. Smith, Ms. Smith writes Jimmy's name on the board. If a bit later, Jimmy sails an airplane to Barb with "I love you" on it (as my husband often did to me in English class), Ms. Smith puts a check next to Jimmy's name. Another check and Jimmy can expect a drastic, standard response: detention or a trip to the office. Assertive discipline was supposed to free teachers for their main task, instruction in subject matter.

My contention is that such instruction is not their main task. It is one task and an important one. As this exploration proceeds, I will ask whether it is helpful to restrict the functions of institutions to one main task. Such restriction is probably a mistake, because all institutions (and people) have multiple goals and purposes, and these shift and take on varying emphases with changes in events. But if the school has one main goal, a goal that guides the establishment and priority of all others, it should be to promote the growth of students as healthy, competent, moral people. This is a huge task to which all others are properly subordinated. We cannot ignore our children—their purposes, anxieties, and relationships—in the service of making them more competent in academic skills. My position is not anti-intellectual. It is a matter of setting priorities. Intellectual development is important, but it cannot be the first priority of schools.

The three approaches I have described to curriculum, instruction, and classroom management illustrate movements guided by an ideology of control and dominated by a search for method. The idea is to make the individual teacher, the individual student, and their relationship irrelevant to the success of instruction, which is posited as the primary goal of schooling. Once objectives are chosen, teachers are not supposed to deviate from them. They are to seek means within a narrowly defined standard form to reach the objectives, and, further, the objectives now established are almost entirely cognitive. The purposes and objectives of students are ignored (indeed denied, as random behavior) unless they happen to coincide with those of the teacher.

Important objections have been raised against this methodical approach to teaching. Early in this century, John Dewey (1902) recommended a mode of associated living as the basis for both education and democracy. He insisted that students must be involved in the construction of objectives for their own learning; that they must seek and formulate problems, not simply solve ready-made problems; that they should work together in schools as they would later in most workplaces; and that there is an organic relation between what is learned and personal experience (Dewey, 1916, 1938). Much of what I will later recommend is compatible with Dewey's thinking, but I go considerably beyond him in advocating new priorities. Dewey could never escape the charge of anti-intellectualism, and much of his educational thought was mustered to defend his recommendations against that charge. Perhaps as a result, he never really challenged the standard subjects, only their overemphasis and their poor pedagogical handling.

Later attempts to change education have suffered much the same fate. In his powerful introduction to *Crisis in the Classroom* (1970), Charles Silberman corrected his own earlier view that emphasized cognitive goals. He says, "What tomorrow needs is not masses of intellectuals, but masses of educated men—men educated to feel and to act as well as to think" (p. 7). Silberman had come to distrust any program of education that posited intellectual development as the only or main aim. Pointing to the German university and the rise of Nazism, he argued that intellectual development could not ensure against moral perversity. He was right.

The vision articulated by Silberman had a short life. A few attempts were made at open education in elementary schools, and some theorists talked about comparable programs at the high school level. But the same question arose in community after community: If we go this way, what will happen to our achievement scores? This question does not, of course, represent genuine intellectual interest as much as the desire merely to appear intellectually competent.

I was a math–science curriculum supervisor (and doctoral candidate) during the heady days when open education seemed to have a chance. Our district was a high achievement one—98th–99th percentile on most tests, and the parents were supportive of education. They were intrigued with their young superintendent's ideas and gave the go-ahead for radical changes to start in grades 4 to 6. However, they entered a caveat: Go ahead, but don't let our achievement scores drop.

Well, of course, they did fall. (They could not very well have gone up.) I can remember vividly the day on which the middle school principal, the school psychologist, the superintendent, and two curriculum supervisors including myself sat around a conference table scoring the tests in great anticipation and anxiety. The scores had definitely fallen.

Why, why, why? And what were we to tell the kindly board that had said go ahead? Reasons were not hard to find, and the board reacted calmly. They accepted our plea that we needed more time. But the parameters were in place; the priorities had been set. Do nothing in education that might result in lower test scores. Do what you like, but only if you can raise them or at least maintain them.

The so-called swings of the pendulum in American education are tied to these basic dos and don'ts. A real change requires a radical transformation in goals or ends, not simply in means, and the American public has never really understood a call for radical changes in ends. Silberman saw the need clearly but was unable to extricate himself or the open education movement from the traditional entanglement with academic goals. He had to insist that children would learn more and better in this new way. Would anyone have listened if he'd said, "Maybe they won't know as much math and history, but they'll be better people"?

Schools today are probably in worse shape than they were when Silberman wrote. We need the changes he explored. Classrooms should be places in which students can legitimately act on a rich variety of purposes, in which wonder and curiosity are alive, in which students and teachers live together and grow. I, too, believe that a dedication to full human growth—and we will have to define this—will not stunt or impede intellectual achievement, but even if it might, I would take the risk if I could produce people who would live nonviolently with each other, sensitively and in harmony with the natural environment, reflectively and serenely with themselves. To make real changes in education and escape the dull tick-tock of pendulum swings, we have to set aside the deadly notion that the schools' first priority should be intellectual development. Further, we must abandon the odd notion that any institution—family, school, church, business—has one and only one stable, main goal that precludes the establishment and pursuit of other goals.

It may seem odd to some readers that I have charged schools with ignoring social change in their educational planning. Many other critics have made opposite claims, and their worry is that schools cannot accomplish their legitimate academic goals because they have to feed, bus, protect, and pursue students. Schools also have to provide driver education, sex education, career education, drug education, and parent education. It is no wonder that students cannot read or solve mathematical problems, these critics argue; there is too little time left for basic skills. Moreover, these extras usually require special administrators, assistants, and loads of paper work, all of which tax the system further.

The system *is* strained, but largely because it knows only one way to do things: to add courses and routinized services. Students are fed, but the rationale for feeding them is not that loving people compassionately feed hungry children but, rather, that "hungry children cannot learn." The academic purpose of the school drives everything. Kids are fed, but educators rarely consider providing adult companionship with food. At home, in the best conditions, an adult shares meals with a child, asks what the forthcoming day will be like, reminds the child that she really does know her seven-times table, that her story for English is in good shape, and that tonight they will talk about the teacher's reaction. Feeding children's bodies is important; feeding their spirits is even more so. Similarly, when we bus students, we are supposedly aiming at the greatest good for the greatest number. We may—or may not—have a lovely ideal in mind. But we rarely provide the community setting that was once available for large numbers of children. Too often, we do not even think of providing it. We think of providing specialists, computers, advanced math, and remedial reading. We could think of providing an adult at each family-sized meal table. We could think of conversation, continuity, encouraging a sense of belonging.

It is a form of civic mindedness to think of children as precious resources. We teach them math and science so as not to waste our resources and endanger our competitive edge in the world market. Years ago America fell in love with Disney-style kids, freckle-faced little rascals who had trouble with arithmetic and grammar and much preferred fishing to figuring. We loved and still love these kids in a world of make-believe, but in the real world, children are too often valued only for their achievement. They become resources.

A child's place in our hearts and lives should not depend on his or her academic prowess. Lots of young people see through today's educational slogans. We preach constantly that "all children can learn"; we even suggest strongly that they all can learn anything the school has to offer if they are taught well and they try. If they don't try, they are made to feel like traitors, even though they might work very hard at tasks over which they have some control and choice. Thus, despite our determined optimism and insistent everyone-can-do-it, students complain, "They don't care!" They suspect that we want their success for our own purposes, to advance our own records, and too often they are right.

It is time to take full account of the social changes that have swept through the second half of the twentieth century. If the traditional family is now an anachronism, or if, for whatever reasons, families cannot meet the needs for caring, other institutions must fill the need. John Silber (1989), the controversial president of Boston University, has written a book purporting to explain *What's Wrong with America and How to Fix It*. Although I disagree with him on a host of matters, I agree with him on this: We must take public responsibility for raising healthy, competent, and happy children. I will argue that the school must play a major role in this task, and I will argue further that the school cannot achieve its academic goals without providing caring and continuity for students.

To fill the need effectively, we need to ask a series of important questions: What does it mean to care? How is care manifested and focused in human life? Can we make caring the center of our educational efforts?

CHAPTER 2

Caring

The German philosopher Martin Heidegger (1962) described care as the very Being of human life. His use of the term is very broad, covering an attitude of solicitousness toward other living beings, a concern to do things meticulously, the deepest existential longings, fleeting moments of concern, and all the burdens and woes that belong to human life. From his perspective, we are immersed in care; it is the ultimate reality of life.

Heidegger's range of meanings will be of interest as this exploration continues, but the meaning that will be primary here is relational. A *caring relation* is, in its most basic form, a connection or encounter between two human beings—a carer and a recipient of care, or cared-for. In order for the relation to be properly called caring, both parties must contribute to it in characteristic ways. A failure on the part of either carer or cared-for blocks completion of caring and, although there may still be a relation—that is, an encounter or connection in which each party feels something toward the other—it is not a *caring* relation. Even before I describe the contributions of carer and cared-for, one can see how useful this relational definition is. No matter how hard teachers try to care, if the caring is not received by students, the claim "they don't care" has some validity. It suggests strongly that something is very wrong.

In *Caring* (1984), I described the state of consciousness of the carer (or "one-caring") as characterized by engrossment and motivational displacement. By engrossment I mean an open, nonselective receptivity to the cared-for. Other writers have used the word "attention" to describe this characteristic. Iris Murdoch (1970), for example, discussed attention as essential in moral life, and she traced the concept to Simone Weil. Weil placed attention at the center of love for our neighbors. It is what characterizes our consciousness when we ask another (explicitly or implicitly), "What are you going through?" Weil wrote:

This way of looking is first of all attentive. The soul empties itself of all its own contents in order to receive into itself the being it is looking at, just as he is, in all his truth. Only he who is capable of attention can do this. (1951, p. 115)

To say that the soul empties itself of all its own contents in order to receive the other describes well what I mean by engrossment. I do not mean infatuation, enchantment, or obsession but a full receptivity. When I care, I really hear, see, or feel what the other tries to convey. The engrossment or attention may last only a few moments and it may or may not be repeated in future encounters, but it is full and essential in any caring encounter. For example, if a stranger stops me to ask directions, the encounter may produce a caring relation, albeit a brief one. I listen attentively to his need, and I respond in a way that he receives and recognizes. The caring relation is completed when he receives my efforts at caring.

As carer in the brief encounter just described, I was attentive, but I also felt the desire to help the stranger in his need. My consciousness was characterized by motivational displacement. Where a moment earlier I had my own projects in mind, I was now concerned with his project—finding his way on campus. When we watch a small child trying to tie her shoes, we often feel our own fingers moving in sympathetic reaction. This is motivational displacement, the sense that our motive energy is flowing toward others and their projects. I receive what the other conveys, and I want to respond in a way that furthers the other's purpose or project.

Experiencing motivational displacement, one begins to think. Just as we consider, plan, and reflect on our own projects, we now think what we can do to help another. Engrossment and motivational displacement do not tell us what to do; they merely characterize our consciousness when we care. But the thinking that we do will now be as careful as it is in our own service. We are seized by the needs of another.

What characterizes the consciousness of one who is cared for? Reception, recognition, and response seem to be primary. The cared-for receives the caring and shows that it has been received. This recognition now becomes part of what the carer receives in his or her engrossment, and the caring is completed.

Some critics worry that my account puts a tremendous burden on the carer and very little on the recipient of care. But we must keep in mind that the basic caring relation is an encounter. My description of a caring relation does not entail that carer and cared-for are permanent labels for individuals. Mature relationships are characterized by mutuality. They are made up of strings of encounters in which the parties exchange places; both members are carers and cared-fors as opportunities arise.

Even in the basic situation, however, the contribution of the cared-for is not negligible. Consider the mother-infant relationship. In every caring encounter, the mother is necessarily carer and the infant cared-for. But the infant responds—he or she coos, wriggles, stares attentively, smiles, reaches out, and cuddles. These responses are heartwarming; they make caregiving a rewarding experience. To see just how vital the infant's response is to the caring relation, one should observe what happens when infants cannot respond normally to care. Mothers and other caregivers in such situations are worn down by the lack of completion—burned out by the constant outward flow of energy that is not replenished by the response of the cared-for. Teachers, too, suffer this dreadful loss of energy when their students do not respond. Thus, even when the second party in a relation cannot assume the status of carer, there is a genuine form of reciprocity that is essential to the relation.

The desire to be cared for is almost certainly a universal human characteristic. Not everyone wants to be cuddled or fussed over. But everyone wants to be received, to elicit a response that is congruent with an underlying need or desire. Cool and formal people want others to respond to them with respect and a touch of deference. Warm, informal people often appreciate smiles and hugs. Everyone appreciates a person who knows when to hug and when to stand apart. In schools, all kids want to be cared for in this sense. They do not want to be treated "like numbers," by recipe—no matter how sweet the recipe may be for some consumers. When we understand that everyone wants to be cared for and that there is no recipe for caring, we see how important engrossment (or attention) is. In order to respond as a genuine carer, one does have to empty the soul of its own contents. One cannot say, "Aha! This fellow needs care. Now, let's see—here are the seven steps I must follow." Caring is a way of being in relation, not a set of specific behaviors.

I have put great emphasis on caring as relation, because our temptation is to think of caring as a virtue, an individual attribute. We do talk this way at times. We say, "He is a caring person," or even, "She is really a caring person, but she has trouble showing it." Both of these comments capture something of our broad notion of care, but both are misleading because of their emphasis on caring as an individual virtue. As we explore caring in the context of caregiving—any long-term unequal relation in which one person is carer and the other cared-for—we will ask about the virtues that support caring. But for now, it is important not to detach carers from caring relations. No matter how much a person professes to care, the result that concerns us is the caring relation. Lots of self-righteous, "caring" people induce the response, "she doesn't really care about me at all."

Even though I will often use the word *caring* to apply to relations, I will also need to apply it to capacities. The uses should be clear in context. I want to avoid a concentration on judgment or evaluation that accompanies an interpretation of caring as an individual virtue, but I also want to acknowledge that people have various capacities for caring—that is, for entering into caring relations as well as for attending to objects and ideas.

When we discuss teaching and teacher-learner relationships in depth, we will see that teachers not only have to create caring relations in which they are the carers, but that they also have a responsibility to help their students develop the capacity to care. What can this mean? For Heidegger care is inevitable; all aware human beings care. It is the mark of being human. But not everyone develops the capacity to care for others in the way described above. Perhaps very few learn to care for ideas, for nonhuman life, for objects. And often we confuse the forms of caring and suppose caring to be a unitary capacity that transfers easily from one domain to another.

Simone Weil is a good example of an outstanding thinker who seems to have believed that intellectual caring and interpersonal caring are closely related. In the essay from which the earlier passage was extracted, Weil observed that the study of geometry requires attention and that attention so learned could increase students' concentration in prayer. Thence, we may suppose, Weil concluded that closer connection in prayer would produce more sensitive interpersonal relations; that is, she believed that intellectual attention could be transferred to interpersonal attention. This is doubtful. Evidence abounds that people can attain high levels of intellectuality and remain insensitive to human beings and other living things. Consider the Nazi high command or the fictional Professor Moriarty (Sherlock Holmes's nemesis) who attended lovingly to his orchids but was evil incarnate in the human domain. So the varieties of care need analysis.

Unequal caring relations are interesting not only in the human domain but also in the realm of nonhuman animals. It is doubtful whether any animal can be a carer with respect to humans (although there are those who have argued the case for dogs), but many animals are responsive cared-fors, and taking care of animals can be a wonderful way to learn caring. In our interaction with animals, we also have an opportunity to study the forms of response that we value. Some animals respond with intelligence, and we usually value that. Some respond with affection; they like to be stroked, cuddled, held, or scratched. Still others respond vocally. All of these responses affect us and call forth a caring attitude. Further, certain physical characteristics that suggest the possibility of a valued response also affect us. Most of us feel sympathy for baby seals threatened by hunters, because they look as though they might respond in the ways mentioned. Creatures that are slimy, scaly, or spiny rarely evoke a sympathetic response in us. The nature of our responses will be seen as important when we consider the roots of ethical life.

In another sense of care, human beings can care about ideas or objects. An approach to education that begins with care is not, as I pointed out earlier, anti-intellectual. Part of what we receive from others is a sense of their interests, including intellectual passions. To enhance a student's understanding and skill in a given subject is an important task for teachers, but current educational practices are riddled with slogans and myths that are not very helpful.

Often we begin with the innocent-sounding slogan mentioned earlier, "All children can learn." The slogan was created by people who mean well. They want teachers to have high expectations for all their students and not to decide on the basis of race, ethnicity, sex, or economic status that some groups of children simply cannot learn the subject at hand. With that much I agree.

But I will argue that not all individual children can learn everything we might like to teach them. Further, the good intentions captured in the slogan can lead to highly manipulative and dictatorial methods that disregard the interests and purposes of students. Teachers these days are expected to induce a desire to learn in all students. But all students already want to learn; it is a question of what they want to learn. John Dewey (1963) argued years ago that teachers had to start with the experience and interests of students and patiently forge connections between that experience and whatever subject matter was prescribed. I would go further. There are few things that all students need to know, and it ought to be acceptable for students to reject some material in order to pursue other topics with enthusiasm. Caring teachers listen and respond differentially to their students. Much more will be said on this highly controversial issue in later chapters. For now it is enough to note that our schools are not intellectually stimulating places, even for many students who are intellectually oriented.

Few students learn to care for ideas in school. Perhaps even fewer learn to care for objects. I am not talking about mere acquisitiveness; this seems to be learned all too well. I am talking about what Harry Broudy (1972) called "enlightened cherishing" and what the novelist and essayist John Galsworthy (1948) called "quality." This kind of caring produces fine objects and takes care of them. In a society apparently devoted to planned obsolescence, our children have few opportunities to care lovingly for old furniture, dishes, carpets, or even new bicycles, radios, cassette players, and the like. It can be argued that the care of many tools and instruments is a waste of time because they are so easily replaced. But one wonders how long a throwaway society can live harmoniously with the natural environment and also how closely this form of carelessness is related to the gross desire for more and more acquisitions. Is there a role for schools to play in teaching care of buildings, books, computers, furniture, and laboratory equipment?

Caring for ideas and objects is different from caring for people and other living things. Strictly speaking, one cannot form a relation with mathematics or music or a food processor. The cared-for cannot feel anything for or us; there is no affect in the second party. But, oddly, people do report a form of responsiveness from ideas and objects. The mathematician Gauss was "seized" by mathematics. The poet Robert Frost insisted that "a poem finds its own way" (see the accounts in Noddings & Shore, 1998). And we know that well-tended engines purr, polished instruments gleam, and fine glassware glistens. The care we exert induces something like a response from fields of ideas and from inanimate objects. Do our students hear enough—or anything at all—about these wondrous events?

Finally, we must consider Heidegger's deepest sense of care. As human beings, we care what happens to us. We wonder whether there is life after death, whether there is a deity who cares about us, whether we are loved by those we love, whether we belong anywhere; we wonder what we will become, who we are, how much control we have over our own fate. For adolescents these are among the most pressing questions: Who am I? What kind of person will I be? Who will love me? How do others see me? Yet schools spend more time on the quadratic formula than on any of these existential questions.

In reviewing the forms of care, it becomes clear that there is a challenge to care in schools. The structures of current schooling work against care, and at the same time, the need for care is perhaps greater than ever.

THE DEBATE IN ETHICS

No discussion of caring today could be adequate without some attention to the ethic of care. In 1982 Carol Gilligan published her now famous *In a Different Voice*, describing an alternative approach to moral
problems. This approach was identified in the voices of women, but
Gilligan did not claim that the approach is exclusively female, nor
did she claim that all women use it. Still, the avalanche of response
from women who recognized themselves in Gilligan's description is
an impressive phenomenon. "This is me," many women said. "Finally
someone has articulated the way I come at moral problems."

Gilligan described a morality based on the recognition of needs, relation, and response. Women who speak in the different voice refuse to
leave themselves, their loved ones, and connections out of their moral
reasoning. They speak from and to a situation, and their reasoning is
contextual. Those of us who write about an ethic of care have emphasized affective factors, but this is not to say that caring is irrational or
even nonrational. It has its own rationality or reasonableness, and in
appropriate situations carers draw freely on standard linear rationality
as well. But its emphasis is on living together, on creating, maintaining, and enhancing positive relations—not on decision making in moments of high moral conflict, nor on justification.

An ethic of care—a needs- and response-based ethic—challenges
many premises of traditional ethics and moral education. First, there is
the difference of focus already mentioned. There is also a rejection of
universalizability, the notion that anything that is morally justifiable is
necessarily something that anyone else in a similar situation is obligated
to do. Universalizability suggests that who we are, to whom we are related, and how we are situated should have nothing to do with our moral
decision making. An ethic of caring rejects this. Next, although an ethic
of care puts great emphasis on consequences in the sense that it always
asks what happens to the relation, it is not a form of utilitarianism; it does
not posit one greatest good to be optimized, nor does it separate means
and ends. Finally, it is not properly labeled an ethic of virtue. Although it
calls on people to be carers and to develop the virtues and capacities to
care, it does not regard caring solely as an individual attribute. It recognizes the part played by the cared-for. It is an ethic of relation.

In moral education an ethic of care's great emphasis on motivation
challenges the primacy of moral reasoning. We concentrate on developing the attitudes and skills required to sustain caring relations and

the desire to do so, not nearly so much on the reasoning used to arrive at a decision. Lawrence Kohlberg (1981) and his associates, following Plato and Socrates, have focused on moral reasoning. The supposition here is that moral knowledge is sufficient for moral behavior. From this perspective, wrongdoing is always equated with ignorance. Gilligan explicitly challenged Kohlberg's scale or hierarchy of moral reasoning (suggesting a powerful alternative developmental model), but others of us have challenged the whole idea of a developmental model, arguing that moral responses in a given individual may vary contextually at almost any age. (The language used to discuss what one is doing and why may, of course, depend on intellectual development, but moral behavior and its intellectual articulation are not synonymous.)

Moral education from the perspective of an ethic of caring has four major components: modeling, dialogue, practice, and confirmation (Noddings, 1984). Modeling is important in most schemes of moral education, but in caring it is vital. In this framework we are not trying to teach students principles and ways of applying them to problems through chains of mathematical reasoning. Rather, we have to show how to care in our own relations with cared-fors. For example, professors of education and school administrators cannot be sarcastic and dictatorial with teachers in the hope that coercion will make them care for students. I have heard administrators use this excuse for "being tough" with teachers—"because I care about the kids of this state"—but, of course, the likely outcome is that teachers will then turn attention protectively to themselves rather than lovingly to their students. So we do not tell our students to care; we show them how to care by creating caring relations with them.

There is a second reason why modeling is so vital. The capacity to care may be dependent on adequate experience in being cared for. Even while a child is too young to be a carer, he or she can learn how to be a responsive cared-for. Thus our role as carer is more important than our role as model, but we fill both simultaneously. We remind ourselves when we are tempted to take short cuts in moral education that we are, inevitably, models. But otherwise, in our daily activities we simply respond as carers when the need arises. The function of modeling gets special attention when we try to explain what we are doing and why in moral education. But the primary reason for responding as carers to our students' needs is that we are called to such response by our moral orientation.

Dialogue is the second essential component of moral education. My use of the term *dialogue* is similar to that of Paulo Freire (1970). It is not just talk or conversation—certainly not an oral presentation of argument in which the second party is merely allowed to ask an occasional question. Dialogue is open-ended; that is, in a genuine dialogue, neither party knows at the outset what the outcome or decision will be. As parents and teachers, we cannot enter into dialogue with children when we know that our decision is already made. It is maddening to young people (or any people) to engage in "dialogue" with a sweetly reasonable adult who cannot be persuaded and who, in the end, will say, "Here's how it's going to be. I tried to reason with you. . . ." We do have to talk this way at times, but we should not pretend that this is dialogue. Dialogue is a common search for understanding, empathy, or appreciation. It can be playful or serious, logical or imaginative, goal or process oriented, but it is always a genuine quest for something undetermined at the beginning.

Dialogue permits us to talk about what we try to show. It gives learners opportunities to question "why," and it helps both parties to arrive at well-informed decisions. Although I do not believe that all wrongdoing can be equated with ignorance, I do believe that many moral errors are ill-informed decisions, particularly in the very young. Thus dialogue serves not only to inform the decision under consideration; it also contributes to a habit of mind—that of seeking adequate information on which to make decisions.

Dialogue serves another purpose in moral education. It connects us to each other and helps to maintain caring relations. It also provides us with the knowledge of each other that forms a foundation for response in caring. Caring (acting as carer) requires knowledge and skill as well as characteristic attitudes. We respond most effectively as carers when we understand what the other needs and the history of this need. Dialogue is implied in the criterion of engrossment. To receive the other is to attend fully and openly. Continuing dialogue builds up a substantial knowledge of one another that serves to guide our responses.

A third component of moral education is practice. Attitudes and mentalities" are shaped, at least in part, by experience. Most of us speak regularly of a "military mind," a "police mentality," "business thinking," and the like. Although some of this talk is a product of stereotyping, it seems clear that it also captures some truth about human behavior. All disciplines and institutional organizations have training programs designed not only to teach specific skills but also to "shape minds," that is, to induce certain attitudes and ways of looking at the world. If we want people to approach moral life prepared to care, we need to provide opportunities for them to gain skills in caregiving and, more important, to develop the characteristic attitudes described earlier.

Some of the most fascinating work in contemporary feminist theory is devoted to the study of women's experience and its articulation. It seems likely that women's traditional experience is closely related to the moral approach described in ethics of care. Women, more often than men, have been charged with the direct care of young children, the ill, and the aged. They have been expected to maintain a pleasing environment, to look after the needs of others, and to mediate disputes in ordinary social situations. If we regard this experience as inseparable from oppression, then we might agree with Nietzsche that what I am describing is merely "slave mentality." But if we analyze the experience, we find considerable autonomy, love, choice, and consummate skill in the traditional female role. We may evaluate the experience as essential in developing fully human beings.

Women have learned to regard every human encounter as a potential caring occasion. In nursing theory, for example, Jean Watson (1985) defined the moment in which nurse and patient meet as a "caring occasion." It is not just that the nurse will provide care in the form of physical skills to the patient. Rather, it is a moment in which each must decide how to meet the other and what to do with the moment. This is obviously very different from defining a medical encounter as a problem-solving event. Problem solving is involved, of course, but it is preceded by a moment of receptivity—one in which the full humanity of both parties is recognized—and it is followed by a return to the human other in all his or her fullness.

If we decide that the capacity to care is as much a mark of personhood as reason or rationality, then we will want to find ways to increase this capacity. Just as we now think it is important for girls as well as boys to have mathematical experience, so we should want both boys and girls to have experience in caring. It does not just happen; we have to plan for it. As we will see, such planning is complex and loaded with potential pitfalls.

Some schools, recognizing the needs just discussed, have instituted requirements for a form of community service. This is a move in the right direction, but reflection produces some issues to worry about. The practice provided must be with people who can demonstrate caring. We do not want our children to learn the menial (or even sophisticated) skills of caregiving without the characteristic attitude of caring. The experience of caregiving should initiate or contribute to the desired attitude, but the conditions have to be right, and people are central to the setting. This is a major point, to which I will return.

Next, practice in caring should transform schools and, eventually, the society in which we live. If the practice is assimilated to the present structures of schooling, it may lose its transformative powers. *It* may be transformed—that is, distorted. If we were to give grades for care-giving, for example, students might well begin to compete for honors in caring. Clearly, then, their attention could be diverted from cared-fors to themselves. If, on the other hand, we neither grade nor give credit for such work, it may inevitably have second-class status in our schools. So long as our schools are organized hierarchically with em-phasis on rewards and penalties, it will be very difficult to provide the kind of experience envisioned.

The fourth component of moral education from the perspective of caring is confirmation. Martin Buber (1965) described confirmation as an act of affirming and encouraging the best in others. When we confirm someone, we spot a better self and encourage its development. We can do this only if we know the other well enough to see what he or she is trying to become. Formulas and slogans have no place here. We do not set up a single ideal or set of expectations for everyone to meet, but we identify something admirable, or at least acceptable, struggling to emerge in each person we encounter. The person working toward a better self must see the attribute or goal as worthy, and we too must see it as at least morally acceptable. We do not confirm people in ways we judge to be wrong.

Confirmation requires attribution of the best possible motive con-sonant with reality. When someone commits an act we find reprehen-sible, we ask ourselves what might have motivated such an act. Often it is not hard to identify an array of possible motives ranging from the gross and grubby to some that are acceptable or even admirable. This array is not constructed in abstraction. We build it from a knowledge of this particular other and by listening carefully to what she or he tells us. The motive we attribute has to be a real, a genuine possibility. Then we can open our dialogue with something like, "I know you were try-ing to help your friend . . ." or "I know what you're trying to accom-plish." It will be clear that we disapprove of this particular act, but it will also be clear to the other that we see a self that is better than this act. Often the other will respond with enormous relief. *Here is this sig-nificant and percipient other who sees through the smallness or meanness of my present behavior a self that is better and a real possibility.* Confirmation lifts us toward our vision of a better self.

It is worth repeating that confirmation cannot be done by formula. A relation of trust must ground it. Continuity is required, because the carer in acting to confirm must know the cared-for well enough to be able to identify motives consonant with reality. Confirmation cannot be described in terms of strategies; it is a loving act founded on a relation of some depth. When we turn to specific changes that should occur in schooling in order to meet the challenge to care, I will put great emphasis on continuity. Not all caring relations require continuity (some, as we have seen, are brief encounters), but teaching does require it.

Confirmation contrasts sharply with the standard mode of religious moral education. There we usually find a sequence of accusation, confession, penance, and forgiveness. The initial step, accusation, causes or sustains separation. We stand in moral judgment and separate the other from ourselves and the moral community. In contrast, confirmation calls us to remain in connection. Further, accusation tends to produce denial or rationalization, which we then feel compelled to overthrow. But the rationalization may in fact be an attempt on the part of the accused to find that possible motive and convey it to us, the accuser. Because we have to reject it in order to proceed with confession, penance, and forgiveness, offenders may never understand their own true motives. This sequence also depends heavily on authority, obedience, fear, and subordination. We can be harsh or magnanimous in our judgment and forgiveness. Our authority is emphasized, and the potential power of the offender's own moral struggle is overlooked.

I do not mean to suggest that there is never a place for accusation and confession in moral education. It is not always possible for us to find a motive that is morally acceptable; sometimes we have to begin by asking straight out, "Why did you do that?" or "How could you do such a thing?" But it is gratifying how often we really can see a better self if we look for one, and its identification is a first step in its realization.

This whole way of looking at ethics and moral education challenges not only parts of the religious tradition but also the ideas of Freud and like-minded theorists. Freud believed that our sense of morality develops out of fear. The superego, Freud said, is an internalization of authority—of the father's voice—and its establishment results from resolution of the oedipal conflict. Sons fear castration by the father if they disobey or compete with him. Resolution of this desire to rebel and compete involves acceptance of the father's power and authority, and the superego (Freud's guide to acceptable behavior) takes up residence within the son. This account of moral development led Freud to conclude that women must be morally inferior to men. Because girls need not fear castration (having been born in that dread condition), their moral voice never attains the strength and dependability of men's.

Recent criticisms of Freud suggest that more attention should be given to the preoedipal period. Nancy Chodorow (1978) has theorized that girls and boys develop different psychological deep structures because females are almost exclusively the primary caregivers for both. Girls can find their gender identity without separating from their mother and, hence, develop a relational personality structure and perhaps even a relational epistemology or way of knowing (Keller, 1985). Boys, however, must construct their gender identity in opposition to all that is female. Here we have the possible roots of the different moral voices described by Gilligan. We will consider other alternatives as well.

Eli Sagan (1988) has also suggested that moral development begins and is strongly affected by preoedipal life. Without rejecting the Freudian framework entirely, Sagan recommends a shift in emphasis. If we give due weight to early childhood, we see that conscience (a sense of right and wrong, not mere internalization of authority) develops as much out of love and attachment as out of fear. Further, the primary fear is not of harm and punishment but, rather, of disappointing a loved parent and, at worst, losing that parent's love. This is a major challenge to masculinist psychology and a suggestion compatible with an ethic of caring and the model of moral education outlined here. Love, caring, and relation play central roles in both ethics and moral education.

I want to suggest that caring is the very bedrock of all successful education and that contemporary schooling can be revitalized in its light. Before describing a broad plan to make caring central in education, I need to explain why the current ideal is inadequate. Liberal education has been the Western ideal for centuries. Even when it is poorly funded in comparison with technical and professional education, it is still the ideal that puts pressure on precollegiate education. It is the form of education—done well or poorly—that most of us experienced. What is wrong with it, and why should it be rejected as a model of universal education?

CHAPTER 3

Beyond the Disciplines:
A Critique of
Liberal Education

Criticizing liberal education within academe is like criticizing motherhood in a maternity ward. Surrounded by the fruits and joys of dedicated labor, one is hesitant to say that something is wrong with the enterprise. Yet, it is not an ideal for everyone. And I will argue that liberal education is a false ideal for universal education.

"Liberal education" describes a set of disciplines designed for general education rather than specific occupations or professions. It usually includes language, literature, fine arts, mathematics, science, and history (or sometimes, more broadly, social studies, but this substitution is controversial). At the college level, it has long been considered the proper education for gentlemen and, more recently, gentlewomen. At the precollege level, where our attention will be concentrated, it comprises the usually prescribed courses for college preparation.

First, I will argue that liberal education is an inappropriate ideal for general education because it draws on only a narrow set of human capacities; hence, prescribing it for all students ensures inequality of outcomes. Second, I will argue that current political rationales for a single-track, liberal arts curriculum are misguided, and that in any case, educational programs need *educational* rationales as well as political ones. Third, I will suggest that the content of liberal studies is not the content that all children need. I will argue that content suggested by my earlier discussion of caring is far more appropriate. Finally, I will look at popular arguments against tracking and show that they suffer from difficulties similar to those raised by rationales for universal liberal education.

Perhaps the best way to proceed is to look carefully at one set of recommendations for universal liberal education. In *The Paideia Proposal* (1982), Mortimer Adler argues that true democracy demands equal education for all children. He says that universal suffrage and universal schooling are "inextricably bound together" (p. 3), and he concludes that unequal education is incompatible with the premises and practices of democracy. Few of us would argue against Adler if he meant that all children—regardless of race, gender, economic status, or ethnicity—should have access to whatever forms of education are available. Most of us would also agree that access involves more than a formal legal right to education; it involves decent schools, adequate coaching, encouragement, and advice.

But Adler construes equal to mean identical. All children, he says, should have exactly the same education at least through high school, and the subject matter of that education should be the standard liberal arts curriculum: language, literature, and fine arts; mathematics and natural science; history, geography, and social studies. All children can learn, Mr. Adler insists. "There are no unteachable children," he says. "There are only schools and teachers and parents who fail to teach them" (p. 8). This is the kind of platitudinous statement I criticized earlier; it inevitably generates enthusiastic applause from unreflective audiences.

To say that there are no unteachable children is trivial until one fills out the statement with what is to be taught to them and at what cost. Of course most children can learn many things. But, as an old math teacher, I am convinced that no matter how fine the teaching, there will be considerable differences between what is achieved in, say, geometry by students most and least interested in mathematics. I suspect also that there are some, perhaps many, who will never understand the logic of mathematical proof or the power and generality of its greatest products. These students should have educational opportunities that credit and enhance their talents, and they should not be regarded as inferior to the mathematically talented. After all, there are also many people who will never understand the techniques of impressionist painting, the structure of a musical fugue, or the fine points of theology.

I do not judge people's worth by their mathematical talent, nor do I believe that mathematics through calculus is somehow necessary for good citizenship. Lots of very nice people, even very good citizens, find mathematics difficult and unpleasant. Why should all students, regardless of their aptitude, interest, or plans for the future, struggle through algebra and geometry? I am reminded here of a wonderful quote from Fran Lebowitz: "Stand firm in your refusal to remain conscious during algebra. In real life, I assure you, there is no such thing as algebra." For the real lives of many people, this is undoubtedly true.

There may yet be some form or body of mathematics that all children should know, but let's put that important question aside for now and return to it later. Surely academic mathematics is not essential for everyone—not even for all college-bound students.

There is another sense in which Adler's generous "all children can learn" is naive and dangerous. Some 375,000 babies annually are born addicted to drugs. It costs $40,000 or so just to prepare a drug baby for kindergarten, and at present 40% or more of children born to drug addicts drop out of school. To suppose that a standard liberal arts education is an appropriate objective for these children is ridiculous. I want to be very careful here. I am not saying that we should decide before individual assessment that all drug babies are incapable of learning mathematics and literature. Some may want and be beautifully capable of such learning. But liberal education is not at the top of the list of what these children need. First, they will need a school environment that teaches them how to accept care and, later, to give it. Second, they will need a curriculum tailored to their individual capacities and interests, one that will provide assurance that there are many respectable and satisfying ways of life. They will need opportunities to succeed at something deemed worthwhile by the people who teach and care for them. These requirements are important for all children, and I am arguing that it is high time we stopped regarding liberal education as the highest form of education, next to which all others seem inferior. We waste both public resources and individual talents when we insist on liberal education for all.

Adler draws his recommendations from Robert Maynard Hutchins's well-known aphorism, "The best education for the best is the best education for all." There are three "bests" to analyze here, and all three invite important objections. So far I've addressed my complaints to the proposition that liberal education is the best education for all. More generally, we can ask whether any one curriculum is or can be the "best education for all."

If we knew and could categorize the full range of human capacities, perhaps we could devise a curriculum that gives reasonable attention to each capacity. Then we could assure parents that their children would all be exposed to, and, we hope, come to value each human capacity, and that they would also be helped to find and develop the one (or more) in which they show special talent. Harvard professor Howard Gardner (1982, 1983) has advanced a theory of multiple intelligences that identifies seven "intelligences" rather than the one or two traditionally recognized in schools. Even this theory, although exciting in its recognition of multiple abilities, raises concerns: Are there exactly seven human capacities? Should schooling be organized around capacities or around something else, such as human problems? Are the capacities equally valued? Should they be?

The capacities that have traditionally been most highly valued in schools are linguistic and logical-mathematical. These are the capacities recognized and drawn upon in the liberal arts curriculum. If these two lie at the heart of liberal education, then students who are best endowed with these capacities and most interested in developing them will succeed and, predictably, students with other capacities will feel inferior, rejected, out of place, bored, and perhaps hostile. Forcing all students through a curriculum designed for the capacities of a few cannot be done in the service of equality. Suppose, in a hypothetical family, we had seven children all equal in status at the outset. By this I mean that each excels in one of Gardner's seven intelligences, and our society values all capacities equally. Now we force all seven to take a curriculum that concentrates on just two of the seven capacities. Surely the results will be unequal, and such a practice would be deemed unfair. But the same could be said if we organized a curriculum around seven capacities and there turned out to be ten or fourteen or twenty. At any rate, it is clear that an education that values and builds upon only a small part of human capacity cannot be the best education for all.

Colleagues who are neo-Marxists or critical theorists might admonish me here, arguing that I have not attended to the political aspects of the issue. Liberal education is the form of education that has been associated historically with the "best." Whether the people who received this education have been in fact the best with respect to any cognitive capacities may be questioned. More likely, they have simply come from families who could afford to give them this kind of education. But as a result of its association with power and privilege, liberal education has become a form of privileged knowledge, reserved for the "best," however that term might be defined. When we look at things this way, they argue, we can see that Adler has a point. Why shouldn't all children have access to privileged knowledge? Especially if it turns out that the talk about capacities is much overrated, why should not all children have the opportunities, the guidance, the forced discipline, and the resources hitherto reserved for the well-to-do?

My response to these sensible and cogent questions has three parts. First, I am not convinced that liberal education as it has been traditionally defined is the best education for anyone, although a modified form may be adequate for those whose talents are primarily linguistic and/or mathematical. I will say much more about possible modifica-

tion in later chapters. If it is not an appropriate model for mass education, or even for elite education, it seems wrong to foist it on students
for political reasons. Educational proposals should have educational
rationales, not just political ones.

Second, if the power structure is as strong as my colleagues suggest,
trying to give all children access to privileged knowledge probably won't
work. There is a charming story by Dr. Seuss that provides a parallel. In
a society of beings called sneetches, there were plain and star-bellied
sneetches. The star-bellied sneetches were the "best" and dominated
the plain-bellied folks. Recognizing the injustice of the situation, the oppressed sneetches decided to paint stars on their own bellies. Now there
was equality! But not for long. The original star-bellied sneetches had
their stars painfully removed and claimed, of course, that plain bellies
were now marks of superiority. Power structures do not crumble easily.

Forms of privilege in schooling also change. Not long ago Susan
Hanson (1985) studied two high schools from a neo-Marxist perspective. She concentrated on honors programs in a wealthy school and in
an inner city school. She expected to find, in agreement with much educational literature, that the wealthier kids would be engaged in more
inquiry, granted more responsibility, treated with greater respect, and
in general involved in more genuinely intellectual activities. Her expectations were not entirely met. Teachers in the poorer school, operating
within a once prestigious model of education, were in fact demanding
much higher levels of thinking and responsibility than the teachers in
the wealthy school. The paradigm of privileged knowledge had shifted.
The knowledge now valued in the wealthy school was cut-and-dried
material to get students into college: lots of tests, lots of memorizing,
great emphasis on conformity, little time devoted to "meaning," and
plenty of homework for discipline. From an educational perspective,
the program at the poor school was in several ways better, except that
the kids were not doing well with it, and their teachers were frustrated.
Privileged knowledge is not necessarily the educationally "best" knowledge—something that can be, theoretically at least, distributed to everyone. It is privileged because privileged people claim it as their own.

But, critics might respond, the core of knowledge was still defined
by the accepted disciplines. The privileged mode of delivery might
change, emphasis might change, but the subjects remain. We still need,
I insist, an *educational* argument for requiring all students to take the
privileged subjects. As Elizabeth Ellsworth (1989) has pointed out, critical theorists—who want to democratize learning by providing equal

access to privileged knowledge—make the mistake of assuming that they know what the end point of dialogue should be. They claim to know in what direction consciousness should be raised. True dialogue is open to the possibility that people will find their own directions and reasons for choosing them.

Third, trying to find ways to give all children privileged knowledge obscures deeper normative questions. We fail to ask why this particular form of knowledge *should* be important. This is a point on which several feminist educators have spoken eloquently. Jane Roland Martin (1984, 1985), for example, has suggested that the ideal of the educated man (as described in liberal education) must be radically revised to include concepts, skills, attitudes, and capacities valued by and traditionally associated with women. Madeleine Grumet (1988) has charged critical theorists and neo-Marxists with sustaining "the very terms and prejudices of the system they were attempting to criticize" (p. xiv). An increasing number of feminists point out the folly of trying to redistribute either monetary or cultural wealth without addressing the basically evil value structure that undergirds structures of domination.

If we rewrite Hutchins' aphorism more honestly, it might read, "The education traditionally given to the most privileged is the best education for all." Stated this way, many of the questions I have raised follow directly. We see that the recommendation cannot be offered seriously because a successful effort would undermine the very privilege this form of education is designed to maintain.

Consider for a moment that all-important question: What would happen if we succeeded? If all people satisfactorily completed the program described in *The Paideia Proposal*, what expectations would they have for their occupational lives? Traditionally, people with this kind of preparation would go on to college and, eventually, to white collar jobs or professions. Would everyone want to do this?

I am not going to argue that we should restrict access to the liberal arts so that our society will be sure to have enough waiters, plumbers, sanitation workers, and hotel maids. My argument is quite different. Under Adler's plan, those jobs would either be filled by those who do least well in the standard curriculum, or much of the nontechnical blue collar work would have to be shared by a society of intellectuals. The latter seems highly unlikely—an unworkable utopian dream. The former seems highly probable, and the objection is that people would land in jobs—as many do now—by default. Nowhere in the standard curriculum would they have opportunities to develop and demonstrate their own strengths and, thereby, to choose a suitable occupation. Nor is it recognized that success comes in many forms and calls on many capacities.

A whole host of respectable jobs are ignored in such an educational scheme. Mr. Adler might respond, of course, that *all* jobs are ignored under his plan. The education envisioned is entirely nonvocational—preparation for citizenship and further learning, not for specific occupations of any kind. But this is, at best, a half-truth. Although liberal education is not preparation for a particular occupation, it is preparation for a class of occupations, and liberal education at the precollegiate level is preparation for college. Hence my claim is that large numbers of children would have neither the technical skills nor an appreciation for the kind of work in which they will eventually engage. On the contrary, they might very well learn contempt for people who work with their hands and contempt for themselves as well.

The test I have suggested, namely, What would happen if we succeed? is one that should be applied to every educational scheme offered. The suggestions I will make concentrate on producing people who have an adequate understanding and respect for themselves, intimate others, distant others, the living environment, and the world of objects and instruments. Their educations should be similar in some respects but very different in others. Some will, for example, develop more fully capacities that emphasize bodily or mechanical skills; others will concentrate more—but not solely—on the world of ideas. The work of the next chapters is to describe such an education, building on the concepts of caring outlined in chapter 2.

But perhaps I have missed something important about liberal education. Perhaps it should not be rejected because it develops only two capacities out of many. What about the content? Does not the traditional content contain much that all people in this culture should know? This is a more familiar argument for liberal education. Let's consider.

If we eavesdrop on a group of art educators, we are likely to hear them deploring the state of ignorance that most people exhibit with respect to art. I heard an argument not long ago that supported the study of mythology because it is necessary to an understanding of much painting. How could people understand what is depicted, the educators asked, if they were not familiar with the relevant myths? How, for example, could viewers appreciate or understand Thivet's or Strathmann's "Danaë" if they did not know the myth of Danaë and Zeus? These educators went on to suggest strongly that people without this knowledge were not really educated. Odd, I thought. Several people I know well and whom I had always thought of as well educated are not so well educated after all. With impressive technical knowledge, these poor folks had never acquired an interest in either classical mythology or painting. Yet they are not uncultured. Some love symphonic music. One studies Middle Eastern textiles. Several read high-grade science fiction. And, of course, I could go on.

Now visit for a while with math educators. Here you are likely to hear an explicit explosion of the following kind: It is *deplorable* that the average high school graduate does not know what a function is! This passionate statement will be augmented by an outpouring of complaints: I have college juniors who do not know the difference between a definite and an indefinite integral! (This is triggered by the comment on functions in a way I need not explain to the mathematically well educated.) Such a group can go on happily for hours, listing the mathematical shortcomings and ignorance of students and the general populace. I know. I've participated in such conversations.

We could continue our quiet visits to groups of historians, literature teachers, grammarians, classicists, geographers, biologists, music teachers, and a handful of favored others. We would hear the same story over and over again. A person is not well educated if he or she is not familiar with the central ideas of art, or literature, or mathematics, or whatever. But, in point of fact, many people who are widely recognized as well educated exhibit the lacks so deplored by specific groups. One can play this game just so long before stumbling on one's own ignorance.

You may grant me a point here but, properly, push me a bit. Suppose a high school graduate cannot do a multistep math problem that involves only the simplest algebra or no algebra at all? It seems that only about 6% of seventeen-year-olds can do problems of the following kind: John borrowed $900 for one year from a finance company. At 12% simple interest, what amount did John have to repay at the end of the year? Or suppose a high school graduate thinks she needs a passport to travel to New Mexico? Or that the Civil War occurred in the sixteenth century? Am I not alarmed by ignorance such as this?

I confess that I am distressed by such revelations of ignorance. But what distresses me most is that *schools are teaching these things* now and students still do not know them. It is not the case that traditional information and skills are absent from the curriculum. They are not attended to or mastered by students who cannot get past the complaint, "They don't care!" Many students cannot find a reason to bother with standard subject matter. With sufficient attention to their own felt needs and interests, most students would pick up items of general culture just as many children do in family life.

On a recent lecture tour, I had dinner with several delightful academic colleagues. One, an English professor, mused with some dismay on a major difference between the attitudes of his current students and his own as a young student at Columbia. He said something like this: I always assumed that whatever my teachers assigned was worth doing. I never questioned why or whether the stuff had relevance. I was a country boy, thrilled to be at a great university, and I believed my professors.

This is a touching and revealing story. He not only believed his professors but he believed *in* them. What they tried to teach had validity *a priori*. I suspect that this attitude of belief and trust started even earlier, in his relations with precollege teachers in his rural community. Probably his rural teachers were no better than mine academically, but they encouraged him and led him to believe that pleasing his teachers was somehow bound up in the good life he hoped to attain.

Students will do things for people they like and trust. This is a fact that we must acknowledge. There is a worrisome side to it. Kids will do dreadful things as well as beautiful ones for leaders they trust; they will do trivial and menial things as well as significant things. And to make matters more complex, they will not *always* meekly follow those they trust; sometimes they rebel. Further, they often transfer love and trust thoughtlessly. Thus there are untrustworthy forms of "love" and even of "trust."

Despite all this complexity, there is a vital nucleus of educational meaning here. Kids learn in communion. They listen to people who matter to them and to whom they matter. The patterns of ignorance we deplore today are signs that kids and adults are not talking to each other about everyday life and the cultural forms once widely shared. How can it be that kids who watch television every night do not know where El Salvador or the Philippines or Israel is? The people telling the news do not matter, and if there is not a caring parent to comment on the news, then none of it matters.

So, at bottom, subject matter cannot carry itself. Relation, except in very rare cases, precedes any engagement with subject matter. Caring relations can prepare children for an initial receptivity to all sorts of experiences and subject matters. Unfortunately, merely contractual relations can keep them busy for a long time at work for which they have no real talent or interest. Many middle- and upper-class kids have plodded wearily through the standard curriculum to please parents or to reap the rewards promised. These are the positive and negative powers of relation. A faithfully caring relation allows children to select and affirm their own interests after initial exposure. It lays heavy responsibilities on carers to manage the trust placed in them wisely. We have to know when to push a little and when to draw back. In many children's lives, however, human relations are simply irrelevant to the knowledge we profess to value. There is no connection at all.

From the preceding discussion, one can see that I mean to leave open the question whether there is some knowledge that all people must have and even whether there is some knowledge that is desirable, if not necessary, for all. The main argument of this chapter centers on the inadequacy of the traditional subject matters (the material long associated with a liberal education) as an ideal for education. Most of what we teach in the precollege liberal arts curriculum is not necessary for everyday life, and much of what is necessary never appears in that curriculum. Further, if we could agree on what is necessary, we could find far more effective ways to teach it.

The preceding discussion underscores another point about liberal education. Its perpetuation has depended on a certain kind of social relations. It has long been associated, as Hutchins' aphorism reveals, with the "best." Young men of well-to-do families were brought up to believe that such an education was the mark of a gentleman. It was never shown, nor can it be shown, that acquaintance with the standard disciplines is necessary for everyday life. Indeed, apologists have rejected such a criterion as wrongheaded. But it has been necessary for membership in a particular class. For this reason, liberal education was long withheld from women, and when women were at last allowed access to liberal education, elaborate arguments were concocted to show that such an education was desirable for wives and mothers—not for women as potential professionals or as self-actualized individuals.

It is understandable that people from oppressed minorities would clamor for access to liberal education, and that many people from these groups would welcome Adler's plan for one curriculum and, presumably, free access for all. They suppose that such an education is either necessary and desirable in itself (that it will unlock the secrets of happy life) or that it will admit them to a more privileged social and political status. The latter has been just true enough—true for a few individuals—that the myth has been sustained.

But the promise—or threat—today is that everyone should have such an education. As I remarked earlier in my criticism of neo-Marxist positions, what is valued or privileged knowledge is likely to change more easily than the power relations that establish what is privilege. I think Adler and his academic supporters may know this. Deep down, I think they know that whatever surface changes in access are made, the winners and losers will be predictable. The race is fixed. This is what must be changed.

Something else is happening as a result of the push to standardize the curriculum. Since it threatens to be no longer the mark of a particular class, more students than ever are questioning its value. In colleges there is a rising demand for courses in non-Western culture, black and women's studies, action research, and other topics of relevance. Understandably, advocates of liberal education feel their precarious hold on prestige slipping. One can sympathize with their fears: If we are no longer the gateway to privilege, we (some of us) can accept that. It is certainly more just that all people share in the treasury of knowledge. But if that's *all* it is—just a hoard of false gold, just a passport to privilege —what does this mean for my life? for my vocation? What it should mean, of course, is just what the choice of any occupation should mean: Here is work I love (or at least do not hate), work in which I feel respected, in which I am competent—work which some find useful, for which I am paid enough that fear for subsistence does not cloud my professional and personal life. This much should be said of any chosen occupation. If it also adds to my spiritual and emotional life, if it somehow serves to integrate my life and make me more nearly whole, then I am fortunate indeed. But to achieve and accept such blessings, I do not have to claim that all people will be similarly blessed by touching the hem of my garment or struggling with the elements of my beloved discipline.

Many of my colleagues might brush aside my arguments as moot, given today's university climate. They could describe quite accurately the lack of prestige in the humanities. What is all this talk about power and prestige and their relation to liberal education? Look for yourself! Professional schools and departments get the money—medicine, law, engineering, business. That's where the power is! We humanities people suffer what was once known as genteel poverty, and it has been that way for fifty years or more.

There is more than a grain of truth in this description. Many of us are moved to take up the cause of liberal studies because we fear the political power of experts, the domination of economic values, and the plain grubbiness of rampant self-aggrandizement. Then we become all warm and sympathetic to the humanities. Surely we want our engineers to be well-rounded human beings; a bit of literature and philosophy will smooth their rough edges. Surely we want business majors to have a social conscience; a bit of history and ethics might enlighten them. And so on. Liberal arts are prescribed to balance, to make whole.

Although the monetary strength and direct power of humanities departments are indeed weak, these departments nevertheless play a vital role in the politics of knowledge. Their willingness to provide courses for students in areas of professional specialization and preparation frees other schools and departments to pursue their own narrow interests with little direct attention to the intellectual breadth of their students or to their emotional or moral development. All capacities, interests, and tasks are neatly compartmentalized, and university personnel are especially respectful of expertise. We defer graciously to each other and bend over backwards so as not to trespass on each other's territories.

The worship of expertise goes too far, and liberal education paradoxically supports such worship. Often we back away from giving advice on matters that any intelligent, morally sensitive person should be willing to address. Deference becomes a cop-out, and the phenomenon is familiar at every level of human affairs from the White House to the schoolhouse. Recently a former undersecretary of state described for me a typical scenario in advising the president: Advisors back off, saying, That's a matter for the economists, or That's something to ask psychologists about, or. . . . As a result, the president is awash in information but impoverished in the kind of advice that requires sound moral judgment—the sort of judgment that any thoughtful, responsible adult should be able to contribute. We have no council of elders, educated for wisdom; we have only experts and managers.

At the public school level, teachers are often unwilling even to talk with their students about moral matters. I have heard teachers say, We're not trained for that. That's a job for psychologists (or counselors, or parents, or pastors). Pressed, many will protest that they do not have a right to impose their values on students, but these same teachers enforce all sorts of rules—sensible and mindless equally—without questioning the values thus imposed. Surely intelligent adults can and should talk to the children in their care about honesty, compassion, open-mindedness, nonviolence, consideration, moderation, and a host of other qualities that most of us admire. This talk need not be indoctrination any more than mathematics teaching need be lecture and rote learning.

Often the argument is made that it is the special function of certain of the liberal arts, say, literature and history, to address the "eternal verities" without indulging in moral instruction, therapy, or some other direct intervention in the beliefs and personal lives of students. That anything of the sort happens at the precollegiate level is doubtful. At colleges and universities, the paradoxically low status of the humanities and their separation from professional studies precludes effects much beyond the accidental.

But for all the hypocrisy revealed in the monetary priorities of universities, one important process still upholds the actual power of liberal studies. They are still thought to be the prerequisites of college or university study. They are the courses that students must present to be admitted, and there are no signs that this demand is weakening. On the contrary, the demand is growing, and the insistence on one-track precollegiate education is part of it. Children are led to believe that only one form of education is valuable and that only one set of occupations is worth aiming at.

For reasons similar to those advanced for universal liberal education, the educational tide has turned against tracking. The practice of assigning some high school students to college preparatory tracks and others to the commercial, industrial, or general is under severe attack all over the country. An argument against tracking is not necessarily an argument *for* a liberal arts curriculum as Adler has described it. Mainly, it is an argument against unequal treatment that includes differences in pedagogy, counseling, school privileges, and all the rest of school life. Whatever subject matter students encounter in nonprivileged tracks is treated poorly. Students are not asked to think deeply to communicate effectively, or to participate fully in the cultural life of the community. If we had to choose between leaving things as they are or putting everyone on the same track, I, too, would probably have to choose the latter.

I say "probably" because which is the greater evil is hard to judge. Many schools have eliminated commercial and industrial tracks and broadened their academic offerings for students who would not have chosen college preparatory courses in the past. In mathematics, for example, we now have tracks within standard courses. Some students take real algebra courses, and others take minimal courses that hardly deserve the name. Although both courses can be offered for college admission, students from the minimal course are not at all prepared for college mathematics. Not only is the equality so achieved a sham, but the loss of something worthwhile compounds the fraud. These students could be studying something in which they are interested and for which they have some talent. They might excel at something. But the school recognizes only what the "best" are doing as important.

Therefore equality comes to mean participation in whatever that is, even if it is participation in name only.

Fortunately, we do not have to decide between leaving things as they are and putting everyone into the "same" courses. John Dewey argued long ago that it is not the particular subject studied that is important but *how* it is studied. Cooking can be studied seriously and in such a way that the student's capacities are finely developed; so can mathematics. But both can be studied frivolously so that capacities are dulled and interests lost. In the next chapter, I will describe some possibilities for various curricula that differ greatly from standard offerings

Oddly, to argue for tracking today is to risk being branded a racist or an elitist. But my argument proceeds from the assumption that there is nothing sacred about the standard liberal arts curriculum. Educationally, it is not demonstrably better to study literature of a particular kind, mathematics of a particular kind, history of a particular kind, and so forth, than to study woodworking, drafting, science fiction, and photography. The arguments against tracking are political and economic, not educational.

Educational concerns today focus on groups instead of individual students. We are concerned, and properly, that a disproportionate number of black and Hispanic children are placed in lower tracks. The dramatic unfairness of this situation obscures our vision as we look for a solution. We strive to place everyone in higher tracks instead of attacking the hierarchy. Suppose, for example, that regardless of what students were studying, they were regularly invited and expected to attend plays, symphonies, lectures, museum programs, and other cultural events. Suppose they were assigned to discussion groups at mealtime, during which some adult from the community would chat with them, help them to acquire or practice the standard ways of behaving, and inform them about a variety of occupations. Suppose that fine occupational models were to accept some students as apprentices and to talk with other students about their options in life. Studying noncollege topics does not have to doom anyone to an inferior occupation or underdeveloped mind. Such results are artifacts of a false hierarchy, not the inevitable outcome of a course of study. To be sure that all groups of children receive a high-quality education means, first, that the needs and talents of individual children are considered in educational planning and, second, that no children are excluded from a form of schooling from which they might profit.

Many thoughtful planners shrink from the notion of "multiple models" of excellence because they believe the schools are already asked to accomplish too much. John Gardner, for example, in his influential *Excellence* (1971), lauded excellence in all its forms at the societal level, but he charged the school with the task of promoting only academic excellence. It seems entirely right in a society such as ours to value "excellent plumbers above mediocre philosophers," but must we not also value the budding plumber? Gardner argued that the schools cannot do everything and that they are best organized to achieve *academic* excellence. This is in itself questionable, but the weakest part of his argument was revealed when he admitted that some youngsters (probably many) would not do well in a program so oriented. They would have to understand, he said, that the failure they had experienced in school was only *one form* of failure, and that they might still achieve excellence in other enterprises. But I ask you this: How is a youngster who has been at the bottom of the heap for twelve years going to understand that his or her failure so far is only "one form" of failure? Surely, if we value plumbing, and farming, and dancing, and writing, and repairing electronic devices at the societal level, we can find ways of valuing the talents that lead to these occupations during the school years. We really *have* to do this if our talk of equality is to be anything more than *mere* talk.

To be reasonable, however, we do have to consider Gardner's concern that demands on the schools have so proliferated that they cannot achieve any sort of excellence. I suggest that it is not the demands of subjects and activities that overburden our schools but, rather, demands to solve the problems of a society unwilling to bear its burdens where they should properly be shouldered. A society unwilling to rid itself of racial prejudice asks the *schools* to achieve desegregation. A society unwilling to talk with its children about love, delight, and commitment asks the *schools* to teach sex education. A society unwilling to recognize the forms of excellence that Mr. Gardner identifies asks the *schools* to teach everyone algebra. The greatest burden of the schools, as a result, is trying to find some way to teach adequately intelligent students things that they do not want to learn.

To provide an equal quality of education for all our children does not require identical education for all. On the contrary, I've argued, to provide identical education is to ensure inequality. This does not mean that schools should provide no common learnings. We will begin to explore the possibilities for common learning in the next chapter. Reading, writing, and arithmetic come readily to mind and are entrenched in our popular vision of schooling. But it seems equally reasonable to suggest that schools teach all children how to care in the domains I have already outlined.

In concluding this chapter, I want to say straight-out that liberal education as it is now defined is not the best education for anyone. First, it puts too much emphasis on a narrow form of rationality and abstract reasoning as the hallmarks of fully human life. It neglects feeling, concrete thinking, practical activity, and even moral action (concentrating instead on moral reasoning). Although I, too, put a high value on reasoning, I want to include all the other aspects of human life. Second, this overemphasis on the life of the mind leads successful students to believe that they are truly superior to those living more physical lives. A balanced curriculum would help all students to find their special talents and also to develop a healthy respect for talents they do not themselves possess. Third, the traditional liberal arts curriculum is largely a celebration of male life; activities, attitudes, and values historically associated with women are neglected or omitted entirely. Hence its perpetuation tends to reproduce a society in which one sex cares for and emotionally supports the other—which, by definition, does what matters in the culture. This objection to liberal education is significant enough in itself to warrant rethinking the whole enterprise.

Before turning to the task of rethinking the goals, content, and processes of education, I want to underscore my point that the standard liberal arts curriculum as it exists in secondary schools is not the best education for anyone. In *Savage Inequalities* (1991), Jonathan Kozol describes the enormous contrasts between rich schools and poor schools. Poor children lack safe and decent school facilities, encounter watered-down curricula, and receive inadequate instruction. To give poor children something close to what wealthier children receive, well-to-do Americans would have to be willing to share their resources, perhaps even sacrifice a bit. Apparently, they are unwilling to do so. Neither prudential nor ethical arguments move most affluent citizens. This state of affairs suggests strongly that there is something radically wrong with the education that produced these citizens. Both wealthy and poor experience a morally deficient schooling. Is there an alternative?

CHAPTER 4

An Alternative Vision

Suppose education had been planned and school systems constructed by people whose interests and responsibilities focused on the direct care of children, the elderly, ill, disabled, and otherwise dependent. Suppose education was planned by people primarily concerned with the kinds of relations we should establish. For the most part, these people have been women—and much that I recommend can be associated with a feminist perspective—but men, too, often initiate and share in an alternative vision.

In *The School and Society* (1902), John Dewey wrote: "What the best and wisest parent wants for his own child, that must the community want for all its children. Any other ideal for our schools is narrow and unlovely; acted upon, it destroys our democracy" (p. 3). But Dewey disagreed with Robert Hutchins and Mortimer Adler on what the best and wisest parents should want for their children. He did not advocate the same education for all children. In his opinion, the best and wisest parents would want for each of their children an education that matched his or her needs, capacities, and interests.

Although he actively opposed the notion that liberal education in the Hutchins/Adler style was the best education for all, he also opposed the kind of differentiated schooling based on societal needs and children's "occupational destinies." This sort of teaching, advocated by such influential thinkers as Charles Eliot of Harvard (see Preskill, 1989), had little to do with children's capacities and genuine interests; on the contrary, it represented an attempt to protect the academic education of elites who might be held back by the intellectual incapacities of those "destined" for labor. Dewey nevertheless admired Plato's educational scheme in which children were to be educated according to their talents and demonstrated interests. However, he noted that Plato had erred in supposing there were only three categories of useful and admirable qualities. Dewey clearly favored forms of education that could be tailored to the child, and he recognized a multiplicity of human capacities.

This chapter invites the reader into a thought experiment. Suppose we were raising a very large family of heterogeneous children with different biological parents, of mixed races, and widely different talents. How would we want them to turn out? What kind of education would we want for them? There is a troublesome difficulty in undertaking this thought experiment. Although all parents of good will can consider how they might educate children with different talents, they will necessarily approach the experiment from various cultural perspectives. They will be concerned not only with "intelligences" as Gardner has described them, but also with knowledge and attitudes held to be important by the groups with whom they are affiliated. Strictly speaking, there is no "we" to represent in this writing. What I want for our heterogeneous family may be different from what you want. As I explore these two questions, then, I must keep in mind that a practical translation of what I say must depend on dialogue. The question, "What kind of education would I want for them?" must be supplemented by the question, "What kind of education would you want for them?"

Many of us would respond first that we want our children to be happy, but having said that, we need to say what we mean by happy. Do we wish for them untroubled lives of hedonistic leisure? Probably not. We hope that our children will escape severe illness and harm, that they will exhibit and develop admirable talents, and that they will be decent, loving people who will receive love and appreciation in family, professional, and community life. Each of these values or hopes is complex and invites extended exploration.

Sara Ruddick (1980) has analyzed the demands children make on mothers and the corresponding maternal interests that arise. (For Ruddick, persons of either sex who do the daily work of attentive love are *mothers*. This work involves direct physical and psychological care, and historically it has been women's work—hence the emphasis on *mothers*. When I use "parental" instead of "maternal," it is with the understanding that a *parent* of either sex will do the work of attentive love.) Ruddick suggests that mothers want to preserve the lives of their children, foster their growth, and shape them according to some ideal of acceptability. Again, each of these basic interests needs analysis. Is one interest more important than the others? At first glance, it would seem that preserving the child's life has to be most important. One can, of course, only foster the growth of a living child. But the interests in preservation and growth may come into conflict. We may have to allow or even encourage our children to take some risks if they are to grow. At the extreme, some mothers have found it preferable for their sons to die in war rather than be branded cowards or traitors. Thus parental interests take on different priorities at different times, and reasonable people differ on what they mean by growth and acceptability.

We have started on a tough task here. Perhaps we can find a way to organize our thoughts. Since no one scheme seems adequate for such a complex analysis, let me suggest several. First, let's use—tentatively and heuristically—Gardner's (1983) seven intelligences as a scheme for discussing capacities; there may not be exactly seven intelligences, but this scheme will help us in guiding the *growth* of our children. Gardner lists logical-mathematical, linguistic, musical, spatial, bodily-kinesthetic, interpersonal, and intrapersonal intelligences. Keeping this set in mind should help us in considering what to emphasize in each child's education and how to prepare each for a desirable vocation, but let us keep the set open. As we establish programs designed for the various capacities, someone may identify a new capacity, and we may want to incorporate it in our planning.

There are at least two ways in which this scheme can be helpful: Different programs—especially at the secondary level (7–12)—can be planned for children with different capacities; subjects that all children must learn—for example, reading—can be taught in ways that capitalize on their special abilities. Keep in mind that we are using this scheme heuristically. I am not eager to promote a new round of testing that will be used to determine children's places in school. If tests are used at all, they should be given at the request of children (or their parents) who want to learn more about their own talents. By and large, interests—not tested capacities—should determine placement.

But, even with care to emphasize interests and not tested capacities, something seems to be missing in this scheme. My concern (and Ruddick's) for moral development and acceptability is not included here. And nothing is said about common human tasks, health and preservation, or spiritual development. So we need, minimally, another set of categories. Franklin Bobbitt (1915), the father of modern curriculum theory, suggested that education be organized around human activities: "religious activities; civic activities; the duties of one's calling; one's family duties; one's recreations; one's reading and meditation; and the rest of the things that are done by the complete man or woman" (p. 20). This second scheme concentrates on activities or behaviors rather than capacities (or intelligences) and reminds us that there are things all of our children must be able to do in order to live productive and acceptable lives.

However, it too is incomplete in a fundamental way. It can easily deteriorate (and historically did) to a long list of specific objectives empty of motivation, feeling, and convincing rationale. Indeed it was the forerunner of the recent behavioral objectives movement. The main difficulty with it is that it assumes not only that there are categories of activities all human beings must engage in, but also that the required skills and knowledge can be transmitted in a "scientific" way. It disregards the deep existential issues that motivate people to do, or not to do, the things so easily listed.

We need a scheme that speaks to the existential heart of life—one that draws attention to our passions, attitudes, connections, concerns, and experienced responsibilities. Here I would like to use the theme of care already developed. Care, as we have seen, can be developed in a variety of domains and take many objects. We will want to consider care for self, care for intimate others, care for associates and distant others, for nonhuman life, for the human-made environment of objects and instruments, and for ideas.

As we consider how education might be organized around domains or centers of caring, we have to recognize that people take different perspectives on each of these domains not only because of individual interests, but also because they belong to different races, nations, sexes, classes, and religions. All of these group associations affect our interpretations of what it means to care in each domain and which domains should have top priority. Therefore we must add a set of "basic affiliations" to our analytic framework.

Armed with these three schemes and Ruddick's maternal interests, let's return to the question of raising and educating our large family. What do we mean when we say that we want our children to care for themselves? From here on, I will have to speak for myself, a white, professional woman with no formal religious affiliation, sharing as best I can my reasons for various choices and inviting readers to continue their own thought experiments as we proceed. Some of the examples I give will be taken from my own actual experience with a large heterogeneous family, and some will be fictional. I will not always say which is which.

In keeping with a basic interest in preserving the lives of my children, I want them educated for physical health and grace. I am using "grace" to emphasize the integration of body, mind, and spirit. It certainly has a physical connotation; we all admire the grace of dancers and gymnasts. But it points also to the spiritual dimension of life, connoting a special relation with spirit. Further, in all its meanings it points to something that is only partly in our control. It recognizes the gifts and limitations with which we are all born, and it draws our attention to appreciative forms of acceptance. It is, especially, an integrative concept. It reminds us that there are mental and spiritual factors in physical grace as well as physical factors in each of the other forms. With this understanding, I will use the word often, and it is a state I hope my children will seek in their educational experiences.

Part of every day should be spent in caring for the physical aspects of self, and this means attention to nutrition, hygiene, exercise, appearance, and all the facets of health care. Some children may have a special capacity for the bodily-kinesthetic, and these youngsters may eventually want extensive experience with athletics or dance. But all children should be helped to adopt a program of exercise that will contribute to lifelong fitness and grace.

I am not assuming any special organization of schooling at this point. Without regard to the standard forms we call subjects, I am simply exploring what should go into an educational program. When I look intensively at caring for self in chapter 6, I will suggest some things we might do within the present structure. This chapter is the place to dream and create, but after this, we will have to deal with reality and the unlikelihood of educational revolution.

Care of the physical self should be a high priority in education. Just throwing students together for forty minutes a day in a game or calisthenics is not what I have in mind. Whatever is done must be integrated with related domains and activities. Teachers and students must talk with each other about health and grace. It may not be necessary, for example, for all children to exercise or participate in games in school. Some children get plenty of exercise outside the school day. I would hope that a teacher or counselor could take note of this possibility and guide children appropriately.

Central to caring for the physical self is understanding and accepting its potential and limitations. Youngsters have all sorts of worries about their bodies, but we rarely approach physical education as a center for care and concern. Instead we vivisect the body and its interests into separate subjects such as physical education (usually sports), health, hygiene, sex education, drug education, and (rarely) nutrition. Although all of these topics are important, they need to be integrated into the central theme. When I was in high school, we spent considerable time studying the various systems of the body. We learned the names of various bones, the parts of the digestive system, and names for the layers of skin. We never talked about the things that actually worry teenagers: complexion, weight, stature, missed periods, unbidden erections, unwarranted melancholy, and a host of other topics. Everything was kept in tidy compartments and, of course, there was no sex education.

Things haven't changed much, despite the addition of sex education. Many schools have added drug education to their curriculum, because drugs are a problem, and our standard approach is given a problem, add a course. But I would like our children to know that human beings have always sought ways to extend life, enhance sexuality, enhance mental capabilities, and increase physical potential. Our children's temptation to use drugs is not an evil unique to them and their time. The history of humankind is replete with fasts and diets, searches for fountains (and mountains) of youth, and prescriptions for mind- and body-altering substances. It is neither wicked nor unusual to have such interests. It is just unwise to subject one's body to substances or practices that may be harmful. There clearly are connections that can be made here to the subjects we call history, geography, literature, and science, but I would like those subjects to contribute to centers of care, not to substitute for them.

The physical self is only part of the self. We must be concerned also with the emotional, spiritual, and intellectual aspects of self, and clearly these are not discrete. We separate and label them for convenience in discussion, but it may be a mistake to separate them sharply in curriculum. Similarly it is not realistically possible to separate care of self from all the other centers of concern, but it is easier to talk about them one by one.

The spiritual aspect of self, for example, gets almost no attention in today's public schools. Most young people have a host of questions that could be discussed without violating the establishment clause: Is there life after death? Is there a god who cares about me? Am I connected to anything beyond the phenomenal world? Are there spirits with whom I can commune? Will such communion enhance my life? And then, of course, there are all the worries some young people experience over rejecting their parents' religion or exploring new alternatives.

Although we cannot, and I would not want to, teach our heterogeneous family a particular religion in school, I would hope that they might learn something about the human longing for god or spirit. I would hope also that they might eventually be able to ask hard and intelligent questions about existing religions and not become mealy-mouthed in their acceptance of nonsense—confusing indifference with respect. Any of Gardner's capacities can be developed with a concentration on spirituality. This transcendent center of care calls upon and can enhance all of the others. A person engaged in a spiritual quest can use and enjoy logic, poetry, fiction, music, art, architecture, archaeology, dance, service, prayer, and introspection.

Another basic interest of the self is occupational. In addition to finding out what kind of people they are and want to become, our children will also have to choose occupations. A parent may be especially concerned for one child whose talents fall within the spatial and bodily categories. Here is a boy who has mechanical aptitude but not much capacity for logical-mathematical or linguistic pursuits. Indeed the school might tell his parents that he suffers from "specific language disability" or some other intellectual ailment. But, the parents protest, this boy can fix things that his parents cannot begin to figure out. Surely this is a bright youngster. How will his talents be cultivated in the system we call education?

Suppose part of every day were spent in technical, mechanical, and manual work of various kinds. Suppose all children learned how to wire lamps, fix common problems with washing machines, repair furniture, hang doors, and the like. These are all tasks required in everyday life, and they fall easily under Bobbitt's "family duties." In all of these activities, children like the boy just described might lead the way, showing others and supervising tasks. How different this boy might feel about himself if he were credited in school for his real talent.

Similarly, I would hope that the talents of all our children would be recognized and developed in a good school. Kids whose main interests are musical or mechanical or kinesthetic need not be subjected to narrow curricula, as Adler and others fear. Those with mechanical interests can learn about the history and development of machinery, build replicas, visit museums, read technical articles and science fiction, be invited to debate problems in the ethics of technology, investigate environmental problems, become involved in conservation efforts, and engage in a host of other activities. Many of the academic skills we deem important can be learned as adjuncts to their central mechanical interests.

So far I have barely scratched the surface in dreaming about what our children might learn in caring for themselves. But, since I will fill the dream out in a realistic way in chapter 6, let's go on to consider caring for intimate others. Clearly, this is not a discrete category because the self is defined relationally. The kind of persons we are at a given moment affects the quality of relations we enter, and our relations continuously develop the self.

Most of us hope that our children will find someone to love, establish a family, and maintain bonds with friends and relatives. This hope is part of our interest in shaping an acceptable child. What kind of mates, parents, friends, and neighbors will our children be? If we, culturally diverse parents, disagree on this important question, can we find a way to include discussion of the issues in school, or must the children who most need this discussion suffer a lack because we cannot agree?

I would hope that all of our children, both girls and boys, would be prepared to do the work of attentive love. In education today, there is great concern about women's participation in mathematics and science. Some researchers even refer to something called the "problem of women and mathematics." Women's lack of success or participation in fields long dominated by men is seen as a problem to be treated by educational means. But researchers do not seem to see a problem in men's lack of participation in nursing, elementary school teaching, or full-time parenting. Our society values activities traditionally associated with men above those traditionally associated with women. (For an extended and powerful argument on this problem, see Martin, 1985.)

The new education I envision puts a very high valuation on the traditional occupations of women. Care for children, the aged, and the ill must be shared by all capable adults, not just women, and everyone should understand that these activities bring special joys as well as burdens. Work with children can be especially rewarding and provides an opportunity to enjoy childhood vicariously. For example, I've often wondered why high school students are not invited to revisit the literature of childhood in their high school English classes. A careful study of fairy tales, augmented by essays on their psychology, might be more exciting and more generally useful than, for example, the study of *Hamlet*. When we consider the natural interest we have in ourselves—past, present, and future—literature that allows us to look forward and backward is wonderful. Further, there are opportunities for lessons in geography, history, art, and music. (For a marvelous glimpse of what can be accomplished with judiciously chosen literature, see Greene, 1988.)

Our children should learn something about life cycles and stages. When I was in high school, my Latin class read Cicero's essay "On Old Age." With all his talk of wisdom, of milk, honey, wine, and cheese, of meditating in the afternoon breeze, I was convinced that old age had its own romance. Looking at the present condition of many elderly, I see more than enough horror to balance whatever romance there may be. But studies of early childhood, adulthood, and old age seem central to education for real life. Further, active association with people of all ages should be encouraged. Again, one can see connections with standard subjects—statistical studies in math; the history and sociology of welfare, medical care, and family life; geographical and cultural differences. We see also that the need for such studies is a result of the social changes discussed in chapter 1. Home life does not provide the experience in these areas that it once did, and yet the need is greater than it has ever been (Gordon, 1991).

Relations with intimate others are the beginning and one of the significant ends of moral life. In supportive environments where children learn how to respond to dependable caring, they can begin to develop the capacity to care. Whether their caring will be directed to the people around them, however, depends in part on the expectations of their teachers—the adults who guide them and serve as models for them. In the past, too many young men have grown up with the expectation that women will continue to care for them and that they have a right to turn their care and concern to ideas, objects, and great causes. The situation is, indeed, so acute that many feminists fear promoting an ethic of care because it may aggravate the exploitation of women. (On this fear, see the essays in *Hypatia*, 1990; see also the debate in DuBois, Dunlap, Gilligan, MacKinnon, & Menkel-Meadow, 1985. For a frightening account of women's exploitation as caregivers, see Sommers & Shields, 1987.)

If we regard our relations with intimate others as central in moral life, we must provide all our children with practice in caring. Children can work together formally and informally on a host of school projects and, as they get older, they can help younger children, contribute to the care of building and grounds, and eventually do volunteer work—carefully supervised—in the community. Looking at Gardner's intelligences, we see that children can contribute useful service in a wide variety of ways, each according to his or her special talents. Looking at our list of basic affiliations, we recognize that some children may properly resist some kinds of service because of their long association with forms of exploitation. As educators, we should be sensitive to this resistance and encourage dialogue on it. Black and Hispanic youngsters may object to cleaning the school and girls may object to regular and automatic assignment to child care. The objections are valid and should be respected, but the tasks themselves are respectable and important, and full discussion should make it clear that we believe this. Better yet, making sure that all youngsters participate in work activities once highly restricted by race or sex will demonstrate convincingly that we do believe it.

Dialogue is also essential in learning how to create and maintain caring relations with intimate others. Unfortunately, there is little real dialogue in classrooms. A typical pattern of talk can be described this way: Teacher elicitation, student response, teacher evaluation. Then the teacher moves on to someone else, and the student—his or her turn over for the hour—breathes a sigh of relief and returns to other thoughts. If dialogue cannot be introduced into formal lesson structures, it must be provided somewhere. There must be time in every child's day for sustained conversation and mutual exploration with an adult.

Part of what is learned in dialogue is interpersonal reasoning—the capacity to communicate, share decision making, arrive at compromises, and support each other in solving everyday problems. The school presently puts tremendous emphasis on logical-mathematical reasoning but almost none on interpersonal reasoning. As we explore this idea more deeply, we will recognize the futility of antidrug campaigns that advise, "Just say no." Kids do not say no to drugs; they have to say no to other human beings. How do they maintain friendships and status in their peer groups and still say no? One has to learn this important and complex skill. It is part of the capacity to care for oneself and for others.

Interpersonal reasoning is necessary in caring that involves associates and members of the community as well as intimate others. Part of the task of shaping acceptable children is deciding on the domain of acceptability. One kind of acceptability is vital for intimate love; we want our children to be acceptable to a loving inner circle. We also want them to be acceptable in a less intimate way to a wide circle of colleagues, friends, and acquaintances. This kind of acceptability requires a description of the groups to which our children will be acceptable and a decision on which groups are worth such preparation. These discussions require, in turn, an adequate level of interpersonal reasoning. Both we and our children need to talk and listen in order to learn what various groups stand for and what they demand by way of acceptability.

It is odd that acceptability is so little discussed even in social studies courses. Students are taught a narrow conception of the rights and obligations of citizens. Even Adler, for all his emphasis on liberal education and citizenship, concentrates narrowly on voting. As a mother

I have never worried much about whether my neighbors voted, although I have a broad, rather abstract concern about participation in voting. I have always been far more concerned about the basic human qualities of my prospective neighbors: Will they rob or harm me? Will they watch out for my children and property as I will for theirs? Will they be reasonably quiet, clean, and cordial? Will my children find friends who have healthy interests? We spend little time in schools talking about civic responsibility at this level, and yet this is the fundamental level of human association.

Part of what children need to learn is that groups need not be accepted or rejected wholly. Something in the way we now educate induces our children to suppose that persons and groups must be either right or wrong—good guys or bad guys. Along with this simplistic notion of human moral status, they often come to believe that loyalty requires total acceptance or rejection. Therefore, if we have pledged our loyalty to one group, perhaps because we believe with good reason that the group generally stands for fine values, then we are inclined to stand with it against all comers. We learn party lines and begin to divide the world into we and they, us and them. One of the school's most serious shortcomings is that it so consistently induces and maintains the creation of rivals and enemies (Noddings, 1989).

If another situation similar to the Vietnam war occurs, I would hope that our children could oppose it more constructively than their earlier counterparts did. I would hope that they would not jeer at nor spit upon young people who found it their duty to serve in a cause considered unjust by those opposed to it. I would hope also that their thoughtful opposition would be regarded as an admirable form of civic responsibility. Further, I would hope that they could see right and wrong when they occur on either side. One can, in an important sense, be on both sides at critical times—working toward more positive relations, refusing to accept intolerable behavior from either group. Why do so few of us ever learn how to assess the groups we encounter critically, appreciatively, and constructively?

Schools today do try to teach something about other cultures, and they often try to promote global awareness. But I am not talking about abstract learning that can dissipate immediately in a crisis. I am talking about an understanding of self and other that recognizes with a heavy heart that we are all vulnerable to error and to evil. I am concerned with reducing the tendency to project evil onto others not only to exteriorize and then destroy it, but also to deny its presence in ourselves. Especially in an era when we almost never hear honest debate in politics, our children must learn how to evaluate their national history and how to use what they learn about history to reflect on current affairs. My reference here to history does not mean that all children should be taught a specific course in history. It means that teachers should be prepared to deal with relevant historical topics as the need arises. I reject the notion that formal study of history will make better citizens or policy makers who will not repeat the mistakes of the past. What children need to learn is how to sympathize and empathize with other people and to understand their own inclinations toward cruelty and violence.

We all need to understand ourselves as individuals and the groups with which we affiliate. We affect the ways in which groups operate, and they press us toward conformity. Our children watch a lot of television, but schools rarely help them to watch intelligently. Recently I listened to a group of people confessing that they bought products endorsed by famous people. On one level I could hardly believe that people would actually choose a motor oil or cereal because it was endorsed by a stock car racer or football player. Surely everyone knows that these "stars" are paid for their endorsement. On another level it was easy to believe. Several critics have been warning us for years that the primary function of literacy in capitalist societies is to increase the number of consumers and the quantity of consumption (Freire, 1970; Illich, 1971).

Learning about human relations is one of the toughest tasks any of us faces. Too often we equate interpersonal skill with smooth talking or a form of one-way influence. Even Howard Gardner (1983, p. 239), in suggesting the sort of occupation one might enter with a high interpersonal intelligence, lists "therapist" and "counselor." People in both these occupations may indeed learn to cultivate receptivity and two-way influence, but often they do not. Too many manipulate and direct instead of working with, cooperating, and serving. Teachers, doctors, lawyers, diplomats, and politicians all need high levels of interpersonal skills, and so do friends, lovers, parents, and co-workers.

In addition to learning to communicate appreciatively with people of good will and effectively with people who may be untrustworthy, I want our children to examine the effects of their own lives on others. I hope our children will not suffer from poverty, but I also hope they will not crave riches. Moderation should be taught and discussed enthusiastically. To embrace moderation as a way of life does not mean to reject and condemn every luxury any more than maintaining a healthy body weight requires ultraslimness or anorexia. I do not want them to judge each other harshly for interests in a swimming pool, or a solid automobile, or nice clothing, or even a medium-sized boat for recreation.

Possessions well earned and well maintained can add much pleasure to life. But I would like to hear them admit that they have more than enough, to watch over their possessions as they do their weight, and to remain healthily moderate. When I suggest a virtue such as moderation, I recognize that some parents may reject it. Some may prefer that our children all aim for great monetary success. Indeed, one version of the American dream would have us all striving to be millionaires. But there are surely many parents who will agree with me when I suggest alternative measures of success and open discussion of them.

I am concerned, too, with how our children relate to nonhuman life. Most of us introduce our children to pets and try to instill a sense of responsibility concerning their welfare. Caring for a pet can be a powerful component in moral education. Children learn to relieve pain and discomfort, not to inflict suffering, and to appreciate a range of responses in living things. Sharing the care of pets can bring delight as well as responsibility to parents and children.

But our relations with nonhuman creatures are complicated, and many issues arise as we explore them. Should we wear furs, for example, or is the whole fur trade immoral? Contrary to simplistic defenses and attacks on the fur business, the question is a complex one. Some of us want to argue that suffering should be minimized or eliminated. That would outlaw steel-jaw traps. Others argue that naturally wild animals should not be raised just for their furs on farms or in cages. But can there be a sharp line between domestic and wild animals? What about the possibility of gradually domesticating useful species? For my own part, I just say, "The animals need their furs more than I do," and reject fur garments. But this is a personal decision. Is it *wrong* to engage in fur trade? I hope that teachers concerned with "critical thinking" will stimulate our children to consider a long list of related questions: What happens to animals when their range is overpopulated? Is there a form of killing for fur that is more humane than the natural processes in a stressed population? What effects would an end of fur trade have on human beings? Should we use the furs of some animals but not others?

Our moral attitude toward animals should be a major center of care and concern. Should we stop killing and eating animals? Do animals have rights? Should they be used in research? If so, should such use be restricted to the demonstrably essential? What does this mean?

Let's consider. Not long ago, in writing about evil (*Women and Evil*, 1989), I discussed three forms of evil: natural, cultural, and moral.

Natural evil comprises all those painful and harmful events that befall us naturally: most diseases; accidents from fires, storms, and earthquakes; the decrepitude of old age; death. Moral evil is the harm we do intentionally or negligently to one another.

Cultural evil is the most complex and difficult. In this category, we find all the harmful practices that are variously accepted or rejected in different times and places. Our treatment of animals might fall under this category. Whether it should or not is a fascinating question. We can rarely identify cultural evils from within the culture in which they appear. The classical Greeks, for example, did not see the evils of slavery, a now obvious example of cultural evil. Some early societies saw nothing wrong with killing wives for adultery while punishing husbands more lightly, provided their illicit partners were not married women. Many societies have glorified war, another phenomenon that most of us would label a cultural evil. Poverty is another cultural evil. All of these examples involve an infliction of suffering that does not transgress the laws of a given society. Individuals participating in these are not thought to be immoral. Indeed, just the opposite is usually the case. A man unwilling to go to war might be considered by many to be not only unpatriotic and cowardly but also a shirker and thus immoral as well.

Now the question arises: How will future cultures evaluate ours in terms of cultural evil? It is conceivable that people living in enormously crowded conditions will find it impossible to raise animals for meat and, as the feasibility diminishes, new ethical rationales for abstinence will develop. People in, say, the year 3000 may look back upon us as red-jawed barbarians and find the eating of meat as disgusting as cannibalism. Or they may still chew happily on spareribs. We do not know.

Practices that are candidates for cultural evil are sometimes identified by a few creative and sensitive members of the group engaged in the practice, but often no one sees what future generations or other cultures can see. Our children should have opportunities to discuss and analyze such possibilities. Who is prophet and who pestiferous crank? Here, again, we have a chance to listen to several sides, to see the dangers of fanaticism, and—hardest of all—to come to appreciate honest and well-meaning people who take the other side. Are there nice folks among fur trappers? Are there decent, friendly people among those who picket the fur trade? When we are touched by people with whom we do not agree, we begin to believe in the possibility of nonviolent resolution of conflicts. At the same time, when we recognize the reality of hate in opposing parties, and our love for both helps us to understand their hatred, we begin to understand a basic tragedy of human life.

Our children should also learn an appreciation for plant life. In the past few years, I have had some young people in my kitchen who did not know a cabbage from a head of lettuce. They could identify a "salad" and "cole slaw" but never saw what preceded either dish in the kitchen. This is frightening and a little sad. If our children have experience growing things and learning the uses of plants, they may have a more vital sense of urgency about the conservation of our forests and other national habitats. Again, there are connections to history, geography, biology, nutrition, art, mathematics, literature, and a host of other subjects. Further, there is something existentially satisfying about growing things.

I'll say much more about caring for living things in the chapter devoted to that topic, but here it is important to stress the difference between the traditional approach and the one I am advocating. Traditionally, if students learn anything at all in school about plants, they learn botany: the parts of a plant, the families, photosynthesis, the chemical constitution of plants, and the like. Plants become abstractions, a lot of concepts and nomenclature. I am talking about *caring for* plants—learning to nurture them, not name them. I'm talking about generating a sense of wonder at the vitality and endurance of plants that break through sidewalks, scatter their seeds to spring up after wildfires, and wrap their leaves about themselves to survive drought. I am talking about developing in children what Evelyn Fox Keller (1983) calls a "feeling for the organism."

Then there are objects and instruments. I've come late to an appreciation of these, and even now I have little understanding of machinery. But I have a mixer in my kitchen that was made in 1957. I still have the book of directions and recipes that came with it, and my husband has made minor repairs on it once or twice. This old machine has become somewhat special, and we have come to look upon it as *deserving* care. There are people who feel that way about old cars, tractors, barometers, saws, knives, and a host of other things. And then there are those who care about nothing. They apparently have never wondered: What would we do if we had to start all over? What marvels human beings have produced! I would like our children to have a feeling for artifacts as well as organisms.

Consider for a moment an instrument well known to every school child: the pencil. How are pencils made? We can picture long semitubes of wood on an assembly line. Into the groove goes a continuous stream of graphite. Then another strip of wood covers the graphite and is sealed. Next the tubes are cut into pencil lengths and a metallic tip with eraser is fastened to one end of each. How is all this done? What sort of wood is used, and how is it prepared for use at the pencil factory? Where does graphite come from? How is it shipped? How is the hardness tested or controlled? What is an eraser? How are erasers formed? For that matter, what sort of machine stamps "No. 2" on the pencil and at what stage of the process? Once we have understood in principle how pencils are made, we can still ask about the wonderful machines that perform all these functions. What did their prototypes look like, and who invented them?

We are surrounded by wonders that we take for granted—wonders that we snap in half, lightly discard, ignore, and throw on rubbish heaps grown so large that we are threatened with inundation. Perhaps we are tackling the problem at the wrong end. Instead of asking what we can do with all our garbage, perhaps we should ask why we have so much of it. Better, we should ask both questions; asked together, the questions point us to a kind of reverence for usefulness and a search for both conservation and innovation.

Having explored very briefly the notion of living things, objects, and instruments as centers of care, I am led back to the central domain of caring—back to the human domain and a concern for one another. My hope is that our children will understand the dangers of extremism. To embrace and revere the living world does not require a total rejection of technology. To be fascinated and engaged by the world of technology does not suggest neglect of the living world. To be against cruelty to animals does not necessarily require condemnation of all those who raise or hunt animals for consumption. Animals, after all, hunt and consume each other. But, having said this, the problem of our moral relations and obligations to animals and plants remains. In fact, the *problem* arises in our realization that no simple response is adequate, and fighting each other introduces an even worse problem.

To complete my sketchy dream of education for our heterogeneous family, I need to consider ideas as a center of caring. Now I am in a domain familiar to my colleagues—the one most academics name as *the* domain of schooling. Obviously this domain is not discrete and entirely walled off from the others we have considered. On the contrary, my discussion so far has concentrated on how ideas are embedded in and connected to the everyday interests of all human beings.

But ideas, concepts, and conceptual systems can themselves be centers of care. Some years ago, I, like most graduate students, took a course in statistics. Most of my classmates complained that there were not enough relevant examples in the course materials. They were going to be educational researchers, and they wanted to apply statistics to the study of education. I could understand their complaint, but I didn't share it. Coming from a mathematical and philosophical background, I was most interested in the proofs of theorems and derivations of formulas. It was annoying to me that we spent so much time on exercises—relevant or irrelevant. There are such odd students here and there who are captivated by the ideas themselves.

Some of the children in our heterogeneous family may be people for whom traditional liberal education is just right in the sense that its topics will fascinate them. (There are still worries from the perspective of parents and teachers who want to raise their children to be kind, moderate, and nurturing.) Several of my own children fell into this category. One spent an entire evening investigating the family tree of Medea—scattering encyclopedias and other reference books all over the living room, directing her mother where to look next, exclaiming with pleasure as the pattern unfolded. Shortly thereafter, she spent weeks studying Troy. She traced the voyages of Ulysses and drew beautiful illustrated maps. Then she read of Schliemann's excavations and drew profiles of the site. My main task as a parent and teacher of this child was to be sure that she did not go to school too often.

I have to explain that paradoxical remark. Schools today are not supportive places for children with genuine intellectual interests. With rare exceptions, they are not supportive places for students with any genuine or intrinsic interests. Dreaming again, I would hope that children like this daughter could be in classes with other people—students and teachers—who shared intellectual interests. There are many youngsters who could do wonderful things in academic courses if their teachers were not bogged down in administrative trivia, in disciplining unruly students, in "motivating" those whose interests lie elsewhere. What would we do with these others? These others were, of course, my first concern. They should be in classes that treat their own centers of care. These classes can be just as exciting for the students who want to be there as the usual academic classes can be for the few.

Allowing the academically talented (that is, those talented in the traditional logical-mathematical and linguistic categories) to move along as rapidly and as deeply as their energies permit is not necessarily elitist. Here the ideals of our dream and the realities of today's schooling clash. In my dream alternative, there is no hierarchy of capacities. We do not value mathematical or linguistic talent above mechanical or musical, and we do not force people to study intensively in any of these areas. But we want these students, like all others, to feel comfortable with their special interests.

In a full discussion of caring for ideas, I will have to face the realities. There are some practical things that can be done to avoid hierarchy and elitism. We could, for example, design open honors courses. I taught such a geometry course for a few years. Any student who had passed first-year algebra could enroll in this class. I carefully explained at the outset that there would be lots of homework, a rapid pace, sophisticated talk about esoteric topics, and challenging tests. But if students wanted to do it, they were welcome regardless of their previous grades in mathematics. We can be consistent in valuing interests over capacities.

In such a setting, one of Mortimer Adler's recommendations becomes wise and useful. He recommends three pedagogical modes: lecture, seminar/discussion, and coaching. Coaching is imperative for mastery, and for youngsters with poor backgrounds it is essential just to stay afloat. But coaches usually work with highly motivated students. The students may vary in natural talent, but most of them want to succeed, and they trust their coach. Adler makes the mistake of assuming that all children want to learn the traditional academic subjects or that, if they do not, a good coach can motivate them to learn anyway. I question whether this is possible. More important, I question the morality of forcing material on people. I would first have to be convinced that there is something wrong with their own interests or that the material under consideration is so vital that everyone must know it. However, I would employ coaching extensively for those who express interest in the subject at hand.

My alternative vision suggests an entirely different organization of schooling. One can only speculate on what the disciplines might have been and how the curriculum would have been constructed if, for example, women rather than men had designed them. Women have traditionally been closer to the everyday cares of life, but their subordination to men has generated twin problems: First, women have not had the power to enact ideas that are generated by traditional female values; second, attributes, values, and tasks associated with women have been systematically devalued—even scorned. If it were possible to redesign education along the lines of our alternative vision, we would see children studying, discussing, exploring matters, and doing things in their various centers of care. Teachers would work with all children on topics of general concern and with small groups of children on more specialized subjects.

The alternative vision, as I have described it, need not be characterized as a feminist or woman's view, although I think a feminist perspective can contribute richly to it. I have already mentioned John Dewey several times. His analysis of schooling suggested almost a century ago that education should begin with and remain closely tied to the actual experience and concerns of students. But his recommendations have been widely interpreted as psychological; that is, Dewey seemed to address questions about how children learn. He did not really challenge the dominance of existing disciplines in the curriculum but, rather, showed how they could be employed in the solution of genuine problems. Indeed, he made strong arguments for science, history, and geography in the school curriculum. He wanted these subjects to serve real human needs and also to be "progressively organized" so that those students who developed interest in them would gradually accept and employ their standard logical organization. My vision, in contrast, assesses the traditional supremacy of the disciplines as fundamentally wrong. Other matters—centers of care—are more important and more essential to full human life.

I have started an argument that I now want to fill out. In its general form, it is an argument against an ideology of control—one in favor of shared living and responsibility. Its first thesis is that there are centers of care and concern in which all people share and in which the capacities of all children must be developed. The second, closely following the first, is that education should nurture the special cognitive capacities or "intelligences" of all children and that this requires a scheme of multiple intelligences resembling that suggested by Howard Gardner. A third is that the focus on centers of care and the development of capacities must be filtered through and filled out by a consideration of differences that are associated with race, sex, ethnicity, and religion. The various perspectives that arise must be treated respectfully, critically, and regularly. Finally, my argument draws on Ruddick's maternal interests. Not only must we respect the various talents of our children and the occupations they will fill as adults but, if we are doing the work of attentive love, we must care deeply for them. We want to preserve their lives, nurture their growth, and shape them by some ideal of acceptability. Our parental interests inevitably guide the choices we make in all the other categories and, indeed, in the categories themselves.

CHAPTER 5

Caring and Continuity

The disciplines will probably remain as the backbone of the curriculum for the foreseeable future, although there have been important challenges to this traditional structure; for example, the National Association for Core Curriculum has worked for more than thirty years to transform what we now call the middle school into a humane center of education with similarities to the one I described in chapter 4 (see Lounsbury & Vars, 1978; *The Core Teacher*). But this curriculum has not swept the nation, nor has it threatened the stability of the secondary curriculum or the hegemony of the disciplines. Further, it represents an interdisciplinary approach, not one that displaces the disciplines. The experience of Core enthusiasts illustrates how difficult it is to make changes in the standard curriculum. Theodore Sizer (1984) has also recommended a shift to interdisciplinary work—work that would allow students to concentrate on problems instead of artificially and rigidly compartmentalized subjects. In recent talks, he has emphasized the moral aspect of this shift. We really *must* do something like this if we are to educate all of our children. Still, there is little movement in the direction Sizer suggests.

However, conditions in today's schools are desperate enough that sensible people may be ready to consider modification along the lines we are discussing here. There are some things we can do without entirely overthrowing the traditional structure. The changes I will suggest in this chapter are feasible, but they also acknowledge and embrace ideas that may seem heretical to some people in the educational establishment.

First, we must understand that the school, like the family, is a multipurpose institution. It cannot concentrate only on academic goals any more than a family can restrict its responsibilities to, say, feeding and housing its children. The single-purpose view is not only morally mistaken, it is practically and technically wrong as well, because schools cannot accomplish their academic goals without attending to the fundamental needs of students for continuity and care. As we saw in chapter 1, social changes over the last forty years have left many young people without a sense of continuity and with the feeling that no one cares. Therefore, although schools should continue to reflect on and pursue many purposes, their first—their guiding purpose—must be to establish and maintain a climate of continuity and care. I mentioned the need for continuity in an earlier chapter. Caring in education differs from brief caring encounters in that it requires strong relations of trust upon which to build. Such relations take time and require continuity. I will discuss briefly four forms of continuity in the education of children: continuity of place, continuity of people, continuity of purpose, and continuity of curriculum.

CONTINUITY

John Dewey (1963) posited continuity as one of the criteria of educational experience. For Dewey, an educational experience had to be connected to the prior personal experience of students and also to a widening or deepening of future experience. Both directions on the continuum are essential, and Dewey gently chided followers who favored one and forgot the other. His child-centered followers, for example, too often concentrated on the child's past and present experience, forgetting that the teacher bears major responsibility for the child's future experience or growth. Others subordinated authentic present experience to a future experience disconnected from prior experience and present interest. Dewey's recommendations are still vital, but today they need to be analyzed more closely and extended.

The structure of social relations has changed dramatically since Dewey wrote. Many children suffer instability in both family and community life. More mothers work outside the home, neighborhoods are less personal, schools are larger, and recreation is often passive—connected to personal experience only by chance and presented with no consideration of what Dewey called "growth."

In such a world, schools should be committed to a great moral purpose: to care for children so that they, too, will be prepared to care. Instead, too many educators, perceiving the general and pervasive deterioration of schooling, have advised that the schools concentrate on academic matters. Some have even said that the schools were designed for academic purposes, but these people are plainly wrong. At least they are wrong historically if we look at the establishment of schools in the United States. Moral purposes have, until recently, been more important than academic ones, and the latter were often frankly designed to serve the former (Tyack & Hansot, 1982). Today it is essential that the moral purposes of schooling be restored.

Continuity of Purpose

Students should be aware that their schools are conceived as centers of care—places where they are cared for and will be encouraged to care deeply themselves. This suggests that the school day should be organized in a way that reflects the primary purpose. We might, for example, organize the day so that half of it is spent on centers and themes of care and the other half on conventional subjects. (I'll say more about this under "continuity of curriculum.")

Looking seriously at the school day from the perspective of caring, we see that lunchtime is usually an educational dead spot. Teachers (except those on lunch room duty) take a break from students, and students all too often take a break from everything civilized. In contrast, families that take personal responsibility for educating their children often make mealtime an important educational event. It is a time when the day's experiences are recounted with enthusiasm or sympathy or apology; when moods are assessed; when world, community, and family affairs are discussed; when family work and vacation plans are debated; and, even, when specific information is proffered and skills demonstrated.

Perhaps mealtime should be such an event in the school day also. I do not mean that this should become another duty for teachers, although teachers might well want to participate at least occasionally. There should be tables at which adults from the community and students might sit together, eat, and engage in civilized conversation. There is no reason why this conversation should be guided by specific objectives or formally evaluated. We do not conduct formal evaluations of family conversation at the dinner table nor of other social events we hold in our homes. This does not mean that we should not talk about how the conversations are going, reflect on them, and improve them. It just means that we should keep our primary purpose in mind and not allow ourselves to distort every activity in the school day in a mistaken quest for a foolproof system of accountability. *Responsibility* is broader, deeper, and more ambiguous than accountability, and it describes commitment in interpersonal relations more accurately.

I have used lunchtime as an example of how differently we might look at the school day if we were committed to schools as centers of care. Clearly, everything we do during the school day would take on new significance from this perspective, and we will consider other important features in the following sections.

To live by our primary purpose, we must make schools far more open places than they are now. Parents and other community members should be free to attend, watch, and help at the invitation of teachers. Parents, teachers, administrators, and students should remind each other of the primary purpose, and they should ask continually why they are engaging in certain activities. Activity should not be mindless for any of the participants.

In the United States today, many students describe themselves as "lost." They are told constantly that proper educational credentials will ensure a "better" life, but when they see that they are not in the top 10 or 20% academically, they fear that there is no place at all for them. The presence of caring adults in regular conversation can assure them that there are many ways to earn a respectable living and contribute to the community; that there is a place for them in the community now and in the future; and that we all recognize the continuity of purpose that guides both the school and the community.

Placing top priority on the moral purpose of caring for students and educating them so that they will be prepared to care does not imply that the school should set no other purposes. Schools, like families, are multipurpose institutions. Of course schools should have academic purposes. It should be expected that all students will find centers of care that will provide occupational and recreational interests, in addition to the personal and moral interests that are central in all lives. The school can also seek purposes that involve specific skills, desirable attitudes, and social interactions. If the purposes chosen are compatible with the primary purpose and pursued in its light, they are likely to be met more effectively than they are now because together they form a consistent pattern of goals that can be sought without contradiction.

Continuity of Place

In order to build a caring community, students need continuity in their school residence. They should stay in one school building for longer than two or three years. Children need time to settle in, to become responsible for their physical surroundings, to take part in maintaining a caring community. When we have to choose between highly specialized programs for a narrow age range and continuity of place, we should choose the latter.

In the past couple of decades, many school districts with declining enrollments have chosen to close schools in order to economize and provide special programs. When our first priority is program—as it has been for more than thirty years—we are inclined to cram students into larger and more specialized schools where we can provide the best and most advanced courses. When our first priority is continuity and care, we may be willing to sacrifice a few advanced courses for the sake of community.

In the future, using the priority of care and community, districts undergoing declining enrollment might keep their schools open and rent space to organizations compatible with education. Once such a decision is made, all sorts of creative opportunities arise. Cooperative deals might be made with child care groups, art and music studios, even veterinary hospitals and florist shops. (I know there are legal problems here, but they are not insurmountable. The problem is more lack of imagination than legal constraint.) The basic guiding idea is to make the school into a family-like center of care. We must stop moving children from place to place in order to solve social problems or "satisfy their developmental needs." One of their greatest needs is stability—a sense of belonging.

There are two cautionary remarks I want to make here about my own advice. First, I am not necessarily arguing for smaller schools. Although I think smaller schools might enhance a caring environment, it may be that smaller classes, or even *some* smaller classes in crucial areas, are more important. I do not intend my examples and suggestions as recipes. Continuity of place might be achieved in a big school, just as some sizable cities manage to maintain a sense of community. It is the guiding idea that I want to emphasize. Second, continuity of school place will not be possible for those youngsters whose families move or break up. So it is certainly not a complete solution. Some day we may have to consider residential public education to meet the needs of transient families, but this is a highly controversial idea that deserves separate and extensive analysis. Suffice it to say here that our inability to provide continuity of place for all children should not prevent our providing it for as many as we can.

The need for continuity of place raises serious questions about junior high schools and middle schools. Preadolescents need opportunities to work with and live with younger children. They also need continuity of place in order to achieve a sense of belonging. Establishing special schools designed to meet their developmental needs may be counterproductive. Children can never be reduced to a set of abstract, discrete, and universal needs isolated from their one obvious need— the need for care; and care requires continuity.

In the United States today, many children are shifted about from year to year to achieve racial balance. This is morally wrong and irresponsible. We are using our children as a means to achieve a desirable social end, but children—or any human beings—ought not to be used merely as means. Further, the people we are supposedly helping are rarely consulted about the means chosen. Using the perspective of caring, we may decide to plan more effectively. We want youngsters to stay in one place (with many of the same people, I will argue next) for a substantial period of time. Then we should plan for racial integration, if this is held to be desirable, early on, project what classes will look like from year to year, and keep the children in one place. To achieve racial and ethnic harmony, it is not sufficient merely to expose children to different groups. They must have time to develop caring relations with particular others. This observation leads logically to our next domain of continuity.

Continuity of People

Children need continuity not only of place but also of people. Students could easily stay with one teacher for three or more years rather than the typical one year. Placement should, of course, be by mutual consent. Some readers may react to this by saying, "That would be great if the teacher is a good one. But suppose my kid has a bad teacher for three or four years?" First, that's one reason why such an arrangement has to be by mutual consent. Second, you should not accept having your child with a bad teacher for even one year. When we do not like or trust our physicians, lawyers, or dentists, we find new ones. Within reason, we ought to be able to do that with teachers, too.

At the high school level, such a system would allow teachers to take responsibility for the entire development of students in a particular subject. I had this experience for many years as a mathematics teacher, and it was wonderful to work with students for several years and watch their growth. Jaime Escalante, the real-life teacher-hero of the movie *Stand and Deliver*, insists that to do the job he has set for himself he needs three years, not just one, with his students. He recognizes the same need I'm addressing: Students need to know someone cares for them as persons. In low moments, even though they can't see the sense in it, they will continue to work on mathematics out of trust and love for their teacher. Then better moments come along.

The heresy in all this is that I am claiming that specialization, a high priority on program, and efficiency are not sacred and not always sensible. It is not necessary to create special schools to provide for the developmental needs of preadolescents. Teachers do not need degrees in counseling to advise students on the usual academic and personal problems. (This does not at all diminish the role of professional counselors, who will still be needed for special problems and to advise other teachers.) Further, teachers should not be allowed to avoid their responsibilities as moral educators by claiming that they are not prepared for this work. All decent adults are, or should be, prepared for this work. It is a human responsibility—one that belongs to all of us. Mathematics teachers (Escalante is a good example) should be concerned with their students' progress in English and science, and in social and moral life, too. They must be *educators* first and mathematics teachers second.

Further, once we have accepted the priority of care, we may be able to weave in the benefits of some specialization. For example, some elementary schools use teams of teachers who stay with children over a period of years. In this arrangement, children will have mathematics and language arts specialists who will provide both continuity and specialized instruction. Another advantage of this system is that children may be able to find their own special teacher and confidante on the team. In some ways, this system is more practical than one that matches children with just one teacher for several years, but both schemes are worth trying.

Before moving on to discuss continuity in curriculum, I want to mention a familiar phenomenon that vividly points up the need for continuity in the teacher–student relation. These days, tragedies strike school campuses fairly often. Children are murdered, killed in accidents, commit suicide. When these tragic events occur, "grief counselors" are dispatched to the affected schools. I am not arguing that there is no need for specially trained people to advise administrators and teachers and, perhaps, to listen to severely disturbed students. But the best grief counseling should come from teachers who know and care deeply for their students. They are the people who should comfort, counsel, and express their common grief. In contemporary schools, teachers and students do not know each other well enough to develop relations of care and trust. Of all the domains of continuity, this is the easiest and, perhaps, most important one to change. Students and teachers need each other. Students need competent adults to care; teachers need students to respond to their caring.

Continuity in Curriculum

Dewey (1963) argued that continuity is the longitudinal criterion of educational experience; that is, material offered in school should pass the important test of being connected to students' personal experience—past and future. When this criterion has received attention at all, it has usually been interpreted to mean that students should be allowed to exercise some choice in their selection of courses. Such choice has also been endorsed as appropriate for participation in democratic life. But choosing one's courses does not ensure continuity unless one also has some choice of course content, and this is rarely allowed. Further, mere choice, unguided by intelligent dialogue with teachers, can lead to chaos rather than continuity. Students wind up with a hodgepodge of unconnected courses, and schools begin to look like shopping malls (Powell, Farrar, & Cohen, 1985)—places where people often abandon themselves to peer pressure and whim. Properly objecting to such haphazard proliferation of courses, Mortimer Adler (1982) and like-minded colleagues have gone to the opposite extreme and want to require that everyone take exactly the same course of study. Both approaches are wrong, and neither is necessitated by our commitment to democracy.

If we were starting from scratch to build a curriculum, I would suggest organizing it entirely around centers or themes of care: care for self, care for intimate others, care for strangers and distant others, care for nonhuman animals, care for plants and the living environment, care for objects and instruments, and care for ideas. But we cannot start from scratch. Further, several centers of care are compatible with existing subjects: There are students who are deeply interested in literature, art, mathematics, or some other academic subject. In the interest of compromise and practicality, then, I would suggest a secondary school curriculum that is divided equally between the subjects as we now know them and courses devoted to themes of care. (I will not discuss elementary school curriculum here because the public has always been reasonably receptive to humane alternatives in the elementary school. It is the secondary school curriculum that most needs reform.)

Suppose, for illustrative purposes, that we consider an eight-period day. I have suggested that it be divided equally between the standard subjects and themes of care. One period designated to the latter would be lunch with conversational groupings. The rest of the time would be devoted to themes of care, and a team of teachers would be available to supervise various projects and discussions. Topics might include health management, sex, child rearing, household technology, driver education and safety, nutrition, drugs and substance abuse, environmental issues, and a host of others that arise in current life. The precise topics discussed in any year would be chosen by students and teachers together. Because students would be enrolled in a class like this for six years (grades 7–12), there would be time to cover a lot of topics. Teachers should, of course, exercise some leadership and be sure that individual students get the information and skills they need in all important areas.

Many themes would draw heavily on literature and history. Instead of analyzing canonical literature and studying chronological history, students might choose from a reasonable variety of important topics those which they would study with care. Possible topics would include childhood and aging, spirituality, moral life and obligation, oppression, and war and peace. Again, teachers would take responsibility for providing some whole-class discussion of essential topics, individual and group coaching on special skills, and an appropriate sequence of topics for each student.

The other half of the day would be spent on more traditional subjects, augmented by special subjects necessitated by our attention to multiple intelligences. These would consist of disciplinary knowledge modified by considerations of care. In this segment of the curriculum, we would rely on revision rather than revolution, and in fact such revision is well under way—much of it inspired by feminist, ethnic, and other critical studies. Eventually, after many years of successful practice, the disciplines might give way entirely to a new mode of curricular organization.

Curriculum planning in this new mode would involve the recognition of multiplicity in human capacities (Gardner, 1982, 1983) and therefore would establish several equally valued programs at the secondary school level. Each of these programs would include the courses, seminars, and workshops devoted to themes of universal care, and each would include specialized courses in the revised disciplines.

Suppose, again for illustrative purposes, we were to establish four equally prestigious programs in our secondary schools: a linguistic/mathematical program that looks somewhat like the present one; a technical one that concentrates on the world of technology; an arts program that includes specialties in music, fine arts, dance, and drama; and an interpersonal program that emphasizes studies of people and their interactions. There could be interesting hybrids, too. For example, students with kinesthetic-spatial talents might want to combine studies in technology and arts; future athletes, physical therapists, and coaches might be attracted to such a combination. The four programs and their combinations could provide for most of Gardner's seven intelligences. This is a realistic suggestion and, so far, not dramatically different from what has been suggested for magnet schools, except that I would like to see all of these programs in one school for the sake of student interaction and easy switches between programs. Further, we would want heterogeneous groups in the care half of the day.

No one program would be "college preparatory." Rather, it should be possible within each specialization to prepare for college or to prepare directly for the job market. Similarly, no program would be vocational in the narrow sense of preparing for a particular job. Here I am in agreement with Adler and his colleagues. The school must do more by way of education than mere job preparation. But there must be opportunities for intelligent choices, and those opportunities must be designed with the full range of human capacities in mind. Each program would provide preparation for a large class of occupations and recreations.

Under this plan, every student would spend part of every day in courses that treat themes of care and part in areas of specialization. Instead of creating a host of disconnected courses, we would integrate departments where feasible and design courses that have continuity in both the subject matter of specialization and the areas of care. Such planning should be cooperative; that is, both teachers and students should participate in the construction of curriculum. Teachers must know their students well enough to connect present interests with prior experience, and they must know the community and subject matter well enough to make connections to future experience. A curriculum of the sort suggested here recognizes both the universality and tremendous variety of possible future experiences.

SUMMARY

To meet the challenge to care in schools, we must plan for continuity:

1. *Continuity in purpose.* It should be clear that schools are centers of care—that the first purpose is caring for each other. This includes helping all students to address essential issues of human caring and, also, to develop their particular capacities in specialized areas of care.

2. *Continuity of school residence.* Students should stay in one school building long enough to acquire a sense of belonging. Although I would prefer smaller schools, it may be possible to create a feeling of community in larger schools if community is made a priority. Children should be in residence more than three and, preferably, for six years.
3. *Continuity of teachers and students.* Teachers, whether singly or in teams, should stay with students (by mutual consent) for three or more years.
4. *Continuity in curriculum.* The idea is to show our care and respect for the full range of human capacities by offering a variety of equally prestigious programs of specialization, each embedded in a universal curriculum organized around essential themes of caring.

I will turn now to a fuller discussion of curriculum organized around centers and themes of care.

CHAPTER 6

Caring for Self

Within each center of care, we can identify many themes. "Caring for self" is a huge topic. In one sense, everything we care about is somehow caught up in concerns about self, and, having posited a relational definition of self, it is even harder to extricate individual selves from the relations in which they are formed. But we do have individual bodies that move about, grow old, suffer pain, are recognized by others, and become associated with particular occupations and recreations. In this chapter I want to concentrate on understanding the self in certain of its most vital concerns: physical, spiritual, occupational, and recreational life. Other aspects of self—for example, emotional and intellectual—will be considered in later chapters. This chapter's categories are chosen because they come closest to ones that can be considered as aspects of individual lives. Even so, many of the topics treated here will be revisited as we discuss other centers of care.

PHYSICAL LIFE

Considering how important our bodies are to us, it is surprising how little attention they get in schools. Since the days of the Greeks, educators have extolled something called the life of the mind, but at least the Greeks recognized the contribution of a sound body to this enterprise. Most modern mothers do, too. We know that children need exercise, rest, and adequate nutrition to remain alert and intellectually lively, but many of us resist the school's construal of the body as a mere means to enhancing mind. We want the body to be treated as important in its own right. Our children are physical entities enlivened with spirit and reason.

As parents, we want to preserve the lives of our children. Some of us watch over the physical lives of our children attentively, and some do not. Because of the social changes noted in chapter 1, it has become increasingly important for schools to be involved in helping children to care for themselves. The topic is so large that we cannot possibly cover it in any one discussion, nor can even a single facet be discussed comprehensively. But let's look at a few central themes and see what might be done with them in schools.

First, it seems that many of the isolated topics we now teach might reasonably be integrated into scientific and technological themes within the care context. I will argue that the courses we now call physical education, home economics, driver education, sex education, drug education, health and hygiene, and parenting ought to be integrated. Teachers who now work in these areas should be encouraged to form one large department that can provide continuous discussion on topics of essential care for the physical self.

Physical "education" departments that limit themselves to the supervision of sports and exercise should be eliminated. In the years after high school, no one forces us to exercise or participate in games. We all have to learn why and how to exercise our bodies and to take responsibility for our fitness. Proper physical *education* would provide open discussion on issues of fitness, monitor the condition of bodies, and prescribe possible modes of exercise and recreation. Secondary school students would then be encouraged to use the various exercise facilities available at schools. Team sports should be offered also, but as part of a complete educational program in which competition and cooperation are discussed and analyzed.

In addition to providing information on why, how, and where to exercise, the school should provide discussion on various social and economic issues on the topic. For example, we are living in a time when fitness is a watchword. More and more adults have taken up running; many people have joined health clubs and engage in weight lifting, rowing, biking, running in place, and games like racquetball. The key is to raise a sweat and the heart-rate. This interest in fitness is, perhaps, a good thing except that, while adults are running around the park, most kids are lying in front of television sets. I suspect kids think that exercise is something people do to stave off old age and fat, and most of them are not worried much about either. They should be, and schools should help them to be concerned.

Exercise in the 1980s took on a selfish and unproductive look. Why not exercise by playing ball with the kids, or by scrubbing the kitchen floor, or by digging a new bed for perennials? Not everyone has kids, of course, but there are children who need the companionship of vigorous adults. Again, not everyone has a yard in which to grow perennials, but there are reforestation programs that welcome volunteers. The purposes of conversation on these possibilities are several: to increase self-understanding, to explore the possibilities of productive exercise, and to consider service as part of our exercise program.

We might also explore the peculiarities of the current fitness craze from another set of perspectives. Must one wear a fashionable warmup suit to run? Must bikers wear tight, shiny pants? What pushes us to the levels of conformity we now observe? It might be a good exercise for students to try an ad-resistance experiment. For one month, we will buy nothing we see advertised. We will deliberately shop for cereals not promoted, brands unknown to television. We'll wear our old clothes biking, running, and digging. The idea is simply to encourage reflection, to get young people to ask: Why am I doing this? How else might I accomplish my purpose? And, of course, at bottom is a marvelous opportunity for humor and satire. A good laugh at ourselves might be one of the best forms of exercise yet discovered. Self-understanding is basic to the entire enterprise of caring for self.

Discussion of exercise can also contribute to an analysis of time management, and adolescents preparing for busy adult lives need frank discussion of this important topic. At home there are many opportunities for exercise, but we are often too tired, or the opportunities seem too much like work. But here is an important area for reality training. Work is a basic, enduring reality, and our health depends, at least in part, on how we regard it. Scrubbing the kitchen floor or the bathroom can be an objectionable chore, or it can provide both intrinsic and extrinsic satisfaction. Most of us recognize the extrinsic satisfaction of admiring the clean floor or the polished fixtures, but how many of us learn to enjoy the process? If we reflect on it, we can bend, stretch, reach, push, and even move fast enough to work up a sweat while scrubbing or vacuuming. But we do not usually look at things this way. Sweating at tennis or running is fun—a break from work—but scrubbing, or digging, or dusting ceilings is just more work. Why do we draw a sharp line between work and recreation?

Combining work, exercise, and play may be a key element in achieving some stability and serenity in young married life. Our children are at present ill-prepared for the rigors of family life. Young men are not often raised to do their share of housework, and young women complain of exhaustion from doing two jobs. It is unlikely that career patterns will return women to full-time housekeeping, and so it is imperative for young people to learn how to manage household tasks without sinking into fatigue and self-pity.

So is the fatigue of manual labor "all in the mind"? I do not want to push that idea. Many young people, especially young mothers, suffer from real physical exhaustion. Further, I am not arguing that scrubbing floors is always fun. I would not want to do this all day long or do it for a living. Coercion and monotony both take their toll. Probably no one should be expected to do this sort of work day in and day out. Pollyanna might see the cheery side of scrubbing floors for a living, but I do not.

The argument is subtler and, I think, more important than superficial advice to think positively. It is one for careful (and somewhat *carefree*) self-analysis. What will my life be like? How can I satisfy the needs of my body without neglecting other aspects of that life? Can necessity sometimes be turned to virtue and, even, fun?

Part of the difficulty in turning housework into exercise, a problem for analysis, and an occasion for sharing and fun is its long association with women and unpaid service. Too many men scorn housework as "women's work"—something beneath their dignity, although the full range of household management is varied and far more challenging than the average paid occupation. It is understandable, then, that women—now able to work outside the home—often also attach low worth to unpaid household jobs. Even when housework is paid, it is low status work, something to be escaped if possible. I am suggesting that the ordinary tasks of life be studied appreciatively and turned to our own individual and collective advantage. They are part of a vital center of care.

Nutrition and substance abuse should be handled in a similar way: open discussion with many opportunities for self-analysis and skeptical examination of current policies and practices. None of this should be allowed to become pedantic, riddled with tests of nomenclature and the like. Emphasis should be on the questions raised by students and teachers as equal partners in the enterprise. Some youngsters might enjoy an aesthetic and historical look at cookbooks. Others might enjoy evaluating meals at various restaurants and fast-food places. All should learn how to preserve the nutritive value of foods in cooking and storing; all should learn to appreciate the celebratory and ceremonial functions of food.

A study of substance abuse should include recognition that the problems are not new, and some humor can be injected into the topic without downplaying its seriousness. People under the influence—like cats with catnip—can be very funny. They can also be dangerous, disgusting, and very sick. It is important to discuss substance use and abuse, not preach on it or merely give information. It is not merely a problem for weak or wicked teens but a long-standing problem for all of humanity.

Closely connected to problems of nutrition and substance abuse are two other topics of keen interest to teenagers: safety (especially automobile safety and safe sex) and appearance. Driver education should include more general discussion of safety and responsibility. It could be connected to a sequence on domestic technology in which students would learn to make minor repairs on household machinery, do safety assessments of their homes, and check for efficiency with respect to utilities. It should also be connected to a larger and more general analysis of personal and interpersonal responsibility. I will save this material for the next two chapters, but I want to remind readers (and myself) that a major effort in this work is to avoid sharp separations between technology and values, thinking and doing, academic courses and nonacademic. All the matters we are discussing here have both intellectual and practical aspects; all require an examination of values, choices, and commitment.

Just as a study of substance abuse leads almost naturally into a discussion of safety and responsibility, so an emphasis on nutrition leads to a discussion of appearance. Schools have always included something on appearance in physical education or hygiene courses. Usually a connection is made between proper nutrition and cleanliness and "clear skin and shiny hair." But far more needs to be said. For example, this topic presents an opportunity to study the social construction of gender. Why has appearance been such an important dimension of femininity? In a devastating critique of society's expectations for females, Susan Brownmiller (1984) lists the topics that "should" matter to women: body, hair, clothes, voice, skin, movement, emotion, ambition. All but the last are to be cultivated; the last is to be shunned. Are those expectations "history"? Such a question can lead to another examination of advertising and to an open debate on what girls and boys look for in each other.

A topic such as appearance might have been discussed some years ago as part of a "life adjustment" course, and some readers may react as essentialists did to those courses by deploring the lack of intellectual content. But there is no lack of such content. On the contrary, it is a topic that can and should lead to historical, philosophical, and literary analysis. Teachers should be prepared to read and discuss selections from Kant, Rousseau, and G. Stanley Hall on women, appearance, and ambition. They should encourage analysis of song lyrics, novels, poetry, and movies. Far from the "life adjustment" approach which might have concentrated on the proper appearance for one's role in professional and community life, this approach uses a topic of general interest to teenagers to launch a critical analysis of culture.

Health management should also be a theme in our center of care. Probably this topic and related matters on all sorts of insurance should be handled in the senior year. Students should learn about costs and benefits, taxes, alternative methods of handling medical costs, the present and coming crises in health management, and whatever related topics may arise. They should also learn how to present their problems to medical personnel, how to press their questions, and how to get information to which they are entitled. There is a personal aspect to this set of topics, and there is a social aspect. Both present opportunities for extended discussion.

In handling a topic such as health management, teachers will have to teach some mathematics, some economics, some ethics, some current events, some sociology, some interpersonal reasoning. Time should be taken to do these things as the need arises. When teacher or students ask how much of one's income goes to medical costs, time should be spent figuring this out. We should not say that arithmetic belongs in math class. Arithmetic belongs where we need it. Teachers can certainly call a temporary halt to discussion and say, "Let's be sure everyone knows how to figure this," and then a few days might be spent on specific mathematical skills. Some readers—especially professional colleagues—may find this recommendation shocking. I am suggesting that non-math teachers teach some mathematics. Yes. I am suggesting that any material *that all students are expected to know* should be part of every teacher's knowledge also. After all, if every component of life knowledge has to be divided among experts, how can we expect students to master all of it? Later, in a discussion of caring for ideas, I will argue that subject matter specialists are indeed vital for the instruction of students who are particularly interested in a subject such as mathematics. But all teachers should be able to handle the mathematics of everyday life, and their own preparation does not have to depend on mathematics courses given by experts. We have to reduce the worship of expertise.

An exploration of health management involves a careful examination of access to medical resources. This exploration is an opportunity to study the problems of racial minorities, the working class, unemployed, and underemployed. Too often these problems are taken up in a few paragraphs in a course such as "Problems of American Democracy," and they lose their pertinence and vitality. In a setting where students will have to examine their own problems of access to health management, social problems should take on dramatic significance. Further, there will be new opportunities to discuss ethical issues and make connections with other centers of care.

Part of caring for self is gaining an understanding of life stages, birth, and death. Many of our children today are isolated from human beings of different ages. Schools exacerbate this isolation by maintaining a system of rigid age-assignment to classes and schools. Further, there are few opportunities to study the problems of children, of parents, or of the elderly except in abstract and uninteresting subtopics in social studies. Yet some of our students come from cultures in which several generations still live together in mutual dependence. Are there valuable lessons to be learned from these arrangements? Are there special problems? Can we extrapolate to invent new forms of family life? Here again, literature, history, sociology, politics, and psychology can all contribute.

Birth is a topic too often restricted to classes for unwed pregnant girls or to brief mention in sex education. It is left out of history, mathematics, science, and literature (as represented in the "canon"). As Sara Ruddick (1989) points out, it is even ignored in philosophy (a subject that allegedly treats universal themes); apparently, it is supposed that human beings "are 'thrown' into the universe somehow" (p. 189). But giving birth is the natural beginning of the preservative love that guides parenting and teaching. We create in real labor new life that gives rise to the great interests of parents and teachers: preservation, growth, and acceptability.

Birth has links with many other topics. For example, all students should be aware of the connections writers have made between birth and war. Ruddick quotes Jane Addams, who compared a mother to "an artist who is in the artillery corps, let us say, and is commanded to fire upon a wonderful thing, say St. Mark's at Venice, or the Duomo at Florence, or any other great architectural and beautiful thing. I am sure that he would have just a little more compunction than the man who had never given himself to creating beauty and did not know the cost of it" (p. 186). By the same logic, mothers should oppose war. Addams consistently opposed even World War I while her otherwise like-minded colleague John Dewey reluctantly endorsed it. Think of the implications for extended exploration that come out of this one paragraph!

Death, too, is largely ignored in schools unless tragedy strikes close to home. Then the school responds compassionately but typically—with expert help to alleviate symptoms. John Silber (1989) advocates teaching children about death as part of "the first objective of early education"—as "training in the reality principle" (p. 4). I think his argument—a typical patriarchal one, by the way—is wrong on almost all counts. He thinks today's children are acquainted only with the make-believe and therefore reversible death seen on television, and he advocates an earlier form of moral education that advised children to earn happiness through virtue and a realization that death awaits us all. This approach is closely connected to the Freudian idea that moral and ethical life begin in fear.

In contrast, contemporary feminists suggest that moral life arises first out of love and attachment (Noddings, 1989; Sagan, 1988). From this perspective, we should concentrate on developing the relationships that provide continuity in children's lives and give them models for their own moral development. I'll say more about this fundamental disagreement later.

But Silber is wrong in his description as well as his prescription. He thinks that today's children have no direct knowledge of death, that in contrast to children a hundred years ago they are less likely to experience the death of a sibling or elder. This may be true of some highly sheltered children, but it is hardly the case for many of our children. When my husband and I were growing up, we never knew anyone who was murdered. In contrast, all of my children have known at least one person who has been murdered, and most of them have known several. Silber is just not looking at the world our children have to live in. He is certainly not looking at the world of inner-city children. He is more guilty of make-believe than they are.

Discussion of death is necessary for self-understanding. Our main motive for discussing it with the young, however, is to preserve their lives, not to rub their noses in reality. Avoiding premature death is properly part of learning to care for oneself and should be considered in a sound education for physical life. But even this aspect need not be entirely grounded in fear. It can also be grounded in the desire to maintain loving relationships, to preserve and protect, to cherish the time that might be given to adventure, achievement, enjoyment, and love. This part of physical life is, obviously, inseparable from spiritual life—our next topic.

SPIRITUAL LIFE

Possibly the greatest lack in modern public schooling is spirituality (see Noddings, 1993). Religion of all kinds is taboo in our schools. The eternal quest of souls for a connection with spirit is ignored as though it never existed. Even when mythology is taught, it is carefully confined to "pagan" myths. Adam and Eve are rarely mentioned lest someone protest, "But that's not a myth!" (Noddings, 1989). That kind of protest should not, logically, deter public discussion. Thorough airing of all sides can be accomplished sensitively and profitably. Why do some of us regard the story of Adam and Eve as a myth? What mythlike qualities does it have? Why do some of us regard it as historical truth? Why do we try to respect each other's views on this when we certainly would not respect a classmate's belief that $2 + 3 = 7$?

An objection might be raised that teachers are not prepared to handle material of this kind. (This is the old specialization argument on which I have already declared myself a heretic.) I would like to see the content of religious study treated in the half day devoted to themes of care, but aspects of spirit should be addressed wherever they arise. Teachers prepared to teach mythology in an intellectually honest way can certainly handle topics in religion. They already understand that myths are not simply untruths or fanciful stories. Rather, myths capture the spirit of a people and encode its deepest fears, hopes, longings, and systems of control. Understood this way, there is no need to fear confusing religion and mythology. They are not synonymous, but all religions invoke and maintain certain myths. An examination of these is part of the school's mission; it demands and exercises critical thinking.

Not only is a study of religion essential in any educational program that purports to induce critical thinking, it is closely connected to our first theme in caring for oneself. Spirit and body are joined, and the quest for grace is an attempt to integrate the self. Topics that can be treated include forms of meditation, prayer, laughter, poetry, ritual, song, and dance. In a profound sense, all of these represent ways of "getting high" without damaging the body. They are possible routes to grace, and they are sometimes products of grace.

My husband and I long ago gave up formal religion, but we still are moved by the hymns we learned as children. Sometimes when we're driving across the country nonstop, on a Sunday morning, the radio yields only religious music. Then we abandon ourselves to singing one old favorite after another. Our children have been astonished. "How do you know so many verses?" they have asked. They might better have asked why we did not teach them these old songs. We had too long supposed that people either learned these things in religious settings (thereby risking all the evils from which we had fled) or they did not learn them at all. Now, older and possibly wiser, we see that matters of the spirit are too important to be confined to centers of indoctrination. They must be part of everyday life and of the most strenuous intellectual efforts.

Few schools teach anything about religion, mistakenly supposing that the separation of state and church requires silence on religion. All it requires, of course, is that public institutions not establish a religious perspective that must be adopted. We cannot indoctrinate in schools. Our national policies have been inconsistent on separation—fussy and pedantic on matters such as public payment for textbooks in parochial schools and the singing of Christmas carols, yet apparently oblivious when "under God" was inserted into the pledge of allegiance (Levy, 1986). I would prefer to eliminate such language because it implies, falsely, that we all accept one god—usually construed as the male god of biblical record—and that we believe our country is under the guidance of this god. Such expressions introduce a religious perspective into official language and should be targets of challenge for those who would uphold the separation clause. But religion—more generally, spirituality—is just too important for schools to ignore, and debates over religious issues should be part of the regular curriculum.

Many theme courses or sequences can be constructed around religion. One might involve conceptions of god and include some of the difficult theological problems that arise when god is defined in particular ways. Another might address religion and politics with sexism and racism as important subtopics. It is particularly important that young women understand the role religion has played in maintaining men's domination over them. If education were to be truly liberal—that is, freeing—the study of religion and politics would be fundamental. (See Ruether, 1983; Spretnak, 1982.) Such topics might be part of a specialty course for students in the interpersonal program and a theme-elective course for others. Similarly, students in the arts program might have courses in religion and art, religion and music, or religion and literature.

Religion is an important theme in black culture, too. Students should come to appreciate the genius of black people in creating black Christian churches out of a religion forced on them as slaves. What could have been a slave mentality became instead a wonderful force for solidarity and liberation (Walker, 1983). Spirituals, poetry, novels, and biographies that describe black Christianity and its influence are plentiful. Many of the same works also reveal other traditions, and these too should be a part of spiritual education.

So much of history and culture is connected to religion that it is hard to imagine people acquiring anything like a cultural or tribal understanding without some knowledge of it. Further, as Carl Jung (1973) insisted, god is a psychic reality; that is, the concept of god seems to be embedded in the human psyche, and the longing for spiritual connection is universal. Acceptance and appreciation of a variety of approaches might have many salutary effects: Students might find a personally satisfying mode of spirituality; they might understand alien others better as they learn about their spiritual commitments; they might develop a genuine and facilitative humility—one that acknowledges both the beauty and the terror of being one tiny manifestation of a universal quest. Extremism may be less likely in children so informed.

Some worry, however, about inducing the opposite of extremism—a form of passive indifference or alienation. This effect is often seen now as students of college age examine their earlier religious beliefs with new and powerful analytic tools. But I would not wait until college age, and I would not encourage the mere application of mathematical-like analysis. The aim is to come to a deeper understanding and appreciation of spirituality, not to reject it entirely. A derivative aim, enormously important in itself, is to understand that we need not believe everything attached to a particular view or group in order to commit ourselves to it. We may be critical adherents, advocates, friends, or supporters.

Among the things I would like our children to learn is how liberation and feminist theologies are restoring an ancient respect for bodies as enspirited beings. In these theologies the body becomes central, and adherents seek redemption and even resurrection in facilitating decent lives for all human beings here and now. They do not treasure the soul as something separate from and higher than the body, and they frankly mourn for the body that is no longer "enspirited" whether through death or collapse into evil or despair. They seek grace through the restoration of spirit in ourselves and others, and in preserving its memory in our narratives. Substantial positions on spirit should be considered as they are suggested by either students or teachers.

In an important sense, study and participation in spirituality is part of the maintenance, restoration, and enrichment of spirit. Children may be inspired by a particular religion or, forsaking such a commitment, they may be deeply affected by the music of Bach, the art of Michelangelo, the majesty of great cathedrals, the power of religion to move armies, the intellectual challenge of theodicies, the pervasive themes of myth, biblical poetry and parable, rituals in both mainstream and pagan religions, or the treatment of women in monotheistic religions. The possibilities are unlimited. The more I think about the centrality of spirituality in our lives, the more concerned I become about its shameful neglect in the public undertaking we call "education." Surely our responsibility to educate includes attention to matters of the spirit.

This is a good place to remind ourselves that we cannot solve the problems of education with only a curricular response. Curriculum is important, and I have acknowledged that fact by organizing many chapters around the topics I would like to see included. But schools have a way of taking vitally important material—exciting material—and reducing it to mush. Discussion and open exploration must be central to spiritual education. It must not be reduced to a set of facts tested "objectively." There might, of course, be common readings that would form the foundation of class discussion, but individual students might satisfy course requirements and earn a grade in a variety of ways: by taking an examination if they are interested in demonstrating their knowledge in the area, by doing a project or term paper, or by undergoing an oral examination on supplementary readings. We must keep our purposes clear. We study spirituality because it matters to us individually and collectively; it is a center of existential care.

OCCUPATIONAL LIFE

In discussing occupational life, I will use "occupation" in much the way John Dewey did. For him, an occupation referred not only to a way of making a living but, more important, to any project or task that fully occupies us; that is, it refers to something that calls forth our wholehearted energies. Individuals are occupied by different projects, and people at different stages of life have different interests. Therefore, although I will discuss preparation for an occupation in the standard sense, I will also be concerned with developmental tasks or those tasks that occupy us by virtue of our age or developmental stage.

There is, of course, a clear relation between the biology of various stages and their characteristic developmental tasks. In an important theme sequence, students would study the developmental tasks of infancy, childhood, adolescence, adulthood, and old age. These stages can be examined from a psychological perspective—as a central concern in caring for self—and also from historical, multicultural, and sociological perspectives. Such study can also include community work that would provide not only service to children or the aged but also supervised laboratory experience to augment what is learned in the classroom.

Along with the social studies aspect of developmental occupations, there could be a wonderful literature component. Many high school English teachers use *The Catcher in the Rye* and *A Separate Peace* to discuss the developmental tasks of adolescence as well as to analyze literature. This use should be extended to a study of fairy tales and children's literature and to works that illustrate the emotional tasks of maturity and old age. One finds superb examples in the novels of Mary Gordon and Doris Lessing and, of course, in biographies and autobiographies. In education, Maxine Greene has illustrated the uses of literature and biography beautifully in work after work. There is no need to sacrifice quality in selecting such works, but they should not be adopted as part of a literary canon, and no one work need be permanently entrenched in the curriculum.

As part of his wide-ranging discussion of occupations, Dewey wrote of the fourfold interests of children: communication, construction (making things), expression (drawing, singing, dancing), and investigation (figuring things out). I can think of no better basis for the elementary school curriculum. If these are things that naturally occupy children, then these are the activities through which children will grow and develop the capacities that will enable them to tackle later developmental tasks. It is clear that all of these interests can be profitably engaged through play, and we need not differentiate sharply between work and play. Indeed, if that separation were not so cruelly and needlessly introduced in elementary school, young adults might not suffer the fatigue we discussed earlier or, at least, the fatigue might not be so acute.

When I was between 4th and 5th grades, a male cousin and I started to play a dice baseball game. We were seriously occupied in this enterprise for about two years. Our parents bought each of us a small metal file box in which we kept the records of our teams and players. He had the National League and I had the American League. (Of course, these teams did not play each other in the regular season, but ours was, after all, a dice game, not the real thing.) We kept the averages of every one of our players. Our method was to divide the number of times at bat into 1,000 and then multiply by the number of hits. In mathematical symbols, we found our averages by converting a fraction such as 9/27 into 333/1,000. Having just completed 4th grade, we knew nothing of decimals, but we were whizzes at dividing and multiplying. As the summer wore on and our make-believe/real players accumulated more and more at-bats, we decided to compose a file card of conversions. We divided everything from 2 to about 50 into 1,000. Then all we had to do was consult the chart of quotients and multiply by the number of hits. We checked results, by the way, and agreed on a rule for rounding off.

Another favorite game was pinochle. My grandmother (his aunt) taught us, and it was a delightfully natural way to learn about negative numbers. We didn't call them that, of course. When a player was "in the hole," he or she had to climb out with a positive score, and another bad hand just sank one deeper in the hole.

Then we played monopoly—my cousin, my sister, and I. Not only did we learn a lot about counting and making deals, we also constructed our own rules for short games and for extended games involving endless borrowing procedures.

Sometimes when we tired of monopoly and baseball, we would sit by the street under my grandparents' beautiful maples and count cars. Jack would have north and I south. All kinds of complications arose. We were very close to a T-corner. Cars emerging from Day Street had to turn either past us or away from us. Was it fair for me to count those that emerged and turned south while those that turned north escaped the count? (No. Jack wouldn't stand for it.) Then we had to decide whether buses and trucks counted. (Yes.) We learned the word *vehicle*. Now, how about bicycles? To make the game more interesting, we started to give extra points for special makes such as Packards.

All of this activity contributed mightily to our mathematical development. Among other things, mathematics involves making distinctions, establishing rules, inventing algorithms, and perceiving order. We were engaged all summer long in such activities. We alternated between real baseball (where I spent most of my time in "fielding practice"—a common plight for girls who played with bossy boys) and the games I have just described. There is little question in my mind as to what these games meant for our intellectual development.

When I had children of my own, we established games in mental arithmetic for "waiting" situations. In the doctor's office, in restaurants, at the dentist's, we did mental arithmetic. The children learned to multiply 4×23 by multiplying 4×20 and adding 4×3. Later when our youngest daughter was doing Advanced Placement calculus, she would call out in the night, "Mom, are you awake?" "Yes." "There's this vector . . ." And she would call out the parts of a problem that we would then solve cooperatively by this telegraphic method.

The children in these stories were *occupied*. They were doing things wholeheartedly, and out of this wholehearted doing came learning. Not all the children in our large heterogeneous family would be interested in the same games or occupations. The important thing is for all of them to have opportunities to become genuinely engaged in activities that contribute to development. Parents and teachers cannot help being more attracted to children who share their own occupations, but this recognition does not imply that occupations must be hierarchically arranged with traditional academic ones at the top. On the contrary, admitting our bias suggests creating a more versatile faculty and deliberate attention to those occupations often overlooked in the standard mode of schooling.

So far I have considered developmental and individual occupations. Attention to both is imperative in coming to understand and appreciate the self. But it is also necessary to plan for the occupation by which one will earn a living. The differentiated programs I have suggested should facilitate such planning. Children would not be "relegated to plumbing" in the 2nd grade as some people fear. I agree with Adler that school should not be preparation for a specific occupation. Rather, children with a real talent for mechanical activities would be encouraged to consider a wide range of possibilities, including that of crossing over to another program. Most important, however, is the value structure behind the construction of these programs. *All* honest occupations are respectable and should be highly valued. One may choose plumbing or diesel mechanics or piano teaching with pride and enter the work wholeheartedly. (Incidentally, one may also do better financially than people who plod through a college course and drift into a tedious office job.)

Part of the specialty courses at the secondary level should be devoted to subject matter counseling. Children enrolled in academic mathematics, for example, should learn something about the psychology of learning mathematics, the fields in which it is a primary tool, and their own idiosyncrasies in doing mathematics. The counseling function should provide the continuity of an apprenticeship, and it should also monitor the student's progress and interests in case a change is required.

With this broad approach to occupation, older people should neither fear retirement nor look upon it as a transition from work to play. It is simply a transformation from one set of occupations to another. When we come to regard wholehearted engagement with respect, we may gradually dismantle the pernicious hierarchy of occupations that stifles both adult and student life, and perhaps we will also find a new appreciation for the occupations of childhood and old age. Although I believe wholeheartedly in what I have just written, I recognize how far we are from its realization. It sounds simple in print. What makes it so difficult? Students and teachers should discuss this problem too. Again, central to my argument for the school as a center of care is that we must talk about these things. Instead of threatening children with a life of menial labor if they do not master academic mathematics, we should inform them honestly about the many ways in which they can develop their own talents, make a living, and earn respect in the community. Growing plants, making things, repairing things, serving people, caring for the young and elderly are all as important as wrestling with ideas and running a company. Students should learn that it is wonderful to be occupied—to be fully engaged in whatever they have chosen to do. The tragedy is that so many fall into "occupations" by default, supposing that their own inferiority has led to their lack of choices.

RECREATIONAL LIFE

Recreational life is closely related to occupational life. We can be as occupied in recreations as we are in our jobs. Indeed many find their recreations much more engaging than their formal occupations. Recreation, it is widely believed, is designed to relieve the fatigue of labor and the boredom of everyday responsibilities. Construed this way, recreation is an escape. But recreation can also be thought of as creating anew, refreshing. In this sense anything we enjoy—even favorite tasks on the job—can be thought of as recreation.

It is important for all young people to discover what refreshes and renews them. A well-integrated life includes intervals of activity that energize and make us feel whole. In helping to preserve our children's lives and physical well-being, we must start them on the road to reflection for self-understanding. One question to ask is, How can our recreation contribute to integration—to filling out our lives? People in sedentary jobs may want to choose recreation involving vigorous physical activity. As we saw earlier, however, some people may want to combine physical activity with productive activity. For example, I get most of my exercise gardening. It is not just that beds and borders need to be dug; I *enjoy* digging, raking, planting, weeding, and I feel better after an hour or two of this activity. Recreation should be both satisfying and satisfactory. It should make us feel good, and it should satisfy a need.

Another important question to ask is, How will our recreation change as we get older? I do not mean to suggest here that children should be encouraged to plan their whole lives or to forsake the recreational joys of childhood in a mistaken quest for grown-up activities. But recreation is an aspect of life that often needlessly separates generations. Of certain activities we say, That's for kids! or, That's for old folks! And, of course, some things are more appropriate for children or for old folks. But much zest for or life and valuable companionship are lost in an unreflective evaluation of activities and stages of life. Why shouldn't grownups play an occasional game of hopscotch? Why shouldn't kids play pinochle with their grandparents?

We can extend the idea of planning for lifetime recreation by noting a parallel between the school's role in occupational preparation and its possible role in recreational education. Instead of grooming children for particular sports or recreations, the school should be concerned with large classes of recreation. We need to plan for lifelong fitness and grace, not merely for current championships, and we need to think about mental, emotional, and social recreation as well as physical exercise.

Most important of all, schools need to help students increase their self-understanding through reflection on their recreational choices. Why do kids hang out at malls? Why do they spend small fortunes on sport shoes and biking outfits? What do they really enjoy? How will they prepare to have fun throughout their lives? This last is a crucial question for adults to consider and explore with young people. It is a great mistake to tell children that they are now living the best years of their lives. What, then, is there to look forward to? Besides, it's rarely true. It is far more honest and reasonable to help children plan for the good times to come, and these should not be described as lazy days of self-indulgence. To convey such messages authentically, we must talk with our children, live with them, and show by our examples that life is both consummatory—to be enjoyed from moment to moment—and instrumental preparation for further activity, enjoyment, and fulfillment.

Now we have completed a slim outline of caring for self. It might look very different if you, the reader, were to construct it, but my object has been to lay out some possibilities and invite dialogue. If all we did was to care for our physical bodies, connect with the spiritual realm, go to work, and catch some recreation on the way home to dinner and bed, we would have covered the main aspects of caring for self. But the self is a relational entity. We cannot care for ourselves in any meaningful way in isolation from others. So we turn next to the important topic of caring for intimate others. In a deep sense, this is an extension of caring for self.

CHAPTER 7

Caring in the Inner Circle

Caring, in both its natural and ethical senses, describes a certain kind of relation. It is one in which one person, A, the carer, cares for another, B, and B recognizes that A cares for B. As described earlier, A's consciousness during the interval of caring is marked by (1) engrossment or nonselective attention, and (2) motivational displacement or the desire to help. A genuinely listens, feels, and responds with honest concern for B's expressed interests or needs. When we say, "B recognizes," we mean that B receives A's caring and reacts in a way that shows it. A relation of caring is complete when B's recognition becomes part of what A receives in his or her attentiveness. A relation may fall short of caring if either carer or cared-for fails in his or her contribution.

The paragraph above describes the basic caring encounter in all circumstances. But the relationships we are most interested in are those that extend over a considerable period of time. These relationships may be equal or unequal. We expect a mature relationship—one, say, between husband and wife—to be characterized by equal relations; that is, the parties alternate as carers and cared-fors. Both stand ready to be carers, and both respond appreciatively as cared-fors. Relations between friends, colleagues, and neighbors are other examples of equal relations.

But there are many relations that are unequal by their very nature. In these relations, one person occupies the position of carer most of the time, and the other is necessarily the cared-for. Some familiar examples are parent–child, teacher–student, and professional–client relations. In all of these, there may be occasional reversals—encounters in which the dependent party cares for the more powerful partner—but for the most part, these relations are stable and unequal.

What do we want our children to learn about caring in the inner circle—caring for intimate others and associates? How should our understanding of caring relations guide what we do in schools? Let's consider equal relations first. Again, what I suggest here is not a recipe. It is what *I* would like for our children. What do *you* want for them?

EQUAL RELATIONS

Among the relations we expect to be equal are those involving mates or lovers, friends, colleagues, and neighbors. In all of these, we find something amiss if one party is expected to be the carer while the other assumes it is his or her right to be cared for. As I mentioned earlier, fear of exploitation is a major barrier for some feminists in considering an ethic of caring. They are rightly concerned that women will become stuck in the position of carer. How can we remove that fear without abandoning caring?

Mates and Lovers

The urge to find a mate is strong in most of us. It is not only sexual desire that impels us; even more, it is the desire for stable connection. Most of us want someone with whom to share the events of our lives. When something interesting happens in my work day, I often think, "Wait 'til Jim hears this!" Part of the joy and vigor of life comes from the retelling and, thus, reliving of events that are important precisely because they can be shared.

It seems evident that females and males have different perspectives on intimate relations and different problems with connection (Belenky, Clinchy, Goldberger, & Tarule, 1986; Gilligan, 1982; Miller, 1976). Theories on why this is so range from the biological through the psychological and cultural. Both sexes long for connection—for caring relations—but women have, until recently, found it more culturally acceptable to express their longing. In a deeply touching PBS broadcast, commentator Bill Moyers explored with the poet Robert Bly the suppressed male desire for emotional connection and expression. The need, Bly said, is for a male mother. Young men need the preservative and attentive love of mother, but they grow best when this love comes from one who can also initiate them into manhood. Where in schools do we acknowledge this need? When will the wisdom of Bly become part of teacher education?

The problems of women are different, but no less acute. For centuries women were expected to seek connection—indeed to put marriage and stable human relations above all else. When I was in high school and college, girls were explicitly advised to hide their intelligence. We were supposed to do well in school but not to outshine the boys. The real test of our success in life was the quality of men we attracted. Girls today should certainly read and discuss extensively the history of female academic and professional life (for a wonderful start on this, see Rossiter, 1982). Some of these accounts, together with full biographies of women who lived early in this century, move me even now to tears. The hardship, the insults, the misunderstandings, the unfairness, the sheer and utter waste of talent! Both girls and boys should be fully acquainted with this history.

But what has this to do with seeking a mate? Today, instead of being pushed to marry and raise a family (be respectable!), many bright young women feel pressed to reject permanent intimate relations in favor of careers. Many of my graduate students think that it is impossible to "have it all"—to do well in two spheres that have for so long represented different worlds. Secondary schools are contributing to this problem, paradoxically, by urging girls to participate more fully in mathematics and science and to plan for real careers. Schools *should* encourage young women to plan careers, but that's only half the job. They must also provide opportunities to explore what these plans mean for human life and connection.

I wonder sometimes what my life would have been like if I had had the "freedom" young women now have to reject family life. As a high school valedictorian who had to cover up intellectual interests by playing tricks on my teachers and cutting study halls, I felt inwardly pushed to prove my feminine worth by marrying early and having children. Notice that I felt inwardly pushed. I was pressed by a way of life that was so completely accepted that I did not even know where the impulse came from. If I were growing up now, I might well choose an academic and professional life without conventional family.

The thought appalls and dismays me. I would have missed what has become for me the very heart of life—the stable love of a good man, the joy of raising children who have become delightful adult companions, a house full of plants and pets and open doors. This is not the only good life, but it has been my good life. The educational question that arises is whether there is some way to share the wisdom of life so that young people will be able to make choices that fulfill their deepest longings. They need to hear stories like mine and stories that are very different.

Increasingly, women are choosing other women as their stable companions. This choice, too, should be acceptable. More than acceptable, it should be celebrated if the choice is loving and well informed. Many women who have made this choice are occupied just as I am at the moment—reading or writing in a sunny study with a cat purring happily in lap (or, more perversely, on the work at hand), and Mozart playing softly in the background.

There is, of course, something culturally specific about the description just given, and I will move beyond it, but before doing so I want to delve more deeply into the problems of young women in academe. In talking with undergraduate women all over the country, I've been dismayed at the depth of their frustration and disappointment with men. (This is not true of all young women but of a significant number.) Many women have simply given up on men. They are not lesbians, but they have decided to find connection with other women or to go it alone. Many point to their mothers' lives with pity and dread. "I can't live that way," they say, and they see no alternative within the framework of marriage. But, I've asked, aren't men becoming more sensitive, cooperative, egalitarian? The answers to this range from "Are you kidding?" to "Not enough."

One incident was especially revealing and will help to illustrate how an ethic of caring can guide our decisions. In a group discussion, someone pointed out something I mentioned in an earlier chapter—that the very language men often use in describing their household participation suggests that housework and child care are the woman's responsibility. They say such things as, "I took the garbage out for you," or "I changed the baby for you," or "Can I help with the dusting?" I remarked that even my feminist husband sometimes talks this way and that I would not call him on it. What would I do? the group asked. I'd wait until something of the sort happened on television or in a story—some impersonal context—and then I'd point it out and encourage dialogue.

The group—both women and men—disagreed with my approach. They found it wishy-washy. How will men ever learn? the women asked. One young man agreed with the women in criticizing my approach and insisted that he wanted to know when he was doing something wrong. They all asserted that we should be open and frank in our personal relations.

Well, maybe. From the perspective of caring, how we behave with intimate others depends on the other's needs as well as on our own. Why would I not tell my husband straight out that his language bothers me? Put simply, because I love him and have no wish to hurt him, and that kind of remark from me *would* hurt him. In caring, we look beyond the principle that sits in judgment of the language to the person speaking. It is clear to me that, when he uses language of the sort under question, my husband really intends to help, and the fact of the matter is that I have taken major responsibility for certain areas of household management. Therefore, in an important sense, he is helping, and I am responsible, although it should always be possible to renegotiate responsibility.

When we live in caring relations, we teach each other gently by example and by confirmation—not by accusation, confession, forgiveness, and penance. There is a possibility that some people—the young man who agreed with the women, for example—want the treatment described by accusation, confession, and so forth. A caring mate would know this, and, if this mode of response were possible for her, she could use it. It is, of course, an empirical question how many people really want this treatment. But the important question is concrete and individual: Does this much-loved other respond with appreciation and growth to my words? We should not use each other to promote causes or illustrate great truths, and yet we must take responsibility for each other's moral growth. I will revisit this seeming paradox again and again.

I am more familiar with the problems of women in academic life than with those in other occupations, but it is obvious that most women do not spend their mornings in sunny studies, inspired by the music of Mozart and Chopin. Yet all young women need to understand how they are pressed by their cultures and subcultures to relate to men and to seek connection. Sociologists and psychologists have suggested that many teenagers have babies to fulfill their longing for intimate connection. A baby represents permanent connection—someone to whom we will be related forever. If other relations have broken down and there seems little possibility of establishing an equal relation with a man, having a baby might very well be a tempting solution. Young women need help in exploring this temptation in depth. Even this seemingly irrevocable and permanent relation can be destroyed or badly damaged by other social and economic factors. Witness how many children are now brought up by grandparents. Adults need at least one strong, equal relation. This relation makes it possible to do the sort of caregiving required in essentially unequal relations such as parenthood.

In seeking such a relation, all young people need to learn how to explore some basic questions. One was nicely illustrated in the film *Shenandoah*. The character played by Jimmy Stewart was approached by a young man who wanted Stewart's permission to marry his daughter. Stewart asked the young man whether he *liked* his daughter. "I know you love her," he said, "but do you *like* her?" Stewart was pointing to a bit of wisdom that all adults should share with the young. To build a stable, equal relationship, we have to like each other. If romantic love fades—or even as it fluctuates—liking each other provides the connection we need to keep growing. We do not want to hurt those we like. Further, there is an important test built into Stewart's question. Generally, we like people who are capable of forms of growth that we admire. We are, in a sense, predisposed to foster their growth because we already see something admirable, likeable about them. This recognition provides a solid base for a truly moral relationship.

Another basic question was illustrated in *The Fiddler on the Roof*. Here the main character, who had been settled for many years in a hard-working marriage, plaintively asks his wife, "But do you *love* me?" Mystified by the ways of the young who have begun insisting on their own choice of mates, he worries that he has missed something. Do you love me? Do I have that special something that makes your eyes sparkle and your heart sing? Ah, what a topic! Surely this should be a major part of sex education, and it can include biography, fiction, poetry, music, art, and history. Surely this would be the place to read the Brownings, *Romeo and Juliet*, *The Scarlet Letter*, *Wuthering Heights*, the story of John and Abigail Adams, of Marie and Pierre Curie; to listen to Berlioz's *Romeo and Juliet*, Wagner's *Tristan and Isolde*, Bernstein's *West Side Story*, Gershwin's *Porgy and Bess*. My point here is, again, that every topic of great existential interest has intellectual possibilities. But we should let the existential concern drive the intellectual. We should not ordain interest in great intellectual works for their own sakes, although such interest may arise in some students.

Finally, serious dialogue on the search for mates and lovers can contribute inestimably to critical thinking. We should spend time helping young people to distinguish between fantasy and thinking that is a prelude to action. When I was in high school, I read some of Freud (on my own, I hasten to add; the curriculum contained nothing so fascinating). It was tough going, but I learned enough to conclude that repression was bad for one's emotional life. I decided that I would think whatever I pleased, and I recall firmly deciding that most fantasizing was an end in itself—that it could be delightfully and sometimes gruesomely satisfying in itself. It was not a prelude to action. Indeed I was astonished at the conclusion of my analysis to realize that I would abhor in real life many of the things I enjoyed in fantasy. This part of my fantasy life was just like a cleansing bath for the mind—a hot, soapy shower instead of the much-touted (and repressive) cold shower.

We have to help young people with the problems known as "lusting in the heart." I have already expressed my own opinion on the topic: think what you please, so long as you can separate such thinking from planning for action. But there are other perspectives. I would present those, too, but I'd include lots of examples of the damage done to mental health when people suppose that their thoughts can by themselves hurt others. (Think of all the children who suppose that their anger or hate killed a loved one.) On the other side of worry, we do not want young people to retreat into Walter Mitty-like lives, getting satisfaction only from fantasy. A free and healthy mind should be able to move from fantasy-thinking to action-thinking without confusing the two.

Although I believe the open discussion of fantasy and its role in sexual and mental health is essential, students should not be induced to disclose their own fantasies. On the contrary, teachers should gently discourage such disclosure. It is not the content of fantasies that needs discussion (at least not in a classroom) but the fact of them. Students should be encouraged to evaluate their own fantasy life, and they should be assured that it is common and natural to fantasize. They need information and criteria by which to judge the health of their own fantasies.

At the acme of mental health, it should become possible to employ fantasy-like thinking in problem solving. Long habits of keeping the two types separate may actually impede intellectual growth. When it is clear that the domain is one safe for action, fantasy as intellectual intuition can be a powerful tool. It puts the mind to play in an intellectual domain.

In concluding this brief discussion of learning to understand love, I want to reiterate the major points: Nothing is more important to most of us than stable and loving connection; caring for this special person takes precedence over promoting causes and principles; learning to care and be cared for takes place by many avenues and is poorly guided by fixed principles; intellectual life is not at all impeded by a concentration on existential concerns; and in intimate life we have an opportunity to learn a fundamental secret of morality—how to promote each other's moral growth.

Friends

We also find caring relations in friendship. This, too, is a topic that has waxed and waned in philosophical and educational interest, but it has never failed to concern actual human beings in their concrete lives.

Friends are especially important to teenagers, and they need guidance in making and maintaining friendships.

Aristotle is one philosopher who wrote eloquently on friendship, and he assessed it as central in moral life. In the *Nicomachean Ethics* Aristotle wrote that the main criterion of friendship is that a friend wishes a friend well for his or her own sake. When we befriend others, we want good things for them not because those things may enhance *our* welfare but because they are good for our friends. Aristotle organized friendships into various categories: those motivated by common business or political purposes, those maintained by common recreational interests, and those created by mutual admiration of the other's virtue. The last was, for Aristotle, the highest form of friendship and, of course, the one most likely to endure.

Students need to understand, as Aristotle did, that friendship can be genuine and yet depend on mutual interests that may be transient. Some friendships do not extend beyond football season, army service, or common work in the same company. They may still be characterized by wishing the best for one's friend. The kind of friendship that grows out of mutual admiration and likeability is rare and beautiful and brings with it a special moral obligation. Among the good things we want for our friends is moral growth, an increase in virtue. Although Aristotle did not employ the word *virtue* in our modern sense, it still makes sense to say that we want our friends to grow both in requisite excellences and in virtue construed as moral virtue. This means that true friends will protect each other not only from external evil but also from evil that arises internally. When we care, as we must about a friend, we continually support the quest for a better self.

How do friendships occur? What draws people together? Here students should have opportunities to see how far Aristotle's description will carry them. They should hear about Damon and Pythias, of course. But they should also examine some incongruous friendships: Huckleberry Finn and the slave, Jim; Miss Celie and Shug in Alice Walker's *The Color Purple*; Lenny and George in Steinbeck's *Of Mice and Men*; Jane and Maudie in Lessing's *The Diaries of Jane Somers*. What do each of these characters give to the friendship? Can friendship be part of a personal quest for fulfillment? When does a personal objective go too far and negate Aristotle's basic criterion?

Students should be encouraged to examine the concept of loyalty. Is there such a thing as unconditional friendship—staying friends no matter what? One aspect of this question concerns exploitation and requires a careful analysis of equal relations and what makes them equal. As I suggested in the section on mates and lovers, we can rarely browbeat others into carrying their share of obligation, and if caring relations are important to us, we can find better approaches. But we need to attend to this set of problems; we cannot depend on good fortune.

Another aspect is perhaps even more troubling for most of us. When should moral principles outweigh the demands of friendship? The question is often cast this way, even though many of us find the wording misleading. What the questioner wants us to consider is whether we should protect friends who have done something morally wrong. A few years ago there was a terrifying local example of this problem when a teenage boy killed a girl and bragged about it to his friends. His friends, in what they interpreted as an act of loyalty, did not even report the murder.

From the perspective of caring, there is no inherent conflict between moral requirements and friendship, because we have a primary obligation to promote our friends' moral growth. But lots of concrete conflicts can arise when we have to consider exactly what to do. Instead of juggling principles as we might when we say "Friendship is more important than a little theft" or "Murder is more important than friendship," we begin by asking ourselves whether our friends have committed caring acts. If they have not, something has to be done. In the case of something as horrible as murder, the act must be reported. But true friends would also go beyond initial judgment and action to ask how they can follow through with appropriate help for the murderer. When we adopt caring as an ethical approach, our moral work just begins where other approaches pronounce Q.E.D. Caring requires staying-with—or what Ruddick has called "holding." We do not let our friends fall if we can help it, and if they do, we hold on and pull them back up.

Friendship, as an equal relation, makes demands on both parties. Young people should understand that it is sometimes necessary to break off a relation in which they are exploited, abused, or pushed to do things they regard as harmful or wrong. Quitting such a relation is not "breaking a friendship" because, in actuality, there is no friendship without mutual acceptance of the main criterion.

Gender differences in friendship patterns should also be discussed. It may be harder for males to reject relations in which they are pushed to do socially unacceptable acts, because those acts are often used as tests of manhood. Females, in contrast, find it more difficult to separate themselves from abusive relations. In both cases, young people have to learn not only to take appropriate responsibility for the moral growth of others but also to insist that others accept responsibility for their own behavior. It is often a fine line, and because there are no formulas to assist us, we remain vulnerable in all our moral relations.

Colleagues and Neighbors

We work with and live near many people who never become our friends. Do we need a different ethical approach to deal with these people? This is a question raised recently by several philosophers in reaction to an ethic of caring. The problem becomes even more acute as we move beyond face-to-face relations into some form of global association.

It is important to understand that caring does not require us to abandon all other guides to moral behavior. Indeed, if we are to be prepared to care for those we encounter, we must give some respectful attention to the social customs and principles they accept. If there is no moral reason for rejecting these customs and principles as rough guides to social interaction, we can commit ourselves to act accordingly. This kind of acceptance and conformity makes everyday life smooth and congenial.

A great difficulty arises when people mistakenly suppose that the ordinary rules and maxims of a culture *are* its morality. In actuality, they are only a reflection of that morality. In problematic situations, they must always be carefully reassessed, or even set aside in favor of a direct meeting designed to create a caring relation. An alternative, preferred by thinkers using a justice perspective, is to reassess relevant principles and try to decide which should govern the situation, given that the supreme principle is one of justice. This alternative is unsatisfactory for reasons I have already stated. It too often leads moral agents to believe that their moral work is finished when a justifiable decision has been reached.

Some years ago my husband and I were asked by a group of neighbors to sign a petition against another family in the neighborhood. Our neighbors, quite reasonably, wanted this family to clean up their property. It was a mess. Everyone agreed to that. But we were concerned about how the family would feel—accused and coerced by their neighbors. What would happen to neighborhood relations?

We did not know the accused family well, even though we were their nearest neighbors, and we did not care enough to use conscientiously the approach I've advocated. Instead we debated whether our aesthetic sensibility or their freedom to do as they pleased with their own property should have priority, and we decided that their freedom was the more important value. We did not sign the petition. We made the same decision we would have made if we had followed up carefully on our initial line of thinking, but because we did not talk to the accused neighbors directly, we never learned how they felt about the events, and they remained isolated from their neighbors, including us. Thus, despite "right" thinking, we failed to accomplish our initial purpose. (So did the petitioning neighbors, for the result was a massive screen of shrubbery, not a change in life-style.)

All students should learn how to reason with principles, assess values, and argue for various positions. But they should also be aware that these activities are only part of moral life, and a part loaded with theoretical and practical difficulties. The biggest part of moral life is living together nonviolently and supportively even in the face of disagreement. This means that we have to ask continually what must be done after crucial decisions have been made. How do we convey our decisions with the least pain? What support do we offer those who need it? How do we go on living and working together?

For students, classmates are colleagues. Besides cordiality and verbal respect, what do classmates owe each other? An exploration of relations among classmates offers an opportunity to analyze the social structures that support or undermine collegial relations. Consider an example that is familiar to all students—competing for grades. Among the issues to be discussed is cheating. Many students deny that cheating is wrong. In part this denial may be a result of teachers and parents saying repeatedly, "When you cheat, you only hurt yourself." Such a statement is clearly false in a highly competitive system. I suppose adults fell into the habit of talking this way as part of a general retreat from moralistic language. But the statement is not only false, it is hypocritical as well, and it reveals a shocking failure to protect students who are committed to fair competition. It could only be true in a noncompetitive situation where the material to be learned is significant to the student's well-being. And this is hardly true of contemporary schooling. Thus, when students cheat, we must help them to understand that they have committed an uncaring act.

But a deeper question arises.

Why do we pit students against each other? Some argue that we do this to prepare students for a competitive culture. Does that mean that competition is in itself something valuable? Whether or not we are enthusiastic about a competitive way of life, as teachers we should reflect on the issues and encourage our students to do so. Competition is sometimes induced by natural scarcities, but there is no natural scarcity of A's and B's. We introduce this scarcity. Why?

Students should learn something about both the pernicious and efficacious effects of competition. A wonderful book that illustrates both is *A Separate Peace* (Knowles, 1975). The book's unhappy protagonist, Gene, gets better and better grades as he becomes more and more competitive. Observing (wrongly) that, in relations with his best friend, Finny, "the deadly rivalry was on both sides," Gene recalls:

> I became quite a student after that. I had always been a good one, although I wasn't really interested and excited by learning itself, the way that Douglass was. Now I became not only just good but exceptional, with Chet Douglass my only rival in sight. But I began to see that Chet was weakened by the very genuineness of his interest in learning. He got carried away by things; for example, he was so fascinated by the tilting planes of solid geometry that he did almost as badly in trigonometry as I did myself. When we read *Candide* it opened up a new way of looking at the world to Chet, and he continued hungrily reading Voltaire. . . . He was vulnerable there, because to me they were all pretty much alike . . . and I worked indiscriminately on all of them. (p. 46)

Besides drawing the conclusion that genuine interest in learning is a handicap in school competition, Gene also began to see competition everywhere—even in his best friend, Finny, in whom it was entirely absent as a motive. The disaster that followed was in part a result of jealous and zealous competition. Reminiscing as an adult, Gene realizes that not only the tragedy of Finny but also the larger tragedy of war might be traced to this "ignorance of the human heart" that sees rivals and enemies everywhere. He and his schoolmates were but samples:

> All of them, all except Phineas [Finny], constructed at infinite cost to themselves these Maginot Lines against this enemy they thought they saw across the frontier, this enemy who never attacked that way—if he ever attacked at all; if he was indeed the enemy. (p. 196)

Students need to consider when cooperation is more appropriate than competition, and teachers need to ask how competition fits the continuity of purpose we discussed earlier. Does it help to produce competent, caring, loving, and lovable people?

Reflecting on the matter, teachers may be tempted to condemn all forms of competition. But this is not necessary. Undergraduates often ask me whether I think all competition is bad. In response I've suggested three tests for healthy competition: Is the enterprise still fun? Can you take some delight in the victories of your rivals? Are you turning in better performances or products as a result? If the answer to each of these questions is positive, competition may be benign and even useful.

I will close this section by considering a question that will pop up again and again. Do we bear responsibility for the moral growth of colleagues as we do for friends and family members? The answer is yes, but the responsibility takes on a somewhat different form. As with intimate others, we must not push colleagues into behavior they will later deplore; we must be careful not to bring out the worst in them. But, by definition, we do not know these people as well as we know friends and family. Therefore, when we try to confirm them, we risk self-righteousness and emptiness. We may come across as busybodies or do-gooders, as people ready with a platitude and empty gesture. If a moral emergency arises, we have to spend time getting to know a colleague—we have to talk, listen, and stay with this other long enough to construct a likely mode of support. Of course, talking, listening, and staying-with *are* forms of support, and with them in place we may not need to give specific advice or further aid.

UNEQUAL RELATIONS

Whereas students need most to learn about equal relations, teachers need most to analyze and reflect upon unequal relations. Some relations are, by definition, unequal, and one party must of necessity be the main carer. Students, too, have to learn how to care in such relations, but their first contributions are as recipients of care. These contributions, as we have seen, are not negligible. As young people learn how to discern and accept care, they can gradually learn also to care for others. Perhaps the best place to practice is with those even younger.

Children

Most of us are naturally protective and tender with children. Even tough male teenagers usually respond to children with gentleness. In some enlightened schools, educators have begun to match potential high school dropouts with elementary school children who need academic help. As these young people help children with schoolwork, they begin to realize their own potential and the value of an education. It doesn't seem to matter too much that they sometimes have to struggle with the material themselves. What matters is that they know more than the children they are teaching, and that by teaching they, too, are learning. In mathematical circles we have long said that the "best way to learn calculus is to teach it." We do not mean, of course, that people can start right out teaching. They have, first, to be taught. But the material is rarely clear until we ourselves teach it to others. Perhaps the best way to summarize and perfect elementary education is to employ postelementary students as teachers of younger students.

There are many reasons for involving teenagers in the lives of children. First, raising children is one of the most significant tasks any adult undertakes, and it requires adequate preparation. Relying solely on parents to provide that preparation was never a good idea, and today it is disastrous. Second, teenagers need to be confirmed in their budding altruism. They naturally have enormous self-interest, but they also have the capacity to be deeply concerned for others, and schools rarely give them a chance to practice the skills needed to develop this capacity. In schools we talk about concern for others and enforce some rules of polite conduct, but we do not identify the best in students and work actively to bring it out. Third, we need the services of energetic and altruistic teenagers. We should confess this need and urge young people to respond generously to it. Every time I hear young people say there is "nothing to do" in their town, I grieve for them and for the "sandwich generation" of which I am a part—vastly overburdened with the work of caregiving while another generation complains of nothing to do.

Fourth, involvement with children can be effective as an integral part of the academic education of teenagers. I want to elaborate a bit on this point. Earlier I suggested that teaching younger children might serve as a means to summarize and perfect elementary education. For years students, teachers, and parents have complained about the endless reviews that occupy much of 7th- and 8th-grade education. In many schools, children at this level are still grinding away at material that they failed to master in 5th or 6th grade, and by now they simply hate the stuff. Why not include tutoring as a systematic part of their 7th- and 8th-grade education? I am not suggesting intermittent, hit-or-miss tutoring sessions but, rather, careful planning among teams of teachers and students. A 7th-grade math teacher might instruct students on the material they will teach to, say, 4th graders the following week. Part of every math period would be devoted to planning and evaluating what goes on in their teaching assignments. Students could be assigned to classes at the edge of their own competence; that is, 7th graders who are fair but not yet really competent at long division could be assigned to help in classes where that is a major focus. Youngsters who have hitherto mastered most material could be assigned either to enrichment classes where they, too, would be challenged intellectually, or to children with special learning difficulties at any level.

A plan of this sort requires restructuring the curriculum and the school day of the 7th and 8th grades. This revision is consistent with the one I recommended for high schools in which part of every day should be directly devoted to centers and themes of care. Here, too, our purposes are multiple. We organize this way because our purpose is to produce caring and competent people, because we recognize the needs of children, because we need the good services of even our youngest citizens, and because we are concerned with academic growth.

The benefits are not only academic. In the teen years, most girls get some experience with children by babysitting. A few boys also do. However, many boys reject such work as unmasculine, and many never get the opportunity because parents are reluctant to entrust their children to male teenagers. In an age in which accusations of sexual abuse are made so frequently, I'm not sure that I would want my sons to risk the usual forms of lonely babysitting. It is far safer for them to get experience with children in publicly supervised situations. But they must have the experience. It is essential to the development of caring adults and to the eventual construction of equal relations with female partners.

A deeper understanding of self is another benefit to be gained from involvement with children. As older children have opportunities to interact with younger children, they should be encouraged to reflect on their own childhood and the special relations that guided their lives. They can also look ahead to the possibility of working closely with children in the future and, perhaps, consider whether children will play a central role in their lives. It should be acceptable for a well-informed older teenager to express preference for a childless future. Such a preference may, of course, change, but in traditional environments most teenagers never get an opportunity to explore their real inclinations. As a result, they may make poor occupational choices and, worse, drift into parenthood even though they are ill suited for it. A responsible adult can support civic concern about children without engaging in the direct care of children, but if one has children of one's own, caring deeply and effectively is a lifelong commitment. We must educate for this commitment.

Girls especially may need help in understanding and rejecting pathological forms of caring—forms characterized by continual self-denial. No one has described the problem more clearly than Ruddick (1989):

> To court self-denial for its own sake perverts rather than expresses attentive love. Mothers are especially prone to this perversion, since they are rewarded for self-sacrifice. They are familiar with the danger of denying their own needs only to find they have projected them onto their children. A person who counts herself as nothing lacks the confidence needed to suspend her own being to receive another's. [Ruddick is here referring to Simone Weil's beautiful comment about emptying one's soul to receive another.] Since her emptiness is involuntary and often frightening, she searches in her child to find the self she has sacrificed. The soul that can empty itself is a soul that already has a known, respected, albeit ever-developing self to return to when the moment of attention has passed. (p. 122)

In this section I have suggested that the study of children should be an important topic in secondary education, and that practice in caring for and teaching younger children should begin in the upper elementary grades. Surely the care of children should be a central topic in the education of all students.

Students

Students are not usually as close to teachers as offspring are to their parents, but the relationship is still, ideally, a close one, and for some students, teachers are more important than parents. A succession of teachers played a central role in my own life, and I cannot imagine what my life would have been like without these people: the 2nd-grade teacher who discovered that I was a good reader and turned me loose to read; the 5th-grade teacher whose youth and vitality encouraged an adventurous spirit (more adventurous than she anticipated); the 7th-grade teacher who made the move to a new community less painful. This teacher, whom I dearly loved, visited me when I had whooping cough and brought a quart of home-canned tomato juice. I had never liked tomato juice, but because it came from her, I loved it. To this day I prefer tomato juice to orange juice. I recall, too, that she came to my high school graduation, and her presence was more important to me than that of anyone else. Then there was my high school mathematics teacher. He was the reason I became a math teacher. In the last months of his life, many years later, I visited him weekly. Losing a parent was not more painful than losing him. And even in graduate school, my advisor was instrumental in my choice of philosophy and the enthusiasm with which I immersed myself in it. As Goethe said, we learn from those we love.

The teacher–student relation is, of necessity, unequal. Teachers have special responsibilities that students cannot assume. Martin Buber (1965) wrote that teachers must practice "inclusion"; teachers must, that is, take on a dual perspective: their own and that of their students. They must try to see the world as their students see it in order to move them from a less to a more satisfactory view. Good teachers do not reject what students see and feel but, rather, work with what is presently seen and felt to build a stronger position for each student. To do this effectively requires the creation and maintenance of a trusting relationship.

Teachers must remain aware that the relation is unequal. In conversation with Carl Rogers, Buber (1964) tried to convey this important notion to the great therapist:

> A man coming to you for help. . . . The essential difference between your role in this situation and his is obvious. He comes for help to you. You don't come for help to him. And not only this, but you are *able*, more or less, to help him. He can do different things to you, but not to help you. And not this alone. You *see* him, *really*. I don't mean that you cannot be mistaken, but you *see* him, . . . he cannot, by far, cannot *see* *you*. (p. 487)

In the same way, teachers can see students and see with them; students, by definition, cannot see in the same way with teachers. Nor should they be expected to. If a teacher–student relation moves in this direction, it becomes one of mature friendship, and the formal relation, the necessary relation, fades away. Students are set free by their teachers' efforts at inclusion to pursue their own growth, and this is exactly the response good teachers seek. They do not want their students to be constrained by the personal or professional needs of their teachers. The responsibility is clearly enormous.

But students have a responsibility too. As recipients of care, they must respond to their teachers' efforts. Usually this happens in a seemingly natural way. Children who have been similarly cared for at home will respond to teachers spontaneously. But if teachers behave in unfamiliar ways, students may have difficulty detecting attempts to care. Cross-cultural teacher–student relations often induce such difficulties (Heath, 1983). Then even more time must be given to the establishment of trusting relations. It is not enough simply to understand another culture, and indeed the assumption of such understanding often masks reliance on stereotypes. Children come from cultures, but they are also special individuals, each in need of a particular relation with his or her teacher.

Students may also have difficulty recognizing care if it comes in forms they have already assessed as not-caring. If parents rationalize abusive behavior on the grounds that it is for the child's own good, a student may well distrust all efforts to improve his or her condition. This puts an even greater burden on teachers to listen, to receive, to respond to what is really there.

One of the greatest tasks of teachers is to help students learn how to be recipients of care. Those who have not learned this by the time they have entered school are at great risk, and their risk is not just academic. Unless they can respond to caring attempts, they will not grow, and they will certainly not learn to care for others. This is the single greatest problem of children born addicted to cocaine. "Response deficit" children cannot react to the normal parental desire to promote their growth. Teachers may need to devote long periods of time to the establishment of caring relations with these children.

All children need to feel safe in their relations with teachers. It must be acceptable to admit error, confusion, or even distaste for the subject at hand. But students must also accept responsibility for communicating their needs to teachers. They must understand that their responses enliven or dampen their teachers' enthusiasm. Students have tremendous effects on their teachers, and these possibilities should be discussed openly. The contributions of teachers and students are necessarily unequal, but they are nonetheless mutual; the relationship is marked by reciprocity. Students cannot be expected to teach their teachers, but they can be expected to respond with growing sensitivity to attempts to promote their own growth. Too often—even at the collegiate level, but especially at the secondary level—students regard their teachers as enemies to be outwitted or as bumbling authorities to be suffered temporarily (Crozier, 1991). What is lost is not only academic knowledge but a relation that might yield a lifetime of friendship and wisdom.

CONCLUSION

We are participating in a challenging thought experiment: How shall we educate our large heterogeneous family? I would like to ask readers to look back briefly over the last two chapters—caring for self and intimate others. Are there not many opportunities for intellectual engagement and the acquisition of cultural knowledge? Are not the matters discussed vital to all lives? Is there not an enormous demand for critical thinking in the areas discussed? Why, then, do we persist in supposing that learning a set of cultural facts, or even the structure of various disciplines, is the proper goal of schooling?

Professional readers may have started to worry about evaluation. If we make centers of care the focus of universal education, how will we evaluate our efforts? The answer has to be that we should look for the positive signs we see in healthy family life: happy, healthy children; cooperative and considerate behavior; competence in the ordinary affairs of life; intellectual curiosity; openness and willingness to share; a confessed interest in existential questions; and a growing capacity to contribute to and thrive in intimate relationships.

CHAPTER 8

Caring for Strangers and Distant Others

We learn a moral way of life in the inner circle. If our parents are good, loving people, we have a fair start at moral life. An ethic of caring puts great emphasis on the loving attachment between parent and child. It rejects the common notion put forward by Freud and others that morality begins in fear. Morality is affected by fear, but it is inspired by love, and it is demonstrated in loving relations. It is therefore essential that children be cared for and that they recognize and respond to care. With relations of trust and care well established, they may be prepared to care in the wider world of casual acquaintances, strangers, and aliens. But such caring is not easy; the difficulties are many. In this chapter I look first at the difficulties second at promising ways in which students might be prepared to care.

DIFFICULTIES OF CARING AT A DISTANCE

In *Caring* (1984), I wrote some paragraphs that upset many readers. I said that we (here in the United States, for example) could not, as individuals, be obligated to care for starving children in Africa because there is no way for most of us to see caring through to its completion. We might sympathetically send $10 to Oxfam or some other relief organization, but we have no reliable method of knowing whether our money will be used to relieve hunger or to enrich greedy politicians. I still think this is an accurate descriptive account of a major difficulty in trying to care at a distance. I did not mean to suggest, however, that because we cannot really care in such situations, we are not obligated to do *anything*.

But what are we obligated to do? Here we must move slowly. Perhaps the greatest danger to moral association with distant others is the tendency to sentimentalize. One feature of sentimentalization is the substitution of speech and public affirmation for effective action. We judge each other by utterance of and assent to expressions such as Life is One; We Are All Part of a Living Cosmos; All Living Things Have a Right to Life; Save the Whales; Save the Redwoods; Earth First; No Man Is an Island. Because such expressions seem lovely and right, we like to identify ourselves with people who affirm them. Teenagers are easily swayed by sentimental approaches, and they are sometimes led to commit offenses against one group out of allegiance to another group. Education must address this tendency and press the questions: What are we obligated to do? What should we refrain from doing?

The temptation is to rely on absolutes or an ethical calculus. In world affairs, we often use an odd mixture of the two. We may begin by supposing that all people seek freedom or happiness and that all people have a right to freedom and happiness. In evaluating situations at a distance, we may be unaware that more immediate ends have higher priority for the people we would like to help. Perhaps they simply want to eat or to live free of fear. Perhaps they define freedom and happiness differently. Perhaps the villains we have identified as obstructing freedom are merely misguided, not evil. Perhaps these villains are themselves pressed by customs and structures they did not invent and are struggling to understand. Perhaps they even want to do better. Or, of course, perhaps they *are* evil. At a distance, we judge not even by appearances but by reports of appearances. It is often so difficult to assess reality that we give up the task and simply take sides.

Usually, if we are well intentioned, we take the side of the oppressed. As we attempt to better their condition (according to our own definition of what would be better), we have to build an argument that will permit the action we endorse. In the last twenty or thirty years, for example, we have often excused the physical violence of oppressed groups on the grounds that they had experienced "economic violence." Therefore, we say, the oppressed did not commit the first acts of violence. We permit protestors in a good cause to do that which we forbid representatives of the oppressor to do. But economic injustice and violence are two different kinds of harm, and we should not blur them. Nor should we excuse random violence committed by those with whom we sympathize.

This is not the place for a full philosophical analysis of these issues, but it is appropriate to say that such issues must be critically discussed in schools. An ethic of care counsels us to meet each living other in a caring relation. Human beings should not be branded evil and therefore expendable because they belong to the side we oppose on a particular issue. When we attempt to act at a distance, we have to ask what effect our acts will have on concrete human beings. As we sentimentalize one group to bring it closer, we may deliberately put another group at a distance. Creating a psychological distance is a powerful mechanism of moral disengagement (Bandura, 1988). We can, with spurious good conscience, permit acts against those distanced that would appall us within our chosen moral community.

A big part of learning to care at a distance is understanding its difficulties and limits. We have to study carefully the language we use. Consider the language used to justify the allied bombing of population centers in World War II. First, there was a language of "supreme emergency" (see Walzer, 1977). Given the state of the "free" world at the time, this rang true. But what does a supreme emergency permit? Suppose the fine young men who participated in the bombing justified by "supreme emergency" had been told something like this: You will disembowel pregnant women, blow the legs off old men, disfigure young girls, castrate firemen trying to protect their city, blind children, drive young and old into mental illness, burn cats and dogs alive. Could they have done such things face-to-face?

But, one might protest, such effects were not the purpose; they were foreseen but not intended consequences. Winston Churchill, however, said straight out that the saturation bombings were making the people of Germany "taste and gulp each month a sharper dose of the miseries they have showered upon mankind" (Walzer, 1977, p. 256). But who had "showered miseries upon mankind"? The children of Germany? Its young pregnant mothers? Its aged, ill, and retarded? Here it was necessary to redefine what was meant by "innocent" in order to escape the charge of waging war on noncombatants and innocents. Many proponents of the bombings declared that no German was innocent because all were involved by association in the Nazi horror. Philosophers, too, have contributed to this abuse of language. Sartre, for example, held each of us responsible for the world we live in. At one level it is true that we each bear some responsibility for the events of our time, but at another level it is totally ridiculous. A child—even had there been a small son of Adolf Hitler—could not be found guilty of Nazi crimes and therefore deserving of horrible retribution.

Closer to home, students need help in analyzing their own use of language and that of groups to which they belong. During my short tenure as a school administrator, I spoke to some middle school students about reports that some of them had stolen things from large local stores. No one said that he or she personally did this, but many confessed that it was true—that "we" do this sometimes. "We rip off some big stores," they said. "Rip off?" I responded, "Why don't you just say, 'We steal'?" Ah. These youngsters had already made a fine and pernicious distinction. "Stealing" is taking from someone who is hurt by the theft—an individual or small storekeeper. Taking from a big, impersonal corporation doesn't hurt anyone. It is "ripping off," not stealing. Again, we see the power of distance in moral disengagement and the central role of language in justifying our questionable acts.

Thus we can locate at least two great difficulties in caring at a distance: First, we cannot be present to those we would care for, and thus we cannot be sure that caring is completed. Second, we may cause suffering to those we hold responsible for the pain we try to alleviate. In both cases we are often ill informed (even when we try to collect adequate information), and we rely on abstract arguments and deceptively pain-free language to promote our causes. The perceived pain of people (or animals, or the earth itself) triggers sympathy. Our inability to care effectively—in direct contact with the sufferers—leads us to think and act according to general principles that might not apply and procedural rules that might inflict further suffering.

One purpose of global education and multicultural education is to supply students with knowledge of other people and their customs. We suppose that knowledge will reduce misunderstanding, stereotyping, and the almost instinctive fear of strangers. But knowledge alone is unlikely to establish caring relations. In fact, a number of studies have shown that qualities such as "counselor relationship" or "teacher relationship" are only slightly correlated with multicultural knowledge. Knowing something about other cultures is important and useful, but it is not sufficient to produce positive relationships.

Persons with multicultural knowledge sometimes overgeneralize. Organizations often contribute to this mistake by giving their workers pamphlets or other brief forms of instruction on various cultural groups. Even great universities have made the error of circulating two or three pages to educate their faculties and staffs on, say, Asian-American students. As a result, many people who should know better suppose that all Asian-Americans hate to be called "oriental," that all Asian-American students study too hard, and that they all defer to their parents on everything. We forget that people vary as a result of a host of group connections and as individuals, too.

The attempt to achieve better relations through knowledge is part of the Cartesian quest for a method that I've been criticizing since chapter

1. There is no recipe-like method for establishing relations of trust and care, Those who would care must attend to the other, must feel that surge of energy flowing toward the other's needs and projects. Caring is a capacity (or set of capacities) that requires cultivation. It requires time.

Knowledge is important, but it is best acquired in relation. It is useful to know something about a group's literature and art, its historical and contemporary sufferings, its myths and images. But students need motivation to undertake such studies energetically. A powerful source of motivation is an invitation from living others. One good reason for studying a particular selection of literature is that people we care about ask us to read it. In relation, we read to find out what people (including ourselves) are going through. In separation, courses incorporating such literature often induce resentment from those who remain outside them and ignorant, and they sometimes result in unwarranted confidence or even deeper prejudice in those who take them.

I have taught a course, Women and Moral Theory, in feminist studies. Although the course has been well received and the content is important, there are things about it that worry me. First, the content is so vitally connected to existential concerns that it should be shared with both women and men, but few men take the course. Second, the content arouses considerable anger in many women who discover that they have been lied to and cheated for years. Many feminists feel that this anger is entirely appropriate and, indeed, necessary to motivate women to act. But anger also induces separation, and separation sets the stage for new rounds of abuse.

Those of us involved in ethnic or gender studies need to examine carefully what we are doing and what happens despite our best intentions. Women, blacks, Native Americans, and other groups need opportunities to study their own histories and celebrate their own cultures. When we study together as an exclusive group, a tremendous feeling of solidarity often grows. Majority groups need help in understanding and accepting the need of oppressed groups to claim their own literature, art, and theories of oppression and political action. These special courses play a significant role in the education of women and minorities.

But shouldn't all students be exposed to these studies? Wouldn't it be better if women's studies and ethnic studies were integrated into a core curriculum? Wouldn't such integration ensure the universal worth of such studies? Integration is a well-intentioned recommendation heard more and more often. But abandoning ethnic and gender studies would be a great mistake unless the core to which they were to be assimilated were also abandoned and a new core constructed. The present core is fashioned by principles and concepts that are antithetical to the new studies, and assimilation would be tantamount to destruction.

Let me try to make this clear. If the curriculum were redesigned around centers and themes of care, matters of interest to women and minorities could be included in a natural way. For example, we might tackle the question: How can we produce a new generation better than the present one? Such a theme promotes discussion of a host of sub-questions: Should boys as well as girls be educated to provide caregiving? What causes racial tensions, and how do people feel when prejudice is directed at them? Why do all (or most) groups see themselves as genuine human beings and outsiders as *others?* What do we mean by "better" when we plan a generation "better" than we are? All of the existing disciplines have something to contribute to the study of such questions, but in the new curricula the disciplines would not themselves be central. They would serve larger purposes. As long as the existing disciplines are central, they will tend to overwhelm material injected to revise them.

But the worry about exclusivity and separation remains. It is precisely this worry—that racial and gender tensions are actually increased by special courses—that drives the well-intentioned recommendation for integration. Perhaps the answer to this worry is to ask participants in minority studies to take on the tasks of inclusion and reconciliation. Teachers of these courses should, for example, make it clear that they will protect majority students interested and courageous enough to take them. Teachers and students together should explore ways in which their activities can be shared with other groups and especially with the groups regarded as oppressors. It is possible for such groups to maintain the exclusivity needed to develop a full sense of belonging and also to reach out in an attempt at partial inclusion. Minorities can do this without raising fears of domination. The majority's attempt at inclusion always, by definition, threatens domination and usurpation.

We have been considering the problems inherent in trying to care at a distance—for those literally removed from us by space or time and for those who may be physically near but are still strangers. At a physical distance the main problem is lack of completion; there is rarely a way for carers to receive the response of those for whom they would care. And so despite the best intentions of carers, the relations themselves cannot be properly assessed as caring relations. Second, when we plunge into attempts to care without building a relation, we must depend on a form of abstract or inert knowledge. Thus we often fail to treat the recipients of our care as individuals. We may also mistakenly suppose that they want to live exactly as we do—that they want the same knowledge, the same kinds of work, the same forms of worship, the same daily customs. Or we may mistakenly suppose that they do not want any of these. Because we are not in relation, our acts can easily degenerate into acts of false generosity. Finally, when we have the power and desire to act at a distance, it is tempting to initiate and control. We are too impatient or too confident or too puffed up with our own righteous sense of responsibility to listen and encourage initiative from the outsiders. We overlook the possibility that others may want most the power to create their own meanings and explore their own possibilities. This is one of the great defects in the present educational effort to give everyone exactly the same education. Reformers assume that they know what others want, or *would* want if they were sufficiently well informed. Caring at a distance is fraught with difficulties.

Before turning to what we might do to help students meet the world prepared to care, we should discuss a great difficulty mentioned earlier: the temptation to sentimentalize. Unfortunately it is as easy to arouse ill feelings toward strangers as it is to induce sympathy—perhaps easier. Years after bitter warfare it is hard to believe how we dehumanized and hated people who were branded enemies. When we are threatened as individuals or as groups, we tend to place those who threaten us outside the moral community. Once we have placed them there, we can do things to them that would be unthinkable if they were members of the community.

Further, naming one group as outcast or enemy tends often to strengthen the feeling of solidarity within both the inside and outside groups. Just recently, news of the desecration of a Jewish cemetery in France outraged the world. Shortly after the event, two Jewish extremists were apprehended and confessed to committing the crime in an attempt to throw the blame on Arabs and thus unify Jews all over the world in a struggle against Arabs. They sought solidarity in hatred. This event triggered sadness in a people long devoted to living nonviolently within societies that inflicted violence on them. What students should learn from such examples—and many more should be given—is that no group is immune from the temptation to abuse others for its own ends.

We tend to associate all that is good and right with *our* side, and all that is evil and wrong with the other side. We project our hostility and a host of personal moral shortcomings onto the now alien other. We exteriorize evil in order to destroy it, and thereby we perpetuate in ourselves and in the angry other the very evil we set out to fight so valiantly (Noddings, 1989).

PREPARING TO CARE

In the face of so many substantial difficulties in caring at a distance, what are we obligated to do, and how can we educate children so that they are prepared to care? I'll handle the two questions together because, clearly, if we are obligated to do something in the direction of caring, we are also obligated to teach our children how to do this. (We need not insist that they are obligated to do exactly what we will decide to do, for even if our current analysis is correct, they are different people with different relations, loves, and projects.)

First, schools should give far more attention to understanding ourselves and our various allegiances. In chapter 6, I discussed physical, spiritual, occupational, and recreational life in the context of caring for self. But I said there that such a discussion was necessarily incomplete and even a bit misleading because the self is not an isolated entity. It is relational—developed continuously in relation with others. It is with this relational self that we are concerned here.

Why do we tend to draw circles around groups to which we belong and attribute uncomplimentary qualities to people outside our circles? One reason is our deep and natural desire to be in caring relations. We want to be cared for—loved in the inner circle, recognized and respected in a somewhat larger circle, and at least safe to move about in huge impersonal circles. Strengthening our circles of love and allegiance gives us the warmth and love we need, and it also provides protection from those who might harm us.

The problem is that most of the people outside our circles feel the same way we do. They, too, cherish caring relations and feel the need to protect themselves against external attack. When we understand why we draw circles and erect barriers, we can begin to explore the differences between belonging and encountering, between established relations and potential relations. Philosophers, social scientists, and educators today are evincing a revived interest in community as opposed to individualism (Bellah et al., 1985). In many ways this is a move in the right direction, but the idea of community has problems, too.

It is right for students to understand the power of community—that we, as members of a community, act to preserve and improve it; that we are both supported and constrained by it; that we are affected by its habits in ways of which we may be unaware; that however much we may pride ourselves on individuality, we bear the marks of the community in which we are raised. All of this is descriptive. It is not so far *prescriptive;* understanding all this does not tell us what to do.

But as we understand, we may assess our allegiance or lack of it and commit ourselves to active and reflective participation in our various communities. Such commitment seems right, and it has long been an important goal of education to induce it. In the language of theologian Paul Tillich (1952), we would hope that each of our students will develop "the courage to be as an individual" and "the courage to be as a part." We want people to be able to resist the demands of the community for conformity or orthodoxy, and we also want them to remain within the community, accepting its binding myths, ideas, and commitments.

The problem is that communities often act like bloated individuals. Just as an individual may have a personal rival or enemy, so may a community or group. But now the situation is more dangerous because we feel safer acting as a group. So long as we are in a positive relation with *some* people, we need not be so concerned about our relations with others. To make matters worse, our relations with an in-group sometimes require us to treat others badly, and we are rewarded for doing things to outsiders that would bring recrimination and punishment if done inside the group.

Self-knowledge of the sort we are discussing is much more powerful than the inert knowledge of others that we gain from books and lectures. We live with ourselves and have many opportunities to check on the accuracy of our knowledge. Further, we can imagine with some degree of correctness how we might behave in various circumstances if the scenario provided is sufficiently detailed and vivid. But students must be invited to ask questions about themselves, not merely about humans in general.

Too often schools ignore this level of questioning and reflection. Students learn about events in their history class, and they learn something about the human condition in their literature classes; they learn about technological advances in their science classes, and sometimes (rarely) they learn how to calculate benefits and losses in their mathematics classes. But they don't get to ask the existential questions that might make a difference in their own lives and those of humankind in general.

Let's return briefly to the example I used earlier in this chapter—the Allied bombing of population centers in World War II. It certainly makes sense for students to learn about the events, to see the human tragedy that occurred as part of a long line of tragedies stretching over all of recorded history. And students should study the rationales that were offered, including the various calculations that might have supported an argument for the "greatest good for the greatest number." But then they should also ask or be asked: How can people do such things? What makes it possible to do such things? Could I do it? Could I disembowel a pregnant woman face-to-face, deliberately? Could I take a chance that I might do it negligently by, say, driving drunk or recklessly? Could I do it by pushing a button if I were sufficiently rewarded by those I care deeply about?

The purpose of such discussion is not to fix blame, nor is it to reject one's own group and embrace another (more moral, more enlightened) group. It is to understand and perhaps to resist pressures that lead us as individuals and groups to perform outrageous acts. We need to press speakers to translate their recommendations into the language of living bodies, and then to ask whether we can participate in the proposed acts. If we are prepared to care, we must say: "Speak to me, if you must, in terms of dollars, of territory won and lost, of cities destroyed, of enemies overcome—but also speak to me in terms of shattered homes, crippled bodies, crazed minds, grieving mothers, and lost children. And ask me, make me think about, what *I* would do—with whom, to whom, why." This is the language of education for caring.

As we struggle with the problems of caring at a distance, we need not only self-knowledge but an appropriate way of gaining knowledge of others. Abstract, bookish knowledge is insufficient. Some of us are working on a simple idea that may be very powerful. *It is imperative to keep the lines of communication open.* At every level—between individuals, groups, and nations—when events take a bad turn, it may be better to go on talking to and associating with opponents, even wrongdoers, than to cut them off and withdraw from them entirely. In international relations especially, it may be useful to change our typical stance from one of moral superiority in which we apply pressures and sanctions to nations that misbehave to one of firm and friendly persuasion. From this perspective, we should saturate the potentially unfriendly nation with our presence. Times of tension call for massive exchanges of students, artists, scientists, and other people who can meet each other in caring encounters. These are not the times to withdraw. Such withdrawal creates greater distance, an emotional and spiritual separation that may eventually encourage us to put the other outside the moral community. When that happens, as we have seen, horrible acts often follow. Keeping the lines of communication open can prevent this separation and provide us with direct knowledge of the others whose behavior concerns us.

An ethic of caring does not simply sit in judgment and proceed by accusation and punishment. It is concerned with raising the moral level of relations. It proceeds, where possible, by confirmation. When we remain in connection, we have opportunities to point out and nurture the best in others, Are there limits? Are there those so evil that we cannot possibly find good in them and can only be dragged down by our association with them? I'm sure there must be limits, but again this is a matter for lengthy and frequent discussions. It is not a matter for one person to answer once and for all. Asking such questions opens the door to understanding the vulnerability of genuine moral life and the basically tragic conditions in which we seek goodness in connection with each other.

We live in an age both blessed and encumbered by a new orthodoxy in speech. Ethnic, racial, and gender jokes are out, and for the most part, that is a good thing. We are properly aware that words can hurt badly and even inflict real and lasting harm. But as our language is purged, our fears, misgivings, and dislikes sink into a layer of the psyche that Carl Jung called the "shadow." This is the individual and collective side we deny. Continuous denial does not destroy the shadow. It stays with us, and sometimes creates a spontaneous explosion of verbal or physical violence.

In schools we more often preach than teach in the areas of race, ethnicity, religion, and gender. Dialogue is required here, and dialogue ends in questions or in great sadness as often as it does in solutions. The reader will notice how often I've ended paragraphs in questions or confessions of uncertainty. When we are struggling to understand, when we are committed to connection but are unsure how to achieve it, we need genuine dialogue with concrete others. Then we may come to a satisfactory resolution governing this time, these people, this place. Even in genuine dialogue, the end is often uncertainty and the sort of tension that will lead to fresh and more vigorous exploration.

Students and teachers need to discuss issues of interpersonal relations, among them the phenomenon of exclusivity. Many groups today are formed so that people sharing a common heritage or, often, a common oppression can live together, study together, and together reclaim the heritage that has been lost to them. Black students on many campuses prefer to live in black houses. Women at women's colleges protest moves to make their colleges coeducational. On almost all campuses there is increasing demand for ethnic and gender studies. And there is a growing unrest among traditional educators, who fear that their own precious heritage will be lost.

I like to start discussion of this sensitive topic with an examination of earned exclusivity. One would not expect to be allowed to join the Cleveland Symphony Orchestra or the San Francisco Forty-Niners on demand. Membership in such organizations requires a demonstrated talent. Similarly, students merit admission to Phi Beta Kappa and other honorary societies. But here many students are themselves uneasy. Some accept membership only to spend most of their lives hiding the fact that they are members. Their selection causes them both pride and embarrassment.

The question arises: Is membership in, say, Phi Beta Kappa anything like having a position with the Cleveland Symphony? In the latter case, participants are expected to continue to perform at a very high level. Phi Beta Kappa members, in contrast, are rewarded for past performance. But is that all? This is what I urge young people to think about. If the exclusive groups to which they belong pass certain tests, they should be proud to belong, and they should participate enthusiastically. Here are some tests to consider: Are its purposes morally acceptable? Does the organization provide an outlet for like-minded people to promote their own growth? (Are participants encouraged to grow intellectually, athletically, spiritually?) Does the organization reach beyond itself to share what it does with interested members of the general public? Does it do so without exclusionary tests? Does it have mutually beneficial connections with other morally thoughtful groups? Does it promote education or training of the young in its area of interest? These questions should, of course, be answered in the affirmative. There are some questions that should be answered negatively: Does the group exclude others on grounds irrelevant to its central mission? Does it espouse projects aimed at harming or preventing the growth of others? All of these questions can and should be used to evaluate membership in street groups (gangs), churches, cults, and recreational clubs as well as honor societies.

Now let's consider groups whose members are not selected by some form of achievement. What shall we say about campus houses for blacks only, colleges for women only, and the like? It would appear on first glance that such organizations might well pass all the suggested tests except one vital one: Does the group exclude others on grounds irrelevant to its central mission? What we see here is exclusion by race, gender, or ethnicity. Can this be acceptable?

I think it can be, but readers and students engaged in this discussion should evaluate my logic. I would argue that we must be aware of power relations in our society as we assess the moral propriety of exclusive groups. When the dominant group tries to maintain its exclusivity, its efforts must be resisted and even precluded by law. But when a minority or oppressed group seeks exclusion, the exclusion may be a necessary part of a morally worthy mission. For example, it seems that many women students do better intellectually, socially, and often even professionally if their colleges are all female rather than coeducational. If the purpose or mission is to promote the intellectual, social, and political growth of women, and if we agree this is a worthy purpose, then the exclusion of persons because they are male may not be exclusion on an irrelevant criterion.

The same sort of argument can be made for the establishment of housing exclusively for black or other racial or ethnic groups. If the presence of people from the dominant white group might work against the growth of blacks, perhaps whites are properly excluded. We do not yet live in an equal society. If we did, exclusion on the grounds of race, ethnicity, or gender would either be unthinkable or of little concern. Under present conditions, the expression "reverse discrimination" is practically meaningless. Discrimination only has practical import when the people discriminating have the power to keep others from sharing in economic and cultural benefits of the larger society. This is often very hard for students from the dominant class to understand. They want to apply the same tests to all groups in the name of equality, but such application can be reasonably demanded only if the groups are substantially equal to begin with.

I would urge minority groups to look seriously at the other questions, however. There should be attempts to reach out, to join with other groups in worthwhile projects, to invite others to celebrations, debates, and evenings of shared cultural events. And, above all, there should be no projects aimed at harming or preventing the growth of others.

So far I have concentrated on problems associated with the sentimental and negative stereotyping of outsiders. I have suggested that much school time be given to the understanding of self, including the groups with which the self identifies. In addition, students must commit themselves to keeping open the lines of communication, for knowledge gained in relation is more powerful and reliable than that gained through second- and third-hand reports.

These two areas of concentration may help students to avoid searching for villains. When we understand that evil in others is often a projection of evil in ourselves, we may exercise patience and choose persuasion over force. When we accept the fact that our second- and third-hand information may be faulty, we may take the time to connect directly and gather a reliable base of information.

The lines between our own group and potential enemies are sometimes drawn tighter by our perception of the others as evil, but sometimes the lines are tightened because our friends have already defined these others as enemies. Our allegiance seems to demand that we do likewise. Students might be encouraged to examine voting patterns in the United Nations. How often do nations (including our own) vote with their friends regardless of the issue? Students should be asked to consider such situations and reflect on whether we are acting as loyal friends when we vote with them no matter what, or whether, as Aristotle suggested, good friends have higher obligations.

Part of becoming prepared to care is learning that one may be on the side of both parties in a dispute. Especially when we attempt to care at a distance, we must resist taking sides out of traditional loyalty. It is entirely possible to set aside the question of who is "right" and say honestly, "Look, I want what is best for both of you." Further we can insist that violence be admonished. "He hit me first" is a reason for violence that we can all understand, but it is rarely a good excuse. Unless an act of violence is employed in defense against an immediate attack, it is at least questionable. Here we see that insisting on clear language—including a translation that describes what happens to human bodies—is essential. It is also essential that we use the same language to describe the acts of friends and the acts of their enemies. If children are mutilated and killed, that fact must be faced no matter who is responsible. But we need not fall into the traditional pattern of accusation, sanction, punishment. We can instead say to our friends: "I see your predicament. I understand what you're trying to do. But these acts are beneath you. They don't measure up to your good motives. Let's find another way."

Now, let's consider what we are—or may be—obligated to do to relieve suffering at a distance. It is not possible to care for starving children in Africa as we can for such children in our own community. What can we do? We can try to find out which relief organizations are dependable and make contributions to the one we most trust. This may involve more than abstract study. It may involve at least enough participation to know firsthand that the organization lives up to its stated mission. But this is neither sure nor easy. Sometimes we are unaware of what even those closest to us are really doing. Further, under some conditions even the best organizations fail through no fault of their own. Thus caring at a distance is hard and uncertain work.

We can encourage caring attitudes at the community, national, and international levels. We can endorse the substantial exchange of people considered earlier, a public accounting of results achieved by relief efforts, the election of officials who seem to care. In all of these efforts we must be wary of mere rhetoric—of settling for sentimental talk.

At a more personal level, students can be encouraged to live moderately. This is a message rarely delivered in schools. More often we try to convince students that they can "make it big in America" if they study and do well in school. I am suggesting that students need to learn how to curb their appetites and to consider the possible effects of their own wealth on the rest of the world. I'll say more about this in the chapter on caring for animals, plants, and the earth.

Before turning to that discussion, we should say something about caring for those who are separated from us by some form of disability. We often experience a sense of distance between "us" and people who are retarded, blind, deaf, mentally ill, immobilized, or otherwise disabled. Here, too, we tend to talk a shallow line—"everybody's equal"—that belies actual conditions and widespread human reactions.

Disabled people may be thought of as "at a distance" because we have difficulty in either eliciting or recognizing forms of response with which we are familiar. A severely mentally retarded person cannot respond to an intellectual discussion, solve mathematical problems, or draw logical inferences. If we try to elicit such responses, they are not forthcoming. Those people who work lovingly and successfully with the severely retarded usually find other forms of human response that are as valuable as reason. (Reason has been traditionally used by philosophers and other thinkers as the distinctively human characteristic.) Laughter, smiles, hugs, and touches of affection are also valuable human responses. So are eye contact and facial recognition. The capacity to feel pain and show relief from pain are important responses. Playfulness; the capacity to make things, however simple; artistic expression; and rhythmic kinesthetic movements are all responses valued by human beings. Beings—human and nonhuman—capable of any of these responses should elicit a corresponding desire in others to make caring contacts.

Nurses and physical therapists could contribute much to the standard education of students and teachers by helping them to understand the wide variety of human responses and how to encourage those most highly valued. Again, there is no fully adequate substitute for direct contact. If our knowledge comes only from books and lectures, it is easy to sentimentalize the disabled and suppose that we need only avoid "prejudice." In actuality the range of disabilities is enormous. Some are so small that we should ask ourselves whether we have invented them to keep our specialists in business. Some, managed sensitively, may be converted into new forms of creativity. Some are so severe and pervasive that most of us would be unable to detect a characteristically human response. Questions arise, then, about the wisdom of sustaining such lives. If we want citizens who can grapple intelligently and compassionately with the horrendous problems of public health that lie just ahead of us, those questions too must be part of an education that accepts the challenge to care.

CHAPTER 9

Caring for Animals, Plants, and the Earth

Our lives are interdependent with those of nonhuman animals and plants. Many of us have come to realize that the quality of human life cannot be entirely separated from the conditions that nurture other living things, and we realize, too, that we still have much to learn about optimal conditions for life. As in the other centers of care, there are conflicts and causes in this one. Some people are still far too uncaring about the environment. Others have taken up environmental causes uncritically and, sometimes, even violently. Too often, the familiar quest for a foolproof method, a recipe, a test of orthodoxy dominates the discussion. People who should be working together because they care for each other fall out over issues concerning care for the environment. What should students learn in this center of care?

CARING FOR ANIMALS

Many parents provide pets for their children because they suppose that caring for a pet will teach their children responsibility. Such experience can indeed be valuable if it is accompanied by parental caring for both animal and child. Too often, the care of a pet degenerates into "cares and burdens," and the child's unreliability in feeding and cleaning up after the pet strains the parent–child relationship.

It is clear that parents in this country do not do an effective job in teaching their children to care for pets. Every year an estimated ten million animals are killed at humane societies and shelters. These animals do not die to provide human beings with food or clothing. They die betrayed by humans who have, tacitly at least, contracted to care for them. Anyone who has had a much-loved pet must feel deep sorrow for these creatures, who experience everything from mild neglect and abandonment to physical cruelty and abuse. What good does it do to have students in biology class draw the digestive system of a mammal and label its parts if they are not taught to have compassion for the animals they study?

Well, biology teachers might say, students should learn compassion for animals, but not in science class. We already have too much material to cover. My argument is, of course, that we "cover" the wrong material. Even my suggested division of the day into themes of care and specialty courses risks an inappropriate emphasis. But dividing the day entirely into centers of care would not eliminate the risk so long as the divided mentality persists. As we have seen, there are no sharp divisions between caring for self and caring for others, between spirituality and social life, between fact and value. Whatever is under study must be followed where its participants need to go, and needs are identified by both students and teachers.

Appropriate experience with animals involves an appreciative study of responsiveness. Here we continue the important exploration started in chapter 4. Sensitivity to the responses of human beings is basic in moral life. Similarly, sensitivity to the responses of animals is basic to the development of compassion for them. Responsible parents teach their children at a very early age how to detect pain and induce pleasure in their pets. "Kitty doesn't like to be picked up by the tail. Poor kitty! Look, ah, kitty, nice kitty," the parent says while demonstrating considerate and affectionate behavior. Children seem to have inborn detectors for attitude in their parents. They feel the difference between authentic care and a cold, dutiful, or impersonal command. When parents and children share affection for pets, taking care of them is not an onerous chore. Caring parents do not let the dog go hungry or flea-ridden until Billy finally does his job. They care for the dog themselves and care for Billy by reminding him of the suffering caused by hunger, thirst, or itch.

Some children are exquisitely sensitive to animal response, especially pain. One of my sons had an accident with his aquarium when he was about eight. There was a loud crash, and when I arrived at his room, there were glass fragments, water, and fish everywhere. My son was bleeding, but I couldn't coax him away from the disaster area. "Don't you understand?" he shouted, "My fish are dying!" I had to pitch in and scoop guppies. Not until they were all saved would he let me patch him up. Many moral debates and much learning in our household centered on animals.

Animal response is a nontrivial, serious area of study. Scientists have learned quite a lot about animal communication, for example.

Parents and children can get satisfaction and do a better job of caring for pets if they learn what various vocalizations and postures mean. I've learned the meanings of a variety of cat vocalizations, for example: a trilled greeting, a question-like request tone (generally repeated), a warning sound (Don't touch me there!), and a help message (very like the ordinary request but louder). In addition, there are bodily communications: rubbing, "making biscuits," extending a paw to caress me, head pressing, gentle nuzzling. Knowing what a pet wants helps enormously in giving it proper care. It also adds immeasurably to the pleasure of living with a pet.

These topics can and should be considered in schools. If we are ever to have competent parents, we *have* to treat these topics in schools. Films on animal behavior are available, and reading material can be obtained from many societies that support studies of animals. Children love to watch dolphins and listen to whale songs. But the most important thing to be learned is how to respond appropriately to the animals in one's own life. Creatures capable of feeling pain should not be made to suffer unnecessarily; those manifesting affection for their young should not be separated from them needlessly; those capable of solving problems should not be placed in environments where this capacity is diminished. A creature's capacity for response in part defines our obligation to it.

Students should be helped to see that there are three significant areas of analysis in our relations with animals. First, there is study of the animals and their behavior; we need to identify their attributes and capacities. Second, there must be a judgment of the value placed on each attribute and capacity; some we value highly, and others we may deplore. I admire my cat's speed and grace, for example, but I deplore her inclination to kill birds and play with her prey. Third, there is analysis of what obligations are induced by a recognition of the attributes and capacities we admire and deplore. This is difficult critical work, and it is central not only to our relations with animals but also to the development of a coherent ethical position on our obligation to human beings exhibiting some but not all of the usual human attributes.

Some matters concerning animals are uncontroversial, and we can teach with the intention to induce certain values unapologetically. For example, no reasonable, caring person could espouse cruelty or object to our teaching against it. But other matters in our relations with animals are problematic and require careful analysis of competing arguments. Teachers need to be able to distinguish between commonly held values and those that are disputable, however passionately held.

I said earlier that I found arguments in favor of raising and killing animals for their fur very weak. I still believe, however, that students should hear those arguments. They should even see films and hear stories in which trappers and furriers are attractive characters. For example, lots of fine western films portray trappers as rugged individualists and nature lovers. Hunting should be examined in a similar way. If schooling is to have meaning for students, controversial issues must be discussed, and they must be discussed with full affect—that is, with attention to the responses of all those involved. The purpose is not so much the development of critical intelligence (although that is certainly one purpose) as it is development of the capacity to hear and respond sensitively.

The toughest issue in our relations with animals is whether we should eat them. There are strong and weak arguments on both sides, and a host of important subquestions arise. Those who argue for vegetarianism make a convincing case against cruelty, but the killing of animals need not be done cruelly. They make another important argument when they point to the tons of excrement that pollute our ground and surface waters, but this point can be better used as a case for moderation. Most organic farming methods require animal manures and decaying animal bodies. Chemical fertilizers also poison our water supplies, and they exhaust our soil as well. Therefore, from a practical standpoint, we might do better to cut our supply of meat rather then eliminate it entirely. Many advocates of vegetarianism also argue that meat animals use too many resources. Land that could be used for human grain production goes to animal grazing, and the practice is enormously inefficient. Again, this perhaps makes a better case for moderation than total elimination.

Some arguments for vegetarianism are too simplistic, and many depend on sentimentalization. Some religious tracts are guilty of this. One suggests that "gentle cows" be allowed to live and give milk—that we accept the gift of milk but refrain from eating beef. The writers do not say what we should do with the calves needed to induce lactation, nor do they say anything about the possibility of chemical induction of lactation. Any method—natural or artificial—of freshening a cow requires human intervention eventually. What should we do with the males produced? To answer, "Just leave them all alone," is unsatisfactory and impractical. Such an answer romanticizes and sentimentalizes the natural lives of animals, and it ignores the kinds of pressures that must eventually cause humans to intervene and manage animal life.

Religious arguments are used sometimes on one side, sometimes on the other. Some writers point to the biblical passage that grants "men dominion over the beasts. . . ." They interpret that verse to mean that all plants and animals are provided for the express purpose of sustaining human life. Indeed these writers tend to think of the earth itself as a home and storehouse for human beings. Others, pointing to the same verse, interpret "dominion" as stewardship, as a requirement to care rather than an invitation to dominate.

Students should also be exposed to arguments for and against the use of animals in research (Regan, 1983; Singer, 1990). What medical advances depend on animal experimentation? Which could be effectively carried out in other ways? Should students replicate experiments using animals or should they learn the results from books, lectures, or films? Before answering any of these questions, students should become well informed on how animals are actually used and how they are treated in laboratories.

There is much collateral learning that can come from an exploration of our relation to animals. From the discussion above, we can see connections to religion and spirituality. Views range from the almost indifferent acceptance of animal pain in St. Augustine to the worshipful refusal, found in some Eastern religions, to take any life. Every view should be treated respectfully; that is, each should be examined critically for insights and for foolishness. It is not respectful to let nonsense stand just because it belongs to a body of religious belief.

An area of life that arouses so much affect poses a spiritual risk to our young people. On the one hand, they must be allowed to feel deeply and respond compassionately to animals. On the other, they must learn to think critically so that they are less vulnerable to the emotional—and often superficial—messages of various cults. People who have never thought through the problems discussed here (and many more) are likely recruits to extremes—sentimental approaches to animal life or cruel indifference.

There are other forms of collateral learning. Most children love animals and are interested in where and how they live. This interest leads naturally to a study of geography and other sciences. I've watched kids pore over maps in utter fascination as they discuss where elephants, koalas, and penguins live. One of my daughters at age five was so captivated by dinosaurs that she learned a string of very difficult names. I'll never forget the sight of that tiny girl running from display to display in the Museum of Natural History shouting, "Stegosaurus! Brontosaurus! Look, Mommy, diplodocus!" Her interest led almost inevitably to one in geology, and one year we could not dislodge her from the section housing gems and minerals. She became a petroleum engineer—a sensitive engineer interested both in mining resources and in preserving habitats.

Most children who become good readers go through at least a phase in which they read avidly about animals. I remember reading Albert Payson Terhune's dog stories, *Black Beauty, Beautiful Joe,* and *A Dog of Flanders.* My children read many of these and *My Friend Flicka, The Yearling, Old Yeller,* and *The Incredible Journey.* We all read *Peter Rabbit, The Musicians of Brementown,* and *The Wind in the Willows,* and I spent a delightful set of winter evenings with one small daughter reading *The Trumpet of the Swan.* These are not books to be read in artificial and piecemeal assignments. They are to be read eagerly until we are too tired to go on or something intrudes on us. Then we look forward to getting back to our book the following day.

Most elementary school classrooms reflect children's interest in animals. There are often live pets and aquariums in addition to pictures and books about animals. But the scene changes in high school. One would think that interest in animals must be childish, and animal stories give way to "serious" literature. Aquariums and pets disappear. This is one more example of blind response in education. Because children are now capable of abstract thought, we remove actual living things from the classroom. But an intelligent response suggests that this is just the time when serious education on animals should be emphasized. I would not take small children to slaughterhouses or to animal shelters to watch (or even hear about) the continuous stream of euthanasias. But I would introduce high school students to these realities. These young people will soon have households of their own, and with only the romantic notions of children's animal stories to motivate them, they are likely to contribute out of well-meaning ignorance to each year's ten million deaths. One has to ask again how it is that people who can name the parts of an insect and differentiate it from an arachnid fail to understand the loneliness and misery of dogs and cats abandoned and ill treated.

In closing this section, I want to emphasize the point that a serious study of animals is clearly not anti-intellectual. Such study draws on literature, science, history, economics, politics, art, mathematics, psychology, and religion, but it concentrates on a center of care—on something that really matters. Further, it presents another opportunity to engage in critical thinking. There are many questions to debate. The larger society fairly shakes with controversies on our relations with animals. Both sound and unsound arguments guide the behavior of animal advocates, and sometimes deplorable acts are committed by extremists. Yet the schools remain silent, constrained by the traditional disciplines.

CARING FOR PLANTS

Plants do not respond to us in the direct and personal way characteristic of animals and other human beings. But they respond to light, water, nutrients, and—some say—to touch. Again, elementary school children are provided opportunities to plant seeds and take care of plants in their classrooms. Children bring bouquets to their teachers, and some schools encourage their students to sell seeds as part of their contribution to school improvement projects. It is almost as if elementary school children were being prepared for something of great importance, but the high school rejects the core of existential studies and concentrates on the periphery—on the skills and incidental information gathered during exploration. It is rather like panning for gold and keeping the mud instead. An opportunity to study response, beauty, and almost mystical interdependence is lost.

Although human life is absolutely dependent on plants, I do not remember any discussion of plant life in my social studies classes beyond mention of, say, grain exports and the like. When we read Caesar's account of the Gallic Wars in Latin class, no mention was made of Caesar's botanical interests or the fact that an herbalist traveled with his legions. Stories of conquest, colonization, and immigration rarely included tales of green immigrants (Haughton, 1978). Yet these stories are fascinating.

Including the study of plant history, distribution, and cultivation would be a significant corrective to the current emphasis on political history. But even here, important and instructive errors are made. *Green Immigrants* (1978) begins with the astonishing statement that before European colonization there were "no gardens or farms in America" (p. ix). What the author means, of course, is that there were no European-style gardens or farms. But the Indians cultivated plants, and there were homes, villages, and farms in many areas. Schoolchildren know that Indians taught colonists how to grow corn and other crops, but much serious history either neglects plants entirely or concentrates on the contributions of Western science and thought to plant cultivation. Regarding plant life as a center of care intimately related to other centers of care gives us an opportunity to appreciate and criticize human interactions as well as human relations to plants.

The connection between plants and spirituality is especially fascinating. Think about the tale of Adam and Eve. Was the tree of knowledge of good and evil an apple tree? Or was its legendary identity disguised because the original plants—perhaps fig trees and branches—figured significantly in goddess religions? (See Stone, 1976.) Does the Christian practice of communion date entirely from the last supper, or does it have earlier origins in the "flesh and fluid of Hathor" referred to in early Egyptian texts? One can read Ezekiel and Isaiah as well as Genesis with new interest when the sacred role of plants is considered. Why such hatred and fear of the *asherah*?

Plants have long served as symbols of all sorts. *Buxus sempervirens* and its relatives have figured in Greek legends (Diana changed a wood nymph into evergreen boxwood to save her from Apollo), and they have been used in Christian rituals as well. St. John's wort was used in early rituals of sun worship. Indeed its genus name, Hypericum, comes from its association with Hyperion, father of the sun god, Helios. As so often happened, early Christians gave a new name and new ritual purpose to an herb that had long been part of pagan rituals. It is worth mentioning, too, that the word *pagan* means country dweller, and country dwellers have often been hard to convert to non-naturalistic religions. To live in the country is to be tempted to worship nature. This phenomenon is also one to be studied appreciatively.

Volumes have been written on plants and spirituality, and it is not my purpose to outline that vast literature. My point is to emphasize the usefulness and excitement of studying plants in connection with other centers of care. All schools should have gardens, greenhouses, and windowsill plants, and students should learn how to nurture plants. Even if they eventually live in the city with no houseplants, such experience should induce a practical appreciation for plants and the people who grow and use them.

The connection to nutrition is obvious. Many children today do not learn how to cook vegetables so as to preserve their nutrients, nor do they learn what nutrients are available in plants. For both boys and girls today this knowledge is essential. I think here of the wise teacher in *To Sir With Love* who sensibly taught his inner-city students how to make a salad.

We are raising children today who do not know why beehives are placed in orchards (if they even know what a beehive is), how new plants are created, or why there is a danger in heaping chemical fertilizers on our fields. When they do find out about the dangers in pesticides and chemical fertilizers, some of them become fanatics—rebelliously rejecting everything associated with technology. Others largely ignore such issues and react only when a specific scare sweeps the nation. Again, a significant opportunity for the development of critical thinking is overlooked.

The study of edible plants is another wonderful way to make connections with other cultures—their foods, eating customs, languages, and habitats. One could tell the whole history of civilization with a focus on plants, referring to political history peripherally. For example, Columbus convinced the sovereigns of Spain to finance his second journey with the promise of establishing orange and sugar plantations in the New World. He carried orange seeds to Hispaniola. The Romans carried apple seeds to Britain and olives to Spain and Portugal. The Spanish carried the wonderful agricultural products of the Incas to both Europe and North America.

Then there is the beauty of plants and the great satisfaction of growing them. Again, the connection to other cultures is obvious. Students can learn how the Japanese use plants, rocks, and water to create serene and beautiful environments, how the aborigines of Australia used plant products to decorate their bodies, how people all over the world plant trees to provide shade and shelter. They should have opportunities themselves to experience firsthand the joy of growing things—of planting seeds, starting new plants from cuttings and air-layering.

In one of her columns, Ellen Goodman wrote of "the urban dweller's pact with nature." She described the urban dweller's spring ritual—carefully planting tomato seedlings in tiny patches and boxes. Describing the gardener's frame of mind, she wrote:

> Digging holes for seedlings, she thinks of a mantra fitting for gardeners. Plant, to remember that things do not just appear in the refrigerator. They grow, slowly. Plant, to repair the nearly severed umbilical cord with the natural world. Plant, to keep the pact of mutual caretaking with nature. (1990, pp. 19–27)

Students should learn to nurture and protect the plants themselves and the soil in which they grow. As Wendell Berry has put it:

> The soil is the great connector of lives, the source and destination of all. It is the healer and restorer and resurrector, by which disease passes into health, age into youth, death into life. Without proper care for it

we can have no community, because without proper care for it we can have no life. (1977, p. 86)

CARING FOR THE ENVIRONMENT

Caring for the soil is one part—a major part—of caring for the environment. We live in an age of increasing concern about air and water pollution, ozone depletion, overpopulation, loss of forests, and extinction of species and subspecies. But our commitment is undermined by a continual press for progress and expansion, by demands for resources, and of course by greed. Schools give some attention to environmental problems, but they are not giving enough to the development of caring human beings. Their curricular treatment of environmental issues is still too abstract, and the extracurricular approach—recycling, for example—is too limited.

Students in today's schools do learn about ecosystems and food chains, about extinction and habitat preservation. But the problems they tackle are often focused on faraway places—the Amazon basin or southeast Asia. Just as we find it more comfortable to attack racism in South Africa than racism at home, we find it easier to discuss distant environmental problems. One result is that the students do not learn how to criticize powerful counterarguments. They do not realize that the opposition has a story to tell, and they do not learn to work through sophisticated political processes to make measurable improvements—sometimes small ones. If they knew how to do this, they might be able to plan for a continuous series of small changes that would make a significant difference.

It is easier, of course, simply to take the side perceived as good. It is satisfying to join a group that works to save trees, and it is difficult to understand that many factors need to be considered: preserving our forests, providing lumber for construction, protecting the incomes of lumber workers, preserving the families and communities involved in lumbering, guarding against overgrowth and fire, protecting habitats, considering alternative means of preserving species, providing recreation.

Further, students need to think on at least two levels, the personal and political. They need to be involved in a personal, concrete way, and they need to know how to vote and which groups deserve support. In this age of extremes on the one hand and empty sloganeering on the other, one has to be ready to shift allegiances and construct compromises in order to accomplish anything. It is not an easy way to work, and people who are insecure in their affiliative needs may be unable to bring it off. Such people join groups more to belong than to accomplish a goal. Others become so fanatical in goal-seeking that they forget to care for the human beings who represent the opposition. This is another center of care in which we have to learn how to be on both sides—to accomplish ends we evaluate as good and to cause as little pain as possible to those who oppose us.

Students should be involved in direct, hands-on environmental projects as part of their practical education. just as they should participate in care of the young, aged, and disabled, so they should contribute to cleaning up streams, planting trees, and maintaining gardens in parks and school yards. Such work may not only induce a lifelong commitment to environmental causes but might even inspire some students to consider related occupations: horticulture, architectural landscaping, city planning, civil engineering, forestry, artistic endeavors such as painting plants and animals, or journalism involving plants, animals, and the environment. Some service activities can be fruitfully combined as older students work with younger ones on various environmental projects.

An extremely important function of formal schooling is to provide a forum for the critical examination of all these informal activities. In their classes devoted to centers of care, students should have opportunities to discuss their service projects, the needs of organizations they serve, and the conflicts that arise in the operation of these services. Out of these discussions should come a host of related academic activities: reading, locating sources and resources, writing, figuring, planning, communicating.

Another important function of the schools is to induce a reflective examination of one's own life—life as an individual, as a member of a particular race, as a member of an economic class, as a member of any particular group. People of all groups need to have a sense of both efficacy and responsibility. People in depressed areas, for example, need empowerment; that is, they need the kind of education that will help them to take responsible control of their own lives as nearly as that is possible. Emphasis should not be on providing information about services, although such information should certainly be available. Emphasis should be on how to organize, how to locate issues, set priorities, compromise to mutual advantage.

Programs such as Freire's (1970) pedagogy of the oppressed can be valuable in both city and rural schools in this country. These programs are compatible with my recommendation that schools be organized around centers of care. In an inner city school, for example, students may generate themes that will occupy working groups for weeks or even months. Themes might include school and street safety, racial tension, providing support for students from dysfunctional families, coping with drugs and alcohol, resisting the pressure of advertising, becoming a savvy and responsible consumer, and creating a mutually supportive relation with law enforcement officers. In Freire's scheme the themes must come from the oppressed themselves. However, as such programs develop in our schools, it should be possible for teachers, as members of the learning community, to contribute themes also. At every stage teachers will suggest resources and help to develop needed skills. They should also evaluate the resources they suggest for their potential in suggesting new themes. Thus teachers accept a responsibility for cooperatively directing growth without imposing a precise form on it.

In addition to a vigorous pedagogy of the oppressed, I have suggested that schools must also develop a pedagogy of the oppressor (Noddings, 1989). Children from middle- and upper-class environments need to become conscious of the possible effects of their lifestyles on the lives of others. They need to know how much of the world's energy and other resources are consumed by a small segment of the population. Such consciousness raising should induce a more careful and conservative way of life.

I think we need to educate seriously and enthusiastically for moderation. I have started this paragraph with "I think" because the recommendation is highly controversial. There are those who will insist that having everyone scramble for more and more wealth sustains all sorts of productivity, creativity, technological progress, and even philanthropy. I think this is dead wrong, but educationally it is important to allow both sides to be heard. One does not have to espouse communism or even formal socialism to advocate moderation. It is a matter of accepting our individual and group responsibility for the welfare of others and also for our own spiritual, mental, and emotional health.

Students need to learn that success comes in many forms and that some forms may be more desirable and admirable than others. A commitment to teaching and learning moderation requires a massive transformation of current ideology. Instead of promoting schooling as the road to higher economic status, we should promote it as the path to wisdom. Instead of painting a hierarchical picture of success in terms of money and power, we should discuss success in terms of loving relations, of growth in individual capacities, of lasting pleasure in various worthy occupations, of satisfying connections with living things and the earth itself. In the past few decades we have prostituted schooling, and it shows in everything from our overemphasis on achievement scores to our concentration on credentialing for "good" jobs.

When we make wisdom an end of education, we encourage people to watch over their wealth as they do their weight. We do not always need more; sometimes, to be all-round healthy, we need less. Further, by doing with less now we may be in a better position to take care of ourselves in later years. Here, too, we should not go on assuming that others must provide for our needs whether or not we have behaved responsibly. We should help those who need help and accept help graciously when we need it ourselves, but accepting this proposition does not mean abdicating personal responsibility for our own welfare.

One can see obvious connections between the above points and the Protestant work ethic. As part of the cultural heritage that has influenced the schools from their inception, it too should be examined critically and appreciatively. Are there insights to be gleaned from it and retained? Are there dangers and delusions in it? How does it contribute to environmental health? How does it contribute to environmental pathology?

Thinking of work, responsibility for ourselves and for others, and committing ourselves to a moderate way of life are vitally connected to caring for the environment. We have to share the limited resources of earth, and, standing ready to help each other, we must also try not to put too great a strain on the contribution of others. This is where the language of care proves itself so much more practical and visionary than the language of rights and justice. If we run out of resources—natural and financial or of human energy and resolve—rights mean nothing. To say that all people have a right to a particular good is ridiculous in the absence of that good. But to recognize need, to respond reasonably and caringly to it, and to commit ourselves to continuing response require us to live moderately, sensitively, and responsibly.

CHAPTER 10

Caring for the Human-Made World

Caring for the human-made world—the world of objects and instruments—is not the same as caring for human beings. There is no immediate moral impact. Objects do not cry out in pain, exclaim in joy, or express love for us. But how we treat things has an impact on both human and nonhuman life. When we are careless with things or become obsessed with gross acquisition, we use far more than our share of the world's resources, so our behavior with objects has moral implications.

There is another sense in which caring for objects and instruments can be thought of as part of moral life. When we want to be moral people, we consider what kind of life we should lead. In an ethic of caring, we never ignore the impact of the life we choose on others, but we may also consider what the ancient Greeks called excellences. We may want to develop some nonmoral excellences of our own, and we may believe that it is morally—and not just aesthetically—desirable to appreciate the excellence of others. Part of this appreciation involves respectful appraisal of the objects that surround us. Who made them? How did their present form evolve? How do we judge their quality? How should we use them?

UTILITY

When most of us think about objects at all, we think about how we will use them. We buy sofas and chairs to sit in, and it annoys us when children jump on them, walk on them, or sprawl on them in dirty sneakers. Knives are provided at the dinner table to cut food, and we frown on those who convey food to their mouths with them. We sometimes misuse objects simply out of carelessness, and sometimes we misuse them out of ignorance.

How important is it that we use objects for their intended purpose? Maria Montessori (1966) made the proper use of objects a cornerstone of her educational method. She insisted that children should be totally free to work with approved objects provided they are using them for their intended purposes. Further, objects should always have a proper place of storage, and they should be returned there when not in use. Montessori believed that a love of order comes naturally to children at a certain critical period and that order "is necessary for peace and happiness" (p. 53). The physical order in Montessori classrooms is designed to induce serenity of the soul, or what Montessori called grace.

Most of us today doubt whether children have the natural sense of order Montessori attributed to them, but we recognize the importance of using objects appropriately and keeping them in their assigned places. Work gets off to a bad start if we cannot find the tools we need or if they are dirty or broken.

We give little attention to facilitative order in schools. This sounds like a contradiction, given the perennial complaint of critics that schools squelch creativity and put too great an emphasis on order. But the order typically emphasized in schools is not facilitative order; it is not order that induces serenity of soul and grace. It is all too often arbitrary and stifling. Sitting in rows, doing seatwork alone, offering up brief answers when the teacher demands them, forced to attend, required to seek permission for a trip to the restroom—students living in these conditions are unlikely to experience order as facilitative of their own purposes.

Facilitative order provides sufficient time, ample space, appropriate materials, and assurance that someone will help in case of need. One's work space and materials should be inviolate. Even the teacher should await an invitation, or request one, before intervening in the serious work of students. This kind of order is cooperatively constructed by teachers and students. The teacher provides parameters within which students must work and, within these parameters, students are free to pursue their own lines of thought. The teacher must also talk to students about order and utility, about the objects around them and their appropriate use. It is not surprising that so many young people have little regard for desks, books, pens, notebooks, and other school objects. Adults punish and scold them for gross abuses, but they rarely engage them in appreciative reflection on the utility of objects.

A careful consideration of utility leads to an examination of form. Why are objects designed as we now see them? Are there alternatives?

Here there are opportunities to trace the development of writing instruments, desks, and books. There should also be opportunities to learn how students in other cultures work and how they often manage without the objects we take for granted.

Students should be invited to examine objects closely. In an array of different brands, which work best—and what do we mean by best? Are some more aesthetically pleasing than others? What do we mean by this? Are some ecologically preferable? Why?

As objects are examined, students are led to examine their own lifestyles. They may begin to see waste and aggressive consumerism as morally repugnant. They may become intelligently resistant to advertising. They may begin to evaluate objects according to several dimensions.

To do any of these things requires a certain level of literacy about objects; that is, students must learn how things work. Not everyone needs to study academic physics, but everyone should know how simple motors work, that a hair dryer needs ventilation just as a clothes dryer does (that means cleaning out the lint), that turning the oven up to 450 degrees will not get it to 250 degrees faster than turning it to 250 degrees. They should see what a fine chisel is designed to do and what happens to it when it is used to scrape paint or pry open metal lids. They should be required to take household appliances apart, clean them, and put them back in working order.

The kinds of objects studied in depth will depend on students' special interests and capacities. Students in the linguistic/mathematical program may take a particular interest in computing devices and measuring instruments. Those in music will obviously want to study musical instruments and their development. In the mechanical/technical program, students will be continuously surrounded with tools, energy sources, and machinery; some may find hobbies in studying old cars, steam engines, or flying machines. In the interpersonal program, students may be interested in the objects used in social rituals, in clothing, in the arrangement of furniture for cordial living, perhaps even in city planning and environments that are conducive to peaceful interactions. Those who incline more toward what Howard Gardner (1983) calls the intrapersonal may take a great interest in religious objects and their arrangement or in physical arrangements that enhance meditation.

Just as we experience ambivalence about order because traditional schools have so distorted the idea, so we often have ambivalence toward objects. They seem to represent materialism and to be alien to a life of the mind. Indeed, well-educated young people sometimes scorn

objects and blame technology for the dismal lack of human spirit in
the modern world. For example, distrust and contempt for technology
characterized the counterculture of the 1960s. But here we see again
the deplorable inclination to divide the world into two parts, one good
and the other bad. If nature is good, then technology must be bad, or
vice versa if you prefer.

A careful study of objects and instruments is required, and this study
has to be related to how we want to live, to the obligations we feel as
moral people, to our sense of beauty, to our desire to preserve the natural world. Students should reject the proposition that technology can
solve all problems, even its own, but they should also reject the silly idea
that there are no technological solutions to anything. The technological
world of objects, instruments, and energy is, like the natural world, awe-
inducing, and our awe increases as we learn to use objects properly.

PHYSICAL ARRANGEMENTS

Children need to know not only how to use various objects but also
something about their arrangement. This topic has already been suggested by our brief discussion of order. The appropriate arrangement
of objects, buildings, and all sorts of human artifacts is part of their
utility, and it may also be important to our health as well as our aesthetic sense.

The Japanese, for example, are well known for their meticulous
arrangement of wood, rocks, plants, and water to produce effects of
peace and serenity. In this country it was once basic in the education
of young women to learn the proper arrangement of everything in a
household: settings at the dinner table, the linen closet, the pantry and
root cellar, herb and floral gardens, clothes storage, the nursery. Most
of us would not want to return to the stuffy formality of Victorian days,
but we recognize that a certain order of things contributes to their efficient use and also to our inner sense of peace. Neither the serenity of
the Japanese garden nor the lavender-scented order of the Victorian
linen closet happens by accident.

Learning to arrange living environments in a pleasing and efficient
way should start in preschool. It is delightful to watch children in a
Montessori school set a table for two to share a "tea party." Often the
children find a flower or two for decoration, and they always have real
food and milk or juice. No pretend pouring or paper food here! They

eat, converse, clean up, and put everything away before choosing another activity.

There are wonderful opportunities in the study of physical arrangements to draw on history, science, and art. Suppose a group started with the study of settlers in this country. How should a family plan for sanitation? Considering the placement of well and outhouse can lead to a study of soil percolation and to contemporary problems of soil contamination. Careful consideration of physical arrangements can help students understand why the poor have so often been victims of disease. And further study may involve religious beliefs and political ideologies that obscured the truth about human suffering. Do such beliefs and ideologies operate today?

This discussion points up how exciting education could be if it were organized around centers of care. Sanitation is a topic of central importance today, and focus on it requires information from science, history, sociology, political science, health, aesthetics, and religion. If the topic were taken up in history (and it rarely is), it would be a mere footnote to some chronological account of political struggle. (The influenza epidemic in World War I is a good example.) But studied as a major concern for all living beings today, sanitation can be a challenge to both practical and theoretical thought. How does a toilet work? (Students should be able to do simple repairs.) How much water does each flush require? Are there safe ways to use less water? Can the gray water from washing machines be used on the garden? Under what circumstances? How would you do this? If there is a baby in the house, which of the following practices is least harmful to the environment: Use disposable diapers and discard them as they come off the baby; use disposable diapers but flush excrement before discarding; use cloth diapers. (Here students should consider all effects, including energy and water use.)

As this unit progresses, students may want to connect sanitation to arguments on raising animals for meat. How do steaming piles of animal excrement pollute water supplies? What waste products result from various slaughtering practices? What valuable by-products result? What fraction of animal products is now used beneficially?

A unit on physical arrangements could start out with a focus on the immediate environment or on one in a distant time or place. But ultimately it involves how we live today and how the people who come after us will live. Students in cities should study their living arrangements inside and out, and they should begin to think about city planning: Are there enough trees? How do we measure air quality? What instruments are used? What kind of plants will thrive in this air? Are there plants that might improve the air? Are there personal practices that might contribute to improvement?

Students who live near an ocean should learn about its health and capacity for self-purification. Using a living metaphor, one might say that our oceans, streams, and forests are suffering. How do we measure that suffering, and how can we relieve it? Students should certainly learn how water samples are taken and studied. What are the *E. coli* measurements that sometimes cause the closing of beaches? What sort of sewage treatment is used in their own municipality and where does the effluent empty into the sea? Is there a better alternative? What would it cost?

The human-made world is, obviously, a center of care—of fascination, genius, corruption, remedy, and concern. It connects with the biological world. It also connects with social and spiritual domains. Humans use objects in religious rituals, and special arrangements of objects play a role in many ceremonies. Goblets, candles, medallions, bits of stick, carpets, embroidered cloth, robes, headdresses, stained glass, arks, scrolls, statues, torches, knives, altars . . . the list is long. Consideration of these objects links us not only to religion but also to art, archaeology, and anthropology. How are "primitive" rituals different from "modern" ones? What role does each object play? Who is allowed to handle sacred objects? Where do people practice these rituals, and what beliefs underlie them? What is the status of the objects as art?

Here again we see that there are many paths to the study of existential questions. As religious objects are examined, some students will want to study religion more deeply; others may want to study art, history, or archaeology. Still others may become interested in the technical production of objects: making pottery, designing and crafting stained glass, weaving, or embroidering—or even learning about mass production.

Social ceremonies should also be studied. How are dishes, eating utensils, and cookware arranged in various ceremonies? How do people dress? How are all these objects produced—the dishes, pots, silverware, clothing? Can there be substitutions? What materials are considered proper in various circumstances? Which are aesthetically pleasing? Are the ceremonies themselves somehow pleasing, or are they silly? By what criteria do we judge them?

As we begin to pay attention to the objects around us and their physical arrangement, we are led to ask questions about ourselves.

One important question concerns our responsibility for care of the human-made world.

MAINTAINING AND CONSERVING

My high school history teacher used to say, "The first duty of a citizen is to keep the place clean." Keeping the place clean is indeed one of the first conscious contributions a child can make to the environment. In the last thirty years or so, however, we have been reluctant to press children on neatness and cleanliness for fear of warping their personalities and destroying their creativity. I confess that I have been inconsistent on this in raising my own children. Because I like order, I insisted that the public areas of the house be kept clean, but I gave them free rein in their own rooms. Only when things got very bad indeed did I threaten inspections, and now and then I hung signs on various bedrooms saying, "Closed by order of the Board of Health." When a child saw this ominous warning, the reaction was usually, "Uh-oh," and a flurry of cleaning occurred.

But this, I now think, was not the best course of action. I should have spent more time teaching them to care for the objects around them, not just for my approval or tolerance. Toys and art materials should be evaluated and the best treasured. There is a fine line here: We do not want our children to spend their days polishing and protecting their possessions, and we certainly want them to use their possessions freely (as Montessori said, freely and properly), but we want them to see that future pleasure or use depends on care. What happened in the past—and caused the permissive reaction of the recent thirty years— was that caring for objects was identified with a superficial morality. Cleanliness was our public face. We were taught to be neat in order to impress people, and we had to take care of certain objects because "Aunt Mary will think you're ungrateful."

What I am suggesting here is that we use different criteria in caring for objects and the human-made world. First, how will our use or abuse affect other people—not just their opinion of us, but their actual welfare? Second, in what ways is the object worth our care? The second is almost entirely neglected in modern education, and I'll say more about it in the section on understanding and appreciating.

In schools, especially during the time devoted to centers of care, many more lessons should begin with objects, and some dialogue should focus on the "needs" of objects for care. Children should also be involved all through school in helping to maintain the physical facilities, and time should be taken to admire the result. The unfortunate message we give now in schools is that students should learn their academic lessons so that they will not have to do menial jobs for a living. Perhaps, as I said earlier, no one should have to work at repetitious, dirty, bone-wearying jobs day in and day out. Yet the individual tasks should not be scorned. They are essential and worth doing well, and children should come to value an admirable result.

As we work together to make our physical environment pleasing and healthful, we come also to a greater appreciation for those who often perform these tasks for us. This is the heart of learning to care: Students must practice in the company of experienced carers. Very few of us come to care for people, their work, animals, plants, or ideas without direct practice. Just as we need direct, hands-on contact with people to develop genuine caring for them, so we need hands-on practice with the objects of modern living.

MAKING AND REPAIRING

Students should have opportunities to make and repair things. Most elementary and middle school children are exposed to at least one semester of "shop" in which they learn to use simple tools and construct, say, a box or a tie rack. But this experience is usually treated as a prelude to the real work of school—abstraction; it is rarely treated as an introduction to more sophisticated work with objects and tools. This is a great pity, for it suggests to children that work with the hands is only for those who cannot do "better" things.

All children should learn how to do simple electrical work safely: to wire lamps, replace frayed cords, test outlets and repair them. They should also learn how to do basic diagnostic tests on household appliances, and they should be able to make basic plumbing and carpentry repairs. As they learn these things, they should also learn the proper use and storage of tools. Both girls and boys should learn these things.

Both should also learn their way around a well-outfitted kitchen. They should know how to check whether an oven is level and whether its temperature is accurate; why cake and cookie pans must be clean on the outside as well as the inside; why woks and frying pans should be maintained in a well-seasoned condition; why vegetables are best cooked quickly in pans with little water and tight-fitting lids. They should learn how to use mixers, blenders, processors, whisks, paring knives, and potato peelers. And they should learn the limits of their appliances. Many people think foods will keep indefinitely in a freezer, for example.

Children can make some simple objects, and those who become interested can develop their crafts more fully. It is odd that basket weaving has become a metaphor for the easy course—something for which no respectable school should give credit. But how many of us can actually weave a serviceable basket? How many of us could find the appropriate natural materials, plan a basket that would serve a particular purpose, and then actually make it? It seems to me that factoring polynomial expressions is far easier! Children should have opportunities to try both and come to appreciate the skill of those who can do either well.

Besides learning how to make simple objects and do basic repairs, students should learn how those operations are performed on a large scale and in complex situations. Further, they should be exposed to the histories of manufacturing and inventing. Notice that I say "exposed." I certainly do not recommend that students be forced to describe the history of lace making or the fundamental mechanics of automation or the principles of shipbuilding unless they are really interested in these things. But almost all children are fascinated by a visit to a colonial village where they can observe tatting, spinning, weaving, and smithing. Most will be intrigued by the operation of an assembly line. Some, after watching a demonstration of Indian canoe building, may want to build their own boats. The history of making things is, for most people, far more interesting and useful than the history of political events, although the latter come to life vividly when they are connected to the world of making things and maintaining control over one's own work and possessions.

Dewey identified making things as one of the four fundamental interests of children. Unhappily, because schools put so little value on making things, most of us grow up with contempt for work done with our hands. Thus we lose on two counts: We become too clumsy to make things for ourselves, and we fail to appreciate the wonderful world of crafts and technology.

UNDERSTANDING AND APPRECIATING

Schools today, especially secondary schools, are thing-poor places. The absence of things—of objects familiar in homes and other work places—is probably a result of long-standing emphasis on something called the life of the mind. As though the mind could have a life separate from its physical body! A person who can concentrate on abstract ideas is thought to be superior to one who works with concrete objects, and our society has never put sufficient value on the work that keeps our day-to-day world running in an orderly fashion.

We need to learn how to care for the world of human-made objects and their arrangement. The Swiss educator Johann Pestalozzi (1746–1827) initiated a form of education that focused on concrete objects, diagrams, and pictures. He developed something called the "object lesson" that actually began with the presentation and examination of an object. My recommendations are similar to Pestalozzi's in the domain of human-made objects. Start with some object, say, a table lamp, and ask, "How does this work?" Students can take it apart and learn a functional answer to the question. They can study electricity and construct a deeper functional answer, and they can begin to develop a theoretical answer. They can explore the history of lighting. Along the way they may run across a reason earlier people had for killing whales. (Was it, even then, an adequate reason?) They can measure the intensity and spread of light from the lamp and learn about the instruments that do this. Perhaps they will be led to consider the physiology of human vision. Perhaps they will ask how this light differs from sunlight and whether it is adequate for plants. They should be urged to consider whether the lamp is beautiful, well balanced, of appropriate size. Where would it look good?

Pestalozzi was also interested in what objects and their use mean for human beings, and his lessons often ended in discussion of such matters. In fact, it is this "moralizing" that we today associate with object lessons. But the more important point, from the perspective of caring, is that object lessons give us an opportunity to focus our care on objects in the environment and then on whatever else seems to be connected in a way that matters to us. As foci of study, lamps and toasters are as important as quadratic equations and complex sentences.

To appreciate the human-made world in which we live, we might pose a thought question for a class of students: What if we had to start from scratch? How much of the human-made world could we thirty people recreate? What would we have to know? We might even try an experiment. Let's all learn from a good book the principles on which an electric motor or internal combustion engine operate. We will work together until we can all pass an orthodox written test on this material. Now. Can we actually build one? What do we need to know that we did not learn in the theoretical discussion?

The above discussion on the domain of objects suggests a powerful analogy for the moral domain of human interaction. There, too, simply learning about theoretical positions and working through hypothetical dilemmas may be insufficient for moral action in the real world. This is an important point that deserves reiteration, but I do not want to reduce the world of objects to a mere metaphor for another, "higher," world. The object world is important in itself.

As students acquire understanding in the world of objects, they may also gain a greater sense of control over their own everyday affairs. It is gratifying to be able to fix things and to be competent enough to judge a repairperson's work. Practical knowledge also gives meaning and importance to theoretical knowledge and can provide the working base needed to extend and generalize one's knowledge.

Finally, the appreciation of crafts and technology—besides being satisfying in itself—tends to block environmental extremism. Looking back on the antitechnology bias that characterized much of the sixties' counterculture, we can see that many of the positions taken were not only extreme but also unrealistic. To transform the current human condition, we need arguments and plans that spread care into every domain of human life, and that certainly includes the sphere of making and using things.

CHAPTER 11

Caring for Ideas

In our discussion so far, I have concentrated on ideas as they are connected to actual life, existential questions, and general education. Now I will consider how we should approach ideas for their own sake. How should we teach students who are passionately interested in a realm of disciplined thought? How should we teach those who have an instrumental interest in a subject? In short, how should we teach the disciplines as long as they remain in the curriculum?

I have already argued that the disciplines as we now know them should not be used as the heart—or organizing organ—of the curriculum. A first step toward weakening the hegemony of the disciplines is to cease teaching them for their own sake except to those who show a passionate interest in them. Everywhere today, educators in the particular disciplines want to teach their subject from the perspective of experts in the field. Students are supposed to learn to think like mathematicians, scientists, historians, literary critics, aestheticians, and ethicists. This attitude is pernicious and actually does violence to the disciplines thus presented. The average student need not think like a mathematician; lots of people other than mathematicians use mathematics effectively, and students should be encouraged to find their own uses for mathematics and choose their own attitude toward it. Pedagogy should begin with the purposes, interests, and capacities of students. But some students have a passionate interest in particular subjects. These students should have an opportunity to learn those subjects in considerable depth.

In this chapter I will look at two subjects from this perspective. The first, mathematics, I have had extensive experience in teaching. The second, art, I will look at as a philosopher and general educator. My major claim in both cases is that students who have passionate interest in a subject should be initiated into the discourse of the disciplinary community; others need not be. Further, beyond providing the best possible education for individual students, a pedagogy that posits different objectives for students with different capacities and interests stands the best chance of meeting our needs as a nation. If we need mathematicians, engineers, and scientists, then we should invite those students who have the appropriate interests and capacities into a rigorous and wondrous working partnership in the relevant disciplines. Otherwise the threat is not just mediocrity but outright intellectual rebellion.

MATHEMATICS

There is now a tremendous push to get more students involved in mathematics. Many colleges and universities require three years of mathematics for entrance, and this requirement presses high schools to increase their enrollments in college preparatory mathematics. Preparation for college is highly standardized. Whether students plan to study art, religion, or engineering, three years of mathematics is supposed to be good for them.

What jobs really require algebra, geometry, and trigonometry? Think of all the things one could do in this society without using algebra. One needs to be literate in numbers, of course, and everyone should be able to compute percents, compare rates, and understand simple descriptive statistics. Beyond such basic skills, people should understand the mathematics involved in their own spheres of interest, but as I said earlier, this mathematics need not be taught by expert mathematics teachers. Indeed, it could be more convincingly taught by people using it in the fields where it is needed. Consider a problem suggested for students in an algebra class. A set of data is presented on soil acidity and plant growth (Goldin, 1990, p. 20). Students are asked to construct a scatter plot and look for trends. No explanation of pH is given, no mention is made of the type of plants, and no other variable is considered. This problem does not belong in a mathematics class. If it is to be treated at all, it should be done in a biology class where, preferably, students will actually grow plants. Students should consider the variables to be controlled (light, heat, water, nutrients) and the type of plants. They should be thoroughly familiar with the pH scale and the range preferred by most plants. They should also know how to change soil acidity. Selecting one kind of plant, they might experiment by varying the pH; then they should try another type of plant. In this context the statistical exercise becomes real. If scientists and science teachers do not use the mathematics described in this exercise, why should students be interested in looking for trends in a meaningless scatter plot?

Mathematics has served as a well-oiled piece of sorting machinery. Many students are discouraged from college preparation because they hate or fear mathematics, and if they drop it in high school and then decide at the community college level that they want a four-year education, they still have to take mathematics even if it's irrelevant to their projected field of study.

The schools are caught in a web of paradox. There is no question that mathematics, foreign language, and laboratory science were thought to be effective testing-sorting instruments for college entrance. Thus there has long been great pressure to make these courses rigorous and demanding. But now there is even greater pressure to give all children—especially minority children—a fair opportunity to get to college. That means enrolling many more children in college preparatory mathematics. One way to force students into algebra and geometry is to offer no alternative mathematics, and schools that make this choice must enroll everyone in college preparatory mathematics. In our eagerness to give everyone "a fair chance," we offer minimal courses—two years of mathematics taken over a three-year period with everything deep and interesting removed. It does not occur to us to change the requirement—to insist that students prepare well for a line of study and to study mathematics only if it is relevant to that line. Such a requirement would mean that students taking mathematics (or any other subject) would usually see the point of their involvement.

At the level of national interest, we are shooting ourselves in the foot with good intentions. Instead of coining slogans—"All children can learn!"—and forcing all children into algebra "for their own good," we should be teaching college preparatory mathematics to fewer students and doing a better job at it. The mathematics supposedly necessary to understand other subjects should be taught there.

I do not mean to suggest that students should be kept out of mathematics classes by grade requirements, or unless they show proof of aptitude. Classes should be totally open—even, as I said earlier, honors classes. Teachers should talk with students about the receptivity required in caring about mathematics. People can become engrossed in mathematics, hear it "speak to them," be seized by its puzzles and challenges. It is tragic to deprive students of this possibility. "Honors" classes should be classes for the passionately interested. Any student who wants to tackle the work and has at least minimal prerequisite experience should be allowed to do so. The key here is that we accept students' legitimate aims and desires.

The complaint has been made against such a mode of operation that some students will short-change themselves. Ignorant or unconvinced of what a rigorous education can mean in their lives, they will choose courses and topics based on how little work they require. But this complaint rests on a misunderstanding. I am certainly not suggesting that some courses be challenging and others "mickey mouse." Nor am I suggesting that students be left alone to choose what they will do on the basis of mere whim. Rather, the idea is for teachers and students to establish relations of care and trust so that valuable information can be effectively exchanged, advice given, and challenging projects undertaken. I do not believe that many teenagers will downgrade their own education. When they seem to be doing that, it is because we have already told them that their interests are irrelevant to schooling and (explicitly or implicitly) that engineers are better than child care workers, physicians better than nurses, lawyers better than policepersons, executives better than cooks, and so forth. In such a system, choosing what one really wants to study can be—by definition—downgrading one's education. However, it need not be so, and it should not be so.

But, perverse as it is, let's face the reality of today's schools. Students who want to "make it" in life have to take academic mathematics. Can we do anything to improve life in mathematics classrooms without changing the whole system?

There is a movement in mathematics education that is growing in influence and popularity. It is called constructivism. (See Davis, Maher, and Noddings, 1990.) I want to say a little about it here because it offers some positive possibilities, but at the same time, it contains the seeds of its own destruction. Unless it is embedded in an encompassing moral position on education, it risks categorization as a *method,* as something that will produce enhanced or slightly modified traditional results.

Constructivism is a cognitive position holding that all mental acts, both perceptual and cognitive, are acts of construction. No mental act is a mere copy or externally imposed response. If you pass some information to me, I must actively listen to make out what you are saying, and then I have to fit what I have heard into what I already know and decide what to do with the new material. What I do with it depends on my purposes. I may respond with a sympathy-like interest because I care about you even though I do not care about the topic you are discussing. Or I may care deeply about the topic and realize that what you are saying suggests that I have been wrong about something. Or I may evaluate your remark and decide that *you* have made a mistake.

Constructivists believe that people are internally motivated and that they construct their own mental representations of situations, events, and conceptual structures. Constructivist teachers, then, usually spend time trying to find out what their students are trying to do and why. They are ready with suggestions and challenges that will help students to make strong and useful constructions.

What motivates constructivist mathematics educators? For the most part, they want to teach mathematics in ways that are compatible with their beliefs about how people learn. They also tend to believe that mathematical thinking is rich, complex, tolerant of ambiguity, filled with attempts that may or may not succeed, and broadly useful in many human activities. Believing all this, they want to promote their students' mathematical growth. This is fine to the degree that students are concerned for whatever reason with their own mathematical growth.

But constructivism as a pedagogical orientation has to be embedded in an ethical or political framework. The primary aim of every teacher must be to promote the growth of students as competent, caring, loving, and lovable people. Teachers with this aim will work flexibly in teaching mathematics—inspiring those who care about mathematics for itself to inquire ever more deeply, helping those who care instrumentally about mathematics to prepare for the line of work they desire, and supporting as best they can those students who wish they never had to encounter mathematics. To have uniformly high expectations for all students in mathematics is morally wrong and pedagogically disastrous. It is part of a sloganized attempt to make our schools look democratic and egalitarian, when in fact they are systems continually struggling for tighter control.

Now I want to describe in detail an actual program that embodies some of the ideas discussed here. First I will describe the program itself, and then I will present an analysis of what could go wrong if the primary aim is forgotten.

The mathematics department of an average suburban high school (about 1,500 pupils) was faced with an increasing number of students enrolled in third-year college preparatory mathematics—"algebra/trig." The school was also pressed for space, and this fact made the plan proposed by the department administratively attractive. They proposed to work with two large classes (seventy-five to eighty students each) taught by a team of teachers in the school cafeteria. Each student could choose a minimum course, a standard course, or an accelerated course. This provision was designed to accommodate students who disliked math but needed the third year to qualify for university entrance, as well as students who loved math and wanted as much as they could get. The syllabi made clear that students could change their minds—slow down or speed up if they preferred. The minimum course covered six chapters of the course text and required students to pass one chapter test each marking period; completing this course would not qualify a student for twelfth-year mathematics. The standard course required completion of nine chapters, and the accelerated course demanded twelve or more chapters. Further, assignments varied. Students in the accelerated course might skip the easy exercises, but they had to do the difficult ones.

A serious attempt was made to reduce test anxiety. Grades were earned cumulatively. Everyone started the marking period with a grade of 50. When a test was passed, the grade became, say, 70; a second test passed meant perhaps an 85; a third test 95. This method reduces anxiety considerably because nothing can be lost by taking a test. The old (almost tribal) fear of entering the last test of a marking period with a 92 and leaving with a 72 is removed. All tests were graded "passing," "not passing," or "passing +1" This last acknowledged a top-notch performance, and the extra point was added to the student's basic grade at the end of a marking period.

The course was designed as a continuous progress program. Students could not move on to chapter 3 until they had passed a test on chapter 2. One teacher, Ms. Jones let us say, would start the whole group off with an introduction to chapter 1, and then the students would work together at tables while the teachers circulated to give help. Fridays were test days, and on the very first Friday there were always some students ready to take the test on chapter 1. Students who passed the chapter 1 test would move on to work with the teacher who had major responsibility for chapter 2. This process continued until some students were ready for chapter 4, for which Ms. Jones again had responsibility. Usually there were still a few students working on chapter 1, so Ms. Jones divided her time between students in chapter 1 and those in chapter 4.

Every week, one day was designated for "enrichment," and one of the team teachers took a group of students to a separate classroom for discussion of some topic that did not appear in the text. Enrichment topics included Diophantine equations, cryptography, abstract algebra, logic puzzles, history of mathematics, and computer problems. Any students could elect to participate. If I were working with such a team today, I would want to introduce topics from each of the centers of care. Possibilities: our own psychology of learning math, effective tutoring, population and hunger studies, animal populations, matrices for agricultural studies, the special contributions of various ethnic groups, women mathematicians, religious interests of great mathematicians.

In the years that I was involved with this program, results—traditionally interpreted—were good. On year-end standardized tests, no student scored in the bottom decile and very few in the lowest fifth. Everyone learned something. The span of achievement in terms of material covered ranged from the minimum six chapters to more than sixteen! Motivation to do mathematics varies enormously.

For me, however, and certainly for our present discussion, traditional results are not the main concern. Our concern should center on what the students are learning about themselves, about helping each other, about contracts and meeting obligations, about the fascinating applicability of mathematics to human endeavors, and—for some students—about the nature and beauty of mathematics itself. Many things can go wrong if the primary purposes are not kept firmly in mind, and it is worthwhile to analyze the program from this perspective because in doing so we can learn much about why educational reforms fail.

One temptation is to overdo the individual, continuous progress aspect of such a program. Our students were encouraged to work together; they were not placed on individualized schedules. Teachers provided mini-lectures, special help, and advice on which other students to consult; they were not bogged down in checking work as often happens in individualized programs. The press to scientize teaching and learning could easily lead to an overemphasis on tests, to isolation in learning, and to standardized roles for teachers. Participants have to remember why they are engaged in a program of this sort and resist that pressure.

When team teaching is used, there may be a move (as mentioned above) to differentiate the functions of team members: a lead teacher to lecture, one to supervise individual tutoring, one to check work, and so forth. This is deadly and works against the primary purpose. Teachers and students must work together cooperatively as whole human beings, not as bits of pedagogical machinery. From the perspective of caring, team teaching can be a wonderful idea; differentiated staffing, however, is a terrible one.

As the year moves along, teachers may question the capacity of students for self-evaluation and self-governance. This actually happened in our program. Sometimes students would achieve their desired grade, say an 85, by the middle of a marking period and prepare to do something other than math for the next two or three weeks. Although

I always tried to persuade such students to try for a top grade, I accepted their decision. After all, we had a contract. One team member, let's call her Ms. Smith, was aghast at this acceptance on my part. She believed that it was our duty to *make* students do their best, and she also believed that they should do nothing but math in math class. Ms. Smith's attitude was thoroughly conditioned by the control ideology that pervades our schools. Students must be controlled—for their own good, of course. To give way to Ms. Smith on this, I now understand even better than I did then, is to distort the whole program.

Another form of distortion is equally troubling. Over the years, a few teachers trying the approach in other courses (algebra 1, for example) interpreted the facilitative function of the teacher to mean that the teacher should only respond to student requests for help. These teachers never intervened and actually let students sit idle for days, even weeks. Nothing could be further from the spirit we are discussing here. Of course teachers should initiate! They should suggest, persuade, inspire, encourage, negotiate compromises, offer concrete help. Above all they should engage students in dialogue so that decisions are well informed. We do not respect students when we leave them alone to make decisions on whim.

Ms. Smith introduced another concern about control. She complained that too many students were electing to take tests on Fridays even though they were unprepared. Clearly many had not completed the assignments and were simply hoping to pass by luck. She insisted that their notebooks should be checked before they were allowed to take a test. Again, there was the need to control. Indeed Ms. Smith honestly felt it was her duty to control student work in this way. She staggered home every Thursday night under a tremendous load of notebooks. I compromised. On Thursday in class I would gather around me those students who wanted to take Friday's test. Then I would choose specific problems in their notebooks and ask how they had been done, why some had been skipped, whether the student had considered an alternative method that seemed important. These sessions were more conversations than quality checks, and other students would regularly chime in with suggestions. This way of operating is compatible with induction into a community of discourse. We ask different questions of students who are passionately interested in mathematics and expect a different level of response from them. From some students an answer that tells "how it works" is entirely adequate; from others we should expect a response that reflects deep structural understanding.

Finally, someone might challenge the whole notion of mixing mini-mum, standard, and accelerated classes in one program for which all stu-dents would get five credits. The question would be raised: Is this fair? My response is that a criterion of fairness is irrelevant here. Needs are being identified and met. That is what matters. One might want to argue that meeting needs is fair, but I have learned to identify that language as a danger signal. It means that the system wants tighter control.

With the ideology of control so firmly entrenched in our profes-sional and personal lives, it is very difficult to move to an approach that emphasizes mutual respect, responsible freedom, self-evaluation, open cooperation, caring, and sharing. Even well-intentioned people can make or accede to decisions that will press promising programs back into the control mode. Constructivists risk having this happen when they insist on *understanding* as a legitimate goal for all students without analyzing the varieties of understanding. The goal should be for students to understand what they are doing and to what end. This need not require a deep structural understanding of mathematics.

Here I want to say a little more about Jaime Escalante, of whom I spoke appreciatively earlier. I cannot admire everything Escalante does. In particular I cannot approve throwing students out of class, browbeating them for not working as hard as the teacher wants, and using sarcasm as a pedagogical strategy. Many of Escalante's students see the caring that lies underneath the surface cruelty, but some prob-ably do not. We have to ask whether getting students to pass an ad-vanced-placement calculus test is an adequate reason for treating them impolitely. On the positive, polite side, Escalante says repeatedly to his students, "You are the best!" But that lovely compliment means, "You can do A.P. calculus!" It also implies that other students (those not studying A.P. calculus) are less than best. My preference is to respect the full range of human capacities and to help students do high-qual-ity work in whatever field they choose. A student should not have to succeed at A.P. calculus to gain a math teacher's respect.

There is another point to consider with respect to Escalante's meth-ods. It is probably true that a majority teacher could not treat minority students so; complaints would be thunderous. Perhaps minority stu-dents and teachers need the freedom to work out methods that are mu-tually acceptable to them. But, as coprofessionals, we should continue to question as we support. Surely not all minority students respond favorably to coercion. Again, it is not a sign of respect to simply shrug and accede. At every stage and in all of our interactions, we must remind ourselves of what we are trying to achieve, and everything else must be examined in light of our major purpose.

Minorities and women, like majority students, may sometimes fall into the passionately interested category. But often their interests are instrumental. Such interests should be respected. Teachers need to experiment with a range of methods that may be especially effective for particular groups. They should be acquainted with works that treat the various ways of knowing (Belenky, et al., 1986; Culley & Portuges, 1985; Bunch & Pollack, 1983), and, where there are mathematical topics of special interest to these groups, they should be offered for study.

Mathematics teachers should also attend to capacities other than the mathematical. Those with linguistic capacities might learn a lot of mathematics through reading and writing. (We seldom spend time on the intelligent reading of math texts, for example.) Those with artistic talent might enjoy mathematical studies of aesthetics, the mathematics of design, or even the aesthetics of mathematics. Those with strong interpersonal skills might learn best through tutoring others. Our methods must vary.

Finally, although we should encourage students to study mathematics if their interests suggest such study, and we should help minorities and women to see themselves as potentially competent in mathematics, we should not create an environment in which mathematical competence defines a student's self-worth. Lots of successful, competent, morally upstanding people hate math and find their passionate interests elsewhere. Rather than press the question, Why aren't more women interested in math?, we should ask what they *are* interested in and why. We can use the answers to those questions both to encourage alternative interests and to design more appropriate math courses.

ART

I cannot examine every subject that appears in the school curriculum in detail. Among the arts, I have chosen fine arts rather than music or drama because its current direction illustrates the major mistakes I have been criticizing throughout this book.

Many art educators are now recommending a curricular approach called Discipline-Based Art Education (DBAE). This approach is highly cognitive and appeals to the same linguistic and mathematical/logical capacities that support the rest of the curriculum. It suggests that art education should comprise aesthetics, art criticism, art history, and art production. (See Getty Center for Education in the Arts, 1985; also *Journal of Aesthetic Education, 1987*). It should, in short, look more like other disciplines in the precollege curriculum and be subject to the same high-powered cognitive teaching and testing.

I think this movement is wrongheaded even though I have a high regard for many of its proponents. (For other criticisms see a collection of articles in *Educational Theory, 1990;* Gehlback, 1990.) I want to start the discussion with some recollections from my early days as a math teacher. Before I became convinced that the major job of every teacher is much like that of a parent—to foster growth and shape acceptable children—I was certainly a discipline-oriented math educator. There's a story to be told about my conversion from that position, but the point I want to make is different; it centers on the place of art as a very special elective in high schools. Year after year there were kids in my math classes who were terrible in math. When a marvelous art teacher joined the faculty, I found out that some of these people were outstanding young artists; art boomed in that school. They became part of what was known as the "art room crowd," and they held a proud position in our high school. I came to know them because there was a "math office bunch," too, and a few students belonged to both groups, one of my own daughters among them. Once I got to know the art room crowd and moved away from the rigidities of my early position on math (a lot of factors were involved here), I started to do a better job as a teacher. I came to appreciate a multitude of talents. My students no longer appeared to me as just good and bad math students.

In that high school, art played a significant role in the lives of a substantial number of young people. It was different from the other subjects, and the "crowd" was different from the other kids. They were serious about their work, had their own jokes, were trusted in the art rooms on their own and for as many hours as they could manage. I know they did art history and criticism—that they watched slides even during lunch—and that they were involved in evaluating and eventually arranging exhibits at the county museum. These young people were aiming at postsecondary schools my math kids rarely considered—Cooper Union, the Rhode Island School of Design, Pratt Institute; they were working hard at assembling portfolios. They had their service projects, too, and were often involved in designing sets for dramatic presentations, preparing posters for various events, and even producing political cartoons.

I don't know whether tests were given on the slides shown, whether student progress was systematically evaluated as we are so fond of claiming today. I doubt it. Students who took four years of art—sometimes the equivalent of six years by packing in extra hours—treasured their status as members of a community. They were learners but not ignorant learners; they were more like talented apprentices, and their talents were cultivated. The cognitive dimension of art grew out of their passionate involvement with art production. I suspect that their knowledge was active and well integrated with their central interests. It was not that flabby stuff Whitehead called "inert knowledge."

So far I have depended on experiential evidence, personal recollection, to initiate an argument. The major concern that emerges is that students who are really talented in art will be disenchanted by the standard cognitive approach. The people who will do well in these courses are just the people who do well generally in academic courses. In her dissertation, Liora Bresler (1987) showed that exactly this occurred in a cognitively oriented music class at a major university. Musically talented and experienced students dropped out or did poorly; the relatively ignorant and untalented did remarkably well. Art educators should launch a careful study of this phenomenon before converting art education to a more heavily cognitive base.

You can see what worries me in the move to DBAE. I am afraid that art will lose its unique place in schools. I understand the political reasons for advocating DBAE. To a large degree, art has lost its place entirely in many schools (what occurred in my old school is no longer so familiar) and so long as it sports an arty look, it will continue to be suspect in its very difference—to be relatively unimportant in college admission, to appeal to a limited number of students, to be at the mercy of the budget ax. DBAE advocates believe that one way to make art important is to make it just like English, math, and science: require it, make it heavily cognitive, sequence it, test the daylights out of it. But I wonder, if you do this, what will happen to all those young people who for years have found the art room the only place in school worth attending, whose interest in art has kept them in school long enough to qualify for a chance at life's standard goods. Of course it is clear by now that I reject the disciplinary approach to general education, but the example of art underscores the features that worry me most.

My concern so far has focused on the possible loss of uniqueness in art education and the effects of that loss on artistically talented students. Now I want to push the argument up a notch and consider the relation between DBAE and societal goals. "A fundamental premise," say Clark, Day, and Greer (1987), "is that general education, to be balanced and complete, must attend to all major domains of human experience, including the aesthetic domain" (p. 139). This sort of statement has a nice ring to it and has appeared perennially in arguments for the advancement of various curricula. The fact of the matter is, however, that education does not attend to all major domains of human experience, nor do many of its practitioners and theorists show signs of wanting it to do so. We have, instead, intellectualized human experience, and we have been so successful at doing this that we really suppose reading and writing about various domains is equivalent to "having experience" in those domains. Attending to all the major domains of human experience has come to mean—for schools, at least—extending the range of intellectual experience. If art educators are serious about introducing students to an experience they might otherwise not encounter in school, they might well emphasize art production, crafts, and decoration of various sorts.

DBAE does, of course, advocate balance, and art production will be given attention, but as I will argue later, balance does not have to mean equal time. Further, balance is not the point here; respect for a unique set of talents is more the point. In casting its program as it has, DBAE clearly places itself in the liberal arts tradition. "Classical approaches to selection of domains as bases for school programs rely on philosophical analysis," Clark, Day, and Greer state. Further, "These analyses identify domains of human experience that should be addressed in a well-rounded education" (p. 139). It is true that programs that use such language—that talk about the ideal of an educated person and a well-rounded education—are accompanied by or undergirded by philosophical analysis. But a philosophical analysis need not of necessity produce such a view of education. It might, as mine attempts to do, support a view of education as learning to care or, alternatively, as self-actualization, or growth, or mere training. Whether or not to speak of the ideal of an educated adult is itself a fundamental choice that must be supported by philosophical argument.

Because DBAE, like so many other curriculum movements, defends requiring art on the grounds that a democratic society wants all its people to be "truly educated," this is a good place to review our initial argument against liberal education. Two very different views of democracy have been prominent in American education: the more or less static Greek view advocated by Robert Maynard Hutchins and the more dynamic one described by John Dewey.

The first lays out a picture of a society already formed and in decent order and asks how it can be kept that way. Its concept of virtue is reminiscent of the Greeks; it depends heavily on a demonstration of excellence in ways of life (Alasdair MacIntyre [1981] calls them "practices") that demand reflection on ends as well as skilled performance. The masses learn virtue from virtuous masters, and indeed virtue itself is ultimately defined this way. It is the constitutive quality of the good (or virtuous) person. Thus the authority of moral experts plays a large role in such a society, and of course moral expertise is coextensive with intellectual expertise in this vision. The "best" in this society are, happily for them, the best in all ways.

Greek democracy clearly was not classless, and the education recommended by its philosophers reflected this fact. In Plato's *Republic* children were to be educated according to their diagnosed abilities for one of three main functions in adult life. The "best" education was reserved for the "best" students—those who would become guardians of the Republic. This society was certainly a democracy of sorts. Those who were citizens were expected to participate appropriately in the affairs of the society, and gaining a position in the ruling class was supposedly a matter of merit.

The Greek notion of an elite education for guardians is retained in the contemporary ideal of an educated person. In the liberal arts tradition, an educated person is described in terms of the content with which he or she has become familiar, the shared language of this content, and the practices open to persons with such preparation. The education of such persons has long been considered the "best education." But notice that there is a good Greek circularity built into this conception. What is the best education? It is the sort that our finest citizens must have had. Look at them to see what is good. How did they get that way? Through the wonderful education provided for them and through their talent and diligence. Thus the education already experienced by the "best" becomes the best education.

The contemporary version of this doctrine was beautifully described by Hutchins in the 1930s and still proficiently advocated, as we saw earlier, by Mortimer Adler in his *Paideia Proposal* (1982). Because our conception of democracy rejects a classed society, Hutchins and Adler insist that, in Hutchins' words, "The best education for the best is the best education for all." In other words, the education once frankly designed for an elite should now be the education offered to everyone.

The static assumptions in this recommendation are obvious. We know what education is best because we have its best products as examples. All we need to do is to replicate their education for each new generation, being careful of course to give each child a genuine opportunity to succeed at it. Operation of the plan must be scrupulously fair. Besides fairness to individuals, we are urged to consider the benefits such a scheme promises for our democracy. From Adler's perspective a democracy cannot long survive unless its citizens share a common heritage—a common language, set of concepts, knowledge of their past, understanding of the finest products of their culture. The society, for Adler, is a given; at least its ideal is given, and this ideal is realized in a nucleus of living experts who manifest the qualities needed in a good society. What we need to do, he suggests, is to maintain and extend this model.

The practicality of Adler's recommendations can safely be ignored for the moment, and I have so far said nothing about the practicality of DBAE either. It is the vision that I ask you to analyze and critique, Are the persons who have governed, produced acknowledged works of art, built fortunes, and conducted military campaigns really our best persons? Did their education produce a goodness we really want to replicate, or has its acquisition merely been the defining mark of those who claimed themselves to be the best? If a different sort of education had been offered, might our best have been a more compassionate, more generous, more open, less judgmental, less acquisitive, and wiser set of persons? These are important questions, and no scheme for general education should be seriously put forward without exploring them. There is enormous arrogance in the *Paideia Proposal*. It says, in effect, "Look at us! We are clearly the best, and our education should supply the pattern for all education. Let us be generous and give all children the opportunity to be just like us." The *Paideia* totally ignores the riches of pluralistic culture—especially those cultures, such as our Native American, that reject the very premises of liberal education as it has been traditionally defined.

In contrast to the static notion of democracy, there is Dewey's dynamic conception. A democracy is not given, nor is it even illustrated in the workings of a cadre of similarly educated elites all capable of discussing the Peloponnesian Wars, Picasso, and nuclear throw weights—thereby demonstrating their competence to govern. Democracy is not the outcome of a common set of words and customs. Rather, it is an achievement—one that depends on the desire to communicate and the goodwill to persist in collaborative inquiry. Common language, customs, and values are the marks of achievement in the effort at building a democracy, not its prerequisites. To achieve a democracy we must try things out, evaluate them without personal prejudice, revise them if they are found wanting, and decide what to do next through a process of reasoned consensus or compromise in which the authority of expertise is consulted but not allowed to impose its views with no discussion of how, why, and on what grounds.

The same advice is applied to education. For Dewey education, too, is a constructive achievement. It is not a matter of absorbing something already laid out, tried and true. It is a matter of trying things out with the valued help of experts (teachers), of evaluating, revising, comparing, sharing, communicating, constructing, choosing. Strictly speaking, there is no end product—no ideally educated person—but a diverse host of persons showing signs of increasing growth. There will be commonalities, of course, but these will have been achieved in the process and not necessarily through exactly similar experiences. Even when common values are achieved by one group, they cannot be simply transmitted to another. The new group can be guided; we can share what we have learned. But as soon as we *impose* our values on a new generation we risk losing those values that are most needed in a dynamic society—those that encourage reflective criticism, revision, creation, and renewal.

Present debate over plans like the *Paideia Proposal* often concentrates on feasibility. Too seldom are we encouraged to think reflectively about the total pattern of education to which we are committed and how any plan under consideration relates to it. Adler himself has discouraged such reflection by glossing over the great differences between Hutchins and Dewey. One would think, to read the *Paideia*, that the two men were both advocates of the Hutchins–Adler program. He says, for example:

> There is no acceptable reason why trying to promote equality should have led to a lessening or loss of quality. Two decades after John Dewey, another great American educator, Robert Maynard Hutchins, as much committed to democracy as Dewey was before him, stated the fundamental principle we must follow in our effort to achieve a true equality of educational conditions. "The best education for the best," he said, "is the best education for all." (1982, p. 6)

From what has already been said, it is clear that this paragraph of Adler's is very misleading; it conveys a monumental distortion of Dewey's position, since Dewey's conception of democracy was very different from that of Hutchins. Further, Adler makes it sound as though the two men never actually discussed these issues, when in fact their published debates make lively reading. My point here is that we live and work in a time when the history and philosophy of education are not regularly drawn upon to enlighten our debates. That Adler could put Dewey and Hutchins into one compartment with respect to their views on democracy and be persuasive to so many people who should know better is a dangerous sign. It is a sign that the curriculum field is still not paying much attention to its own history. (This is not a reason for forcing all education students to study curriculum history. It is, rather, part of an argument for extended dialogue between professors and students.)

Now what has all this to do with DBAE? Several paragraphs of the monograph suggest that DBAE does hold an ideal of the educated person, that education in art is thought to be necessary for an educated or enlightened citizenry, and that education in the four art disciplines should provide the basis for advanced study in art. This is part of an old and time-honored position in education, but it is one we have good reasons to reject.

There is a tone in DBAE suggesting that persons unfamiliar with, for example, Botticelli's *Birth of Venus* fall somehow short of the ideal of an educated person. As I mentioned earlier, I have colleagues in math education who feel the same way about people who do not know the difference between a definite integral and an indefinite integral. At most meetings of such professional groups, lots of speeches include the words "It is deplorable that . . . ." Now, surely in a complex society such as ours, we cannot insist that every person attain even a minimum level of sophistication in every discipline for which there are living advocates. To insist on this is to have a faulty (static) vision of what it means to be educated. There just *are* well-educated people who have never heard of Botticelli, and there *are* well-educated people who know nothing whatever of integrals, definite or indefinite. There is nothing deplorable in this state of affairs. What would indeed be deplorable is a society in which no one cared enough to make these things available to those who might like to learn them. DBAE is a bit ambivalent on the issue of access versus compulsion. It seems right, for example, to take the position that "DBAE is based on the assumption that all members of society, not only the wealthy or elite, deserve access to the visual arts" (p. 42). I have no quarrel whatever with this. But if "access" means required study, I fear that the objective is to make competency in art a component of the static ideal so widely embraced by advocates of a host of disciplines—each seeking its own place in the educational sun. Neither the worth of persons nor their educational attainment should be measured by whether or not they can appreciate a joke involving Botticelli's Venus—or one, however improbable, involving definite and indefinite integrals.

DBAE draws in a balanced fashion from aesthetics, art criticism, art history, and art production. This tells us the domains from which content will be extracted, but it does not tell us how that content will be presented. Even if we look at the suggested three dimensions of each discipline—the community of scholars/artists, methods of inquiry, and conceptual structure—we find little help in deciding on methods of instruction. Talking about methods of inquiry, for example, is quite different from employing those methods of inquiry. Do people best learn methods of inquiry by actually inquiring and being pressed to evaluate both methods and results, or do they learn best by being given an explicit mode of inquiry and lots of practice in its use? Should the method of instruction vary, depending on the age of the learners and the method of inquiry under consideration? These are crucial questions for curriculum developers, because we know from experience that curriculum and instruction cannot be neatly separated.

I am sure that advocates of DBAE want to respect the autonomy of teachers; one of the contrasts listed between the 1960s discipline-centered reform and DBAE is that the former "attempted to make 'teacher-proof' curricula," whereas the latter "recognizes essential roles of teachers and administrators in curriculum implementation" (Clark, Day, & Greer, 1987, p. 132). But this contrast, though capturing a good intention, is not exactly accurate. Some curricula developed in the 1960s were in fact designed to be teacher-proof, but most were not. They embodied the more fundamental error of ignoring instruction entirely. The new math was notorious in this respect. In many versions it left an absolutely crucial pedagogy at an implicit level. Its makers took for granted that teachers who understood the new material would also see that the old methods were not adequate for this new material. To this day, math educators argue over whether more blame for the failure of new math should be charged to teachers' lack of understanding of the content or their failure to adopt an appropriate pedagogy. A deeper point that I have emphasized repeatedly is that student interests, capacities, and purposes were ignored.

Consider the matter of structure. An emphasis on structure was paramount in new math, and it seems to be in DBAE also, in spite of a contrast explicitly made—"Focused on structure of disciplines as content source" versus "Focused on dynamic view of art disciplines including concepts, methods of inquiry, and communities of scholars" (Clark, Day, & Greer, 1987, p. 132). There is an admirable breadth here—roughly comparable to that of Harvard Project Physics over the Physical Science Study Committee (PSSC)—but the emphasis on conceptual structure is still clear. Therefore, essential pedagogical questions arise: Should an understanding of the fundamental concepts and structure precede the manipulation of objects in the disciplinary domain? Or is this understanding a developmental outgrowth of long years of manipulative work in the field? Is knowledge of structure necessary for all students?

Another great error in the new math seems now to have been the assumption that we could teach children effectively something about the structure of mathematics before they had learned the usual algorithms. Indeed the claim was that children might then invent their own algorithms and would in any case not require hours of practice on routine computations, because they would know what to do as a result of their basic understanding. There may still be something true in this claim, but by failing to consider the sort of pedagogy that would replace didactic instruction in routine practice, we missed an opportunity to validate the claim in any form. Most of us now think that structural understanding is a product of growth through manipulating objects and applying skills rather than a prerequisite or substitute for either. Thus I think it is essential for art curriculum makers to study problems of instruction carefully. Curriculum implementation is part of curriculum making, not a totally separate enterprise.

The problem discussed here is related to the one with which I started out. It seems to me that many children and adolescents are drawn to art by a desire to *do* art; in earlier discussion, I worried over the possible loss of art's unique place in the high school curriculum. The preservation of electives emphasizing art production might relieve this worry, provided the electives do not have heavily cognitive prerequisites. But a basic issue for art curriculum makers remains. It may be that the only sound mode of curriculum and instruction requires placing art production at the center of the enterprise; instruction in aesthetics, art criticism, and history might then grow out of and serve this central function. Art education should serve the artistically interested or talented. Where else in school do they get the respect they deserve?

Advocates of DBAE discuss the necessity of informing students about the social, historical, intellectual, and psychological contexts in which art is produced and critiqued. (See Clark, Day, & Greer, 1987.) Issues that arise here should be considered by specialists in all disciplines, because every discipline has an aesthetic dimension, a history, and a mode of evaluation or criticism, and all of these activities are conducted in and help to define a variety of contexts. Art educators should be applauded, then, for emphasizing these connections. These dimensions are central to caring for ideas.

When we decide to include such matters in our curricula, however, it becomes necessary to consider ideological biases and preferences. There is a temptation to teach a particular view of aesthetics, to teach history as a set of facts quite apart from the set of conflicting interpretations that characterize historical research, and to lay out criteria for criticism without engaging in real evaluation of those criteria. I see no reason to accuse advocates of DBAE of making these errors, but I want to ask how they will avoid them.

The program as it is now outlined assumes a continuous chain of instruction from kindergarten through grade 12. Quite apart from my earlier objections to *requiring* art, the likelihood of such universal continuity must now be considered. If all students were to study art in the fashion advocated for twelve or thirteen years, curriculum makers could plan for progressive involvement with controversial matters of interpretation and the politics of art. Without this continuity, instruction in these highly complex domains might do more harm than good. Even carried through the 12th grade, there should be legitimate concern about the scope and purposes of such instruction. Concentration on the aesthetic can induce an odd and frightening form of amorality, even immorality, as Kierkegaard (1959) so dramatically reminded us. The Nazis were, for example, possibly among the best educated generation—from an aesthetic perspective—the world has yet produced.

Proceeding by example might be useful here. In a powerful historical work, Bram Dijkstra (1986) demonstrates how intimate the connection between art and immorality—in this case misogynism—can be. His opening words are these: "This is a book filled with the dangerous fantasies of the Beautiful People of a century ago. It contains a few scenes of exemplary virtue and many more of lurid sin" (p. vii). He shows convincingly that works of art, art criticism, and versions of art history have all contributed vigorously to the oppression and exploitation of women. "This book," he asserts, "amply demonstrates that there is cause to assume that works of art are by no means beyond involvement in the dominant ideological movements of the time in which they were created" (p. ix). None of us, I am sure, would deny this, but there remains the tough educational question of when and how we introduce such material to students. If, for example, we simply talk about the depiction of historical events in art or, acknowledging the ideological aspect of art, we even discuss the antiwar sentiments of a famous painting, we have not come close to the sort of influence Dijkstra documents so well. Only if education is organized around centers of care are we likely to avoid the domination of groups in power.

Feminist scholars are among those deeply concerned with these issues. This is because the masculinist ideologies pervasive in the disciplines are only now being uncovered and studied. Merlin Stone (1976)
has documented the bias in archeology and religious history in her fascinating study of the ancient Goddess religion. Nina Auerbach (1982)
has shown how both the literature and art of the Victorian age revealed
or held hidden awaiting interpretation a combination of awe, fear, and
hatred for the ancient power of the feminine. Her study focuses on
the latent power of the feminine. "The mermaids, serpentwomen, and
lamias who proliferate in the Victorian imagination suggest a triumph
larger than themselves, whose roots lie in the antiquity so dear to nine-
teenth-century classicists" (pp. 8–9). Dijkstra, as already noted, focuses
on the misogyny and evil in these and other images of the fin de siè-
cle. His themes of therapeutic rape, extinguished eyes, clinging vines,
the nymph with the broken back, maenads of decadence, and many
others are persuasively and heartbreakingly documented with art. In
many cases, the art—both visual and literary—used as documentation
has been greatly admired even though both creators and critics were
aware of its dreadful endorsement of misogyny. Octave Mirbeau, for
example, is quoted by Dijkstra as saying the following in his commentary on Remy de Gourmont's *Lilith:*

> The symbolic genesis of woman, as interpreted by Remy de Gourmont,
> corresponds exactly with the conclusions of anthropological science.
> Woman does not have a brain; she is simply a sexual organ. And that
> is the beauty of it. She has but one role in the universe, but that is a
> grandiose one: to make love, that is to say, to perpetuate the species.
> According to the irrefutable laws of nature, of which we feel rather
> than perceive the implacable and dolorous harmony, woman is not fit
> for anything that does not involve love or maternity. Certain women,
> very rare exceptions, have been able to give, either in art or literature,
> an illusion of creative energy. But those are either abnormal creatures,
> in revolt against nature, or simply the reflections of males, of whom,
> through sexual dysfunction, they have been able to maintain certain
> characteristics. (Dijkstra, 1986, p. 182)

This is not an isolated or unusual case. The world of art and literature
is filled with such material. Marina Warner (1976), in her study of the
Virgin Mary and Mariology, comments on the horror and significance of
paintings of Mary crushing the serpent's head beneath her foot. The serpent, after all, was once a symbol of immortality, knowledge, and feminine power. Mary Daly (1984) also comments on the importance of this

self-destroying act depicted in religious painting. Many other examples of the association of women with dragons, serpents, evil, and death are described in J. A. Phillips' (1984), *Eve*. He, too, discusses the significance of Mary—as the second Eve—crushing the serpent.

As we consider in some depth the treatment of women in art, we uncover related ideologies in religion, psychology, anthropology, literature, philosophy, and even science. The present revival of interest in Jungian psychology, for example, is accompanied by new interpretations of old symbols, legends, and art. Here, too, we see interest in both the alleged power of the feminine and fear of its reputed dark and evil side.

Art educators are in a better position than I to know whether the profession is prepared to cope honestly with these matters. Are there texts that discuss the treatment of women in art openly? The issues that I have pointed to clearly go well beyond current concern about pornography. They appear everywhere in the history of art and literature. In general education, my preference would be to make these matters of central interest in themes of care and to draw on the disciplines in connection with them. But so long as art is a separate subject and discipline-based, these matters must be incorporated.

Just as not all students are interested in mathematics, not all are interested in art. My preference would be for "aesthetic education across the curriculum." All subjects have an aesthetic aspect that should be considered. But if art must be taught as a separate subject to those uninterested, it should be designed to capitalize on the capacities and affiliations of students. It should be possible for students to study engineering or mechanistic art, religious art and its themes, the art and crafts of various racial and ethnic groups, the aesthetics of motion, environmental art, political art, and the like. In response to this recommendation, many educators will say: But shouldn't all students have experience X? And, isn't X especially important for just those kids who would never choose it? By now, you (the reader) know my answer: probably not. It does no harm to suggest, to invite. But we need to entrust students with important choices concerning their own education. Indeed, helping them to choose intelligently is education, and we must reject the pernicious notion that some areas of study are intrinsically more valuable than others.

CONCLUSION

I have argued that caring for a set of ideas such as mathematics or art has much in common with caring for people. We can be engrossed—

passionately interested—in ideas, and schools should make it possible for students to become so engrossed. However, this level of interest cannot be demanded, and students whose interests lie elsewhere should be respected and encouraged to choose what is useful for them in each subject.

We should expect a very different level of performance from the passionately interested. They should be introduced to the full rigor and beauty of the disciplines they study. Hard questions should be asked, and epistemologically excellent responses should be expected. For other students the level of performance and understanding might well be instrumentally defined. They should be able to do and to explain whatever is required by their own purposes. This level is not necessarily *lower*; it is just different.

Devising educational programs along the suggested lines requires a careful analysis of levels of understanding. Understanding does not have to refer to *structural* understanding; it does not have to be tied to the basic nature of the discipline. Rather, it is properly defined with respect to legitimate purposes, capacities, and interests.

CHAPTER 12

Getting Started in Schools

The traditional organization of schooling is intellectually and morally inadequate for contemporary society. We live in an age troubled by social problems that force us to reconsider what we do in schools. At a time when thinkers in many fields are moving toward postmodernism—a rejection of one objective method, distinctively individual subjectivity, universalizability in ethics, and universal criteria for epistemology—too many educators are still wedded to the modernist view of progress and its outmoded tools. Too many of us think that we can improve education merely by designing a better curriculum, finding and implementing a better form of instruction, or instituting a better form of classroom management. These things won't work.

We need to give up the notion of an ideal of the educated person and replace it with a multiplicity of models designed to accommodate the multiple capacities and interests of students. We need to recognize multiple identities. For example, an 11th-grader may be a black, a woman, a teenager, a Smith, an American, a New Yorker, a Methodist, a person who loves math, and so on. As she exercises these identities, she may use different languages, adopt different postures, relate differently to those around her. But whoever she is at a given moment, whatever she is engaged in, she needs—as we all do—to be cared for. Her need for care may require formal respect, informal interaction, expert advice, just a flicker of recognition, or sustained affection. To give the care she needs requires a set of capacities in each of us to which schools give too little attention.

I have argued that education should be organized around themes of care rather than the traditional disciplines. All students should be engaged in a general education that guides them in caring for self, intimate others, global others, plants, animals, and the environment, the human-made world, and ideas. Moral life so defined should be frankly embraced as the main goal of education. Such an aim does not work against intellectual development or academic achievement. On the contrary, it supplies a firm foundation for both.

How can we begin? Here's what I think we must do:

1. Be clear and unapologetic about our goal. The main aim of education should be to produce competent, caring, loving, and lovable people.
2. Take care of affiliative needs.
   a. Keep students and teachers together (by mutual consent) for several years.
   b. Keep students together where possible.
   c. Keep them in the same building for considerable periods of time.
   d. Help students to think of the school as *theirs*.
   e. Legitimize time spent in building relations of care and trust.
3. Relax the impulse to control.
   a. Give teachers and students more responsibility to exercise judgment.
   b. Get rid of competitive grading.
   c. Reduce testing and use a few well-designed tests to assess whether people can handle the tasks they want to undertake competently.
   d. Encourage teachers to explore with students. We don't have to know everything to teach well.
   e. Define expertise more broadly and instrumentally. For example, a biology teacher should be able to teach whatever mathematics is involved in biology.
   f. Encourage self-evaluation.
   g. Involve students in governing their own classrooms and schools.
   h. Accept the challenge to care by teaching well the things students want to learn.
4. Get rid of program hierarchies. This will take time, but we must begin now to provide excellent programs for *all* our children. Programs for the noncollege bound should be just as rich, desirable, and rigorous as those for the college bound.
   a. Abandon uniform requirements for college entrance. What a student wants to do or to study should guide what is required by way of preparation.
   b. Give all students what all students need: genuine opportunities to explore the questions central to human life.
5. Give at least part of every day to themes of care.
   a. Discuss existential questions freely, including spiritual matters.

    b. Help students to treat each other ethically. Give them practice in caring.

    c. Help students to understand how groups and individuals create rivals and enemies. Help them to learn how to "be on both sides."

    d. Encourage a way of caring for animals, plants, and the environment that is consistent with caring for humans.

    e. Encourage caring for the human-made world. Help students to be at home in technical, natural, and cultural worlds. Cultivate wonder and appreciation for the human-made world.

    f. Help students to care deeply for the ideas that engage them.

6. Teach them that caring in *every* domain implies competence. When we care, we accept the responsibility to work continuously on our own competence so that the recipient of our care—person, animal, object, or idea—is enhanced. There is nothing mushy about caring. It is the strong, resilient backbone of human life.

To implement the program I have described requires a change in the way we conceive curriculum and instruction. The sharp separation of the two—a product of the ultrascientific thinking of the last few decades—must be rejected. What is to be studied often suggests a mode of instruction, or even learning without formal instruction. And instruction often gives rise to new topics—new "stuff" for the curriculum. This integrated way of looking at curriculum and instruction is not new. It was well described by John Dewey years ago.

The criticisms and concerns that were directed against Dewey's views will be revived against the suggestions made here. Indeed they may even be angrier and louder, because I have dared to suggest that the disciplines themselves should play a peripheral or instrumental role in the education of most students. Objections that are basically ideological can rarely be met to the satisfaction of the objectors.

There are, however, several legitimate, nonideological objections that can be raised, and these should be answered as adequately as possible. In general these objections take the form of questions in three large categories: curriculum planning, teacher preparation, and evaluation. I'll conclude by saying a little on each.

CURRICULUM PLANNING

Some of the best planning for curriculum and instruction that I have observed has been at the nursery–kindergarten level. Here teachers work together to create and gather resources, plan options for developmental growth, and allocate tasks so as to capitalize on their own individual strengths. At the high school level, this kind of planning is almost unheard of, but it can be done. My description of a math team operating in algebra/trigonometry is an example of what can be done with a largely prespecified curriculum within a particular discipline.

The planning necessary for general education—the centers of care—is even more difficult. Here curriculum will be cooperatively constructed by teachers and students. Teachers will have to predict what students may want to study. Some money will have to be set aside for midyear allocation to resources that could not be ordered ahead of time. Patterns of spending will shift from an emphasis on textbooks to one on paperbacks, kits, charts, tools, art implements, excursions, and museum minicourses.

Cooperative planning does not imply that teachers give up the responsibility to initiate. It might help teachers starting out to suggest alternating units of work: teacher choice, student choice, teacher choice, etc. In planning units of teacher choice much thought should be given to likely student interests as well as to needs that teachers have evaluated, and within teacher-choice units there should be many options for students to study in ways that build on their special capacities and affiliations. Similarly, when units are chosen by students, teacher guidance should remain strong. Teachers have to guide in a way that ensures continuity. At the end of a teacher-choice unit, teachers might say, "Here's what seems to me to come out of this. What do you think?" Then students and teachers together can make a list of worthwhile topics and questions to pursue next.

Students should also be invited to contribute suggestions on classroom organization. Some student choices will lead to individual projects, some to group projects, some to supraclass forums. This kind of participation is not only conducive to intellectual development, but it is essential to the development of citizens who can participate intelligently in democratic processes. Issues of control and power arise here and must be resolved in favor of *empowerment.* Not long ago, Seymour Sarason (1990) predicted the failure of school reform on the very grounds I have been discussing. School reform will fail, Sarason says, because we fail to recognize schools and classrooms as political organizations. Students must participate responsibly in constructing the rules and arrangements under which they will work, play, and share their interests and resources.

At the beginning of the school year, then, high school teachers planning the "caring" part of the day will have to ask such questions as these: What do these particular students need? (This implies that at least one of the teachers actually knows at least some of the students.) What are they likely to be interested in? (Better, call some students in and ask them.) What resources should be available if they choose A, B, or C as options? What can each of us contribute given our varied backgrounds in discipline and general life experience? Whom can we call on in the community to help us evaluate what students are learning? How can we help students to evaluate their own work? (I'll say more on these two questions in a bit.) What will they be studying in their morning classes? What does the class profile look like by way of special capacities and affiliations? How can we plan for inclusive experience as well as experiences that center on particular affiliations?

Teachers will also have to build in time to talk to each other about their own growth as well as that of students. They will have to offer each other moral support, intellectual/academic help, and solid friendship. In discussing students—and this discussion should take place regularly—they will have to help each other to keep the talk caring and professional. The pernicious gossip that corrupts so many discussions in teachers' rooms should be anathema to teachers. As teachers, we must become more like parents who are engaged in the task of raising a huge heterogeneous family.

TEACHER PREPARATION

Teachers provide for many if not most students their only model of what it means to be an educated person. But what do teachers know? High school students are expected to master several subjects each year. Those subjects are supposed to be important; they are supposed to be part of what every well-educated person knows. But if a student asks her English teacher for help with an algebra problem or her math teacher for help interpreting *Billy Budd,* she will probably be told, "That's not my field." If teachers do not know this supposedly essential material, why should all students be forced to learn it?

There are at least two ways to react to this state of affairs. One is to say, "It is deplorable that . . ." and insist that all teachers should be able to help with all standard subjects. Another is to recognize the legitimacy of forgetting large parts of an irrelevant curriculum and try a different approach. Teachers, like students, need a broad curriculum closely connected to the existential heart of life and to their own special interests. They should be able to provide an intelligent approach to the legitimate needs and questions of students.

How should teachers be prepared for a program of this sort? Perhaps the most fundamental change required is to empower teachers as we want them to empower students. We do not need to cram their heads with specific information and rules. Instead we should help them learn how to inquire, to seek connections between their chosen subject and other subjects, to give up the notion of teaching their subject only for its own sake, and to inquire deeply into its place in human life broadly construed.

This does suggest a different form of education. Teachers need an integrated form of education, not a highly specialized education concentrating on one discipline. The current emphasis on a major in the liberal arts (Carnegie Task Force, 1986; Holmes Group, 1986) could be a great mistake. One aim seems right: to prepare teachers who have a broad knowledge of their subject including its history, epistemology, aesthetics, and practical applications. The difficulty here is that liberal arts departments are not organized to do this. The very best teachers' colleges used to operate this way, but their lack of prestige made professors eager to assimilate into "real" departments. So there is a genuine dilemma.

A second aim, however, seems wrong: to strengthen the role of the disciplines in both collegiate and precollegiate education. This move can only lead to greater isolation, increased narrowness of focus, and further territorial battles. Although I agree that teachers need to know much more than most currently do, I have argued that the worship of expertise must go. In its place we should strive for a superbly well-trained capacity for inquiry and a Socratic willingness to pursue wisdom. This means that teachers have to know their subjects so well that they can spot and encourage promising approaches in their students and not be overcome, out of ignorance, by the need to control. It means also that teachers should be willing to discuss matters on which they have had no specific training—all the matters pertaining to human existence—and help students to create and learn powerful methods of investigation.

John Goodlad's (1990) recommendation for a preeducation curriculum comparable to premedicine or prelaw could be valuable if the content of that education were designed along the lines we have been discussing. But if it merely reproduces existing courses—perhaps choosing them based on rigor and prestige—we will accomplish at best a form of professionalization corrupted by all the faults of medicine and law. We will have sold our educational souls for a portion of professional porridge.

The needs of students must drive our plans for teacher preparation. We have to stop asking: How can we get kids to learn math? How can we make *all* our kids ready for college? How can we keep kids in school even though they hate it? And how can we prepare teachers for the real world of teaching? Instead we have to change that world. We have to ask: How can my subject serve the needs of each of these students? How can I teach so as to capitalize on their intelligences and affiliations? How can I complete the caring connection with as many as possible? How can I help them to care for themselves, other humans, animals, the natural environment, the human-made environment, and the wonderful world of ideas? As we ask these questions, we may find an authentic way to prepare teachers.

EVALUATION

Critics are sure to ask how we can measure what has been accomplished. Perhaps we should bracket the word *measure* and just ask how we might evaluate such a program. In the caring segment, we should move away from the question, Has Johnny learned X? to the far more pertinent question, What has Johnny learned?

In answering this question we need to depend more on Johnny; that is, we have to encourage responsible self-evaluation. In his work, William Glasser (1990), too, emphasizes self-evaluation. We all need to learn how to assess our own work and how to draw on peer evaluation intelligently. A general education program organized around centers of care would also encourage members of the community to participate in evaluation. Nurses, mechanics, ministers, carpenters, police officers, accountants, salespeople, cooks, and horticulturists—all people interested in the welfare of children can be involved. After a general briefing on what students have been studying, they could meet with small groups of students and examine the materials they have produced. (In preparation, students would do considerable self- and peer-evaluation.) The community examiners should also ask questions arising out of their own line of work. Nurses can ask questions about health habits and help students learn how to interact with health professionals. Mechanics can assess whether students are gaining a practical knowledge of everyday technology. Police officers can check on attitudes toward civic responsibility and knowledge of safety. Horticulturists can check on understanding of the plant world and attitudes that enhance or impede the beauty and healthfulness of our environment. The possibilities are endless.

When deficiencies are identified, teachers and students together will have to ask which of these are most vital to remove and for whom. Is it acceptable that Dan can't tell a cabbage from a head of lettuce? Is it okay that Mary doesn't know how to fix a frayed electrical wire? Is it possible that many of our students never visit a dentist? Is there a dangerous parochialism developing in one segment of our class? Should we try to interest these kids in Shakespeare?

This kind of evaluation is much harder than giving a multiple-choice test, but if giving multiple-choice tests were central to the assessment of human growth and development, we parents would administer them regularly at home. Instead we lie in bed at night asking ourselves and our mates exactly the kinds of questions I've suggested above, and then—together with our kids—we decide, and we roll up our sleeves and work together to accomplish what we deem important. We should operate the same way in schools. Earlier in this book I quoted John Dewey as saying, "What the best and wisest parent wants for his own child, that must the community want for all its children. Any other ideal for our schools is narrow and unlovely; acted upon, it destroys our democracy" (1902, p. 3).

He was right. But now we must not think narrowly about what we might want for this particular child of our own and then extrapolate that to all children. Rather, we must start with a vision of ourselves as wise parents of a large heterogeneous family and ask, What do I want for all of them? For each of them? Then we can commit ourselves to enacting this vision for all our children.

References

Adler, Mortimer J. (1982). *The paideia proposal.* New York: Macmillan.

Anton, Anatole, Fisk, Milton, & Holstrum, Nancy (Eds.). (2000). *Not for sale: In defense of public goods.* Boulder, CO: Westview Press.

Aristotle. (1985). *Nicomachean ethics* (Terence Irwin, Trans.). Indianapolis, IN: Hackett.

Auerbach, Nina. (1982). *Woman and the demon: The life of a Victorian myth.* Cambridge, MA: Harvard University Press.

Bandura, Albert. (1988). Mechanics of moral disengagement. In W. Reich (Ed.), *The psychology of terrorism: Behaviors, world-views, states of mind.* New York: Cambridge University Press.

Belenky, Mary F., Clinchy, Blythe M., Goldberger, Nancy R., & Tarule, Jill M. (1986). *Women's ways of knowing.* New York: Basic Books.

Bellah, Robert N., Madsen, Richard, Sullivan, William M., Swidler, Ann, & Tipton, Steven M. (1985). *Habits of the heart.* Berkeley: University of California Press.

Berry, Wendell. (1977). *The unsettling of America.* San Francisco: Sierra Club.

Bloom, Allan. (1987). *The closing of the American mind.* New York: Simon & Schuster.

Bobbitt, J. Franklin. (1915). *What the schools teach and might teach.* Cleveland, OH: The Survey Committee of the Cleveland Foundation.

Bresler, Liora. (1987). *The role of the computer in a music classroom.* Unpublished doctoral dissertation, Stanford University.

Brock, William. (1990, July 23). [Interview]. *Time,* pp. 12, 14.

Broudy, Harry. (1972). *Enlightened cherishing.* Urbana: University of Illinois Press.

Brownmiller, Susan. (1984). *Femininity.* New York: Linden Press/Simon & Schuster.

Bruner, Jerome. (1960). *The process of education.* Cambridge, MA: Harvard University Press.

Bruner, Jerome. (1971). The process of education reconsidered. In Robert Leeper (Ed.), *Dare to care/dare to act* (pp. 19–32). Washington, DC: Association for Supervision and Curriculum Development.

Buber, Martin. (1964). Dialogue between Martin Buber and Carl Rogers. In Maurice Friedman (Ed.), *The worlds of existentialism.* Chicago: University of Chicago Press.

Buber, Martin. (1965). Education. In Martin Buber, *Between man and man* (pp. 83–103). New York: Macmillan.

Bunch, Charlotte, & Pollack, Sandra (Eds.). (1983). *Learning our way.* Trumansburg, NY: Crossing Press.

Carnegie Task Force on Teaching as a Profession. (1986). *A nation prepared.* New York: Carnegie Forum on Education and the Economy.

Chodorow, Nancy. (1978). *The reproduction of mothering.* Berkeley: University of California Press.

Chubb, J. E., & Moe, Terry M. (1990). *Politics, markets, and America's schools.* Washington, DC: Brookings Institute.

Clark, Gilbert A., Day, Michael D., & Greer, W. Dwaine. (1987). Discipline-based art education: Becoming students of art. *The Journal of Aesthetic Education, 21*(2), 129–193.

Comer, James P. (1988). Is "parenting" essential to good teaching? *NEA Today, 6,* 34–40.

Conant, James B. (1959). *The American high school today: A first report to interested citizens.* New York: McGraw-Hill.

Conant, James B. (1967). *The comprehensive high school: A second report to interested citizens.* New York: McGraw-Hill.

Crozier, Louis (Ed.). (1991). *Casualties of privilege.* Washington, DC: Avocus.

Culley, M., & Portuges, C. (Eds.). (1985). *Gendered subjects: The dynamics of feminist teaching.* Boston: Routledge & Kegan Paul.

Daly, Mary. (1973). *Beyond God the father.* Boston: Beacon Press.

Daly, Mary. (1984). *Pure lust.* Boston: Beacon Press.

Darling-Hammond, Linda. (2004). From "separate but equal" to "no child left behind": The collision of new standards and old inequalities. In Deborah Meier & George Woods (Eds.), *Many children left behind* (pp. 3–32). Boston: Beacon Press.

Davis, Robert B., Maher, Carolyn A., & Noddings, Nel. (Eds.). (1990). *Constructivist views on the teaching and learning of mathematics.* Reston, VA: National Council of Teachers of Mathematics.

Dewey, John. (1902). *The school and society.* Chicago: University of Chicago Press.

Dewey, John. (1916). *Democracy and education.* New York: Macmillan.

Dewey, John. (1963). *Experience and education.* New York: Collier Books. (Original work published 1938)

Dijkstra, Bram. (1986). *Idols of perversity: Fantasies of feminine evil in fin-de-siècle culture.* New York: Oxford University Press.

DuBois, Ellen, Dunlap, Mary, Gilligan, Carol, MacKinnon, Catherine, & Menkel-Meadow, Carrie. (1985). Feminist discourse, moral values, and the law—a conversation. *Buffalo Law Review, 34*(1), 11–87.

Eisner, Elliot W. (1969). Instructional and expressive educational objectives: Their formulation and use in curriculum. *AERA Monograph Series in Curriculum Evaluation, 3,* 1–18. Chicago: Rand McNally.

Ellsworth, Elizabeth, (1989). Why doesn't this feel empowering? Working through the repressive myth of critical pedagogy. *Harvard Educational Review, 59*(3), 297–324.

Fowler, James. (1976). Stages in faith: The structural developmental approach. In T. Hennessey (Ed.), *Values and moral development*. New York: Paulist Press.

Freire, Paulo. (1970). *Pedagogy of the oppressed* (Myra Bergman Ramos, Trans.). New York: Continuum.

Galsworthy, John. (1948). Quality. In J. D. McCallum (Ed.), *The college omnibus* (pp. 466–469). New York: Harcourt Brace Jovanovich.

Gardner, Howard. (1982). *Art, mind and brain*. New York: Basic Books.

Gardner, Howard. (1983). *Frames of mind*. New York: Basic Books.

Gardner, John. (1971). *Excellence: Can we be equal and excellent too?* New York: Harper & Row.

Gehlback, Roger D. (1990). Art education: Issues in curriculum and research. *Educational Researcher, 19*(7), 19–25.

Getty Center for Education in the Arts. (1985). *Beyond creating: The place for art in America's schools*. Los Angeles: J. Paul Getty Trust.

Gilligan, Carol. (1982). *In a different voice*. Cambridge, MA: Harvard University Press.

Girl Scouts of the United States of America. (1989). *Girl Scouts survey on the beliefs and moral values of America's children*. New York: Author.

Glasser, William. (1990). *The quality school*. New York: Harper & Row.

Goldin, Gerald A. (1990). *A rationale for teaching probability and statistics in primary and secondary schools*. New Brunswick, NJ: Rutgers University Center for Mathematics, Science, and Computer Education.

Goodlad, John I. (1990). *Teachers for our nation's schools*. San Francisco: Jossey-Bass.

Goodlad, John I., & McMannon, Timothy J. (Eds.). (1997). *The public purpose of education and schooling*. San Francisco: Jossey-Bass.

Goodman, Ellen. (1990, May 31). The urban dweller's pact with nature. *San Francisco Chronicle*.

Gordon, Suzanne. (1991). *Prisoners of men's dreams: Striking out for a new feminine future*. Boston: Little, Brown.

Greene, Maxine. (1988). *The dialectic of freedom*. New York: Teachers College Press.

Grumet, Madeleine R. (1988). *Bitter milk: Women and teaching*. Amherst: University of Massachusetts Press.

Gutmann, Amy. (1987). *Democratic education*. Princeton, NJ: Princeton University Press.

Hanson, Susan. (1985). *The college preparatory curriculum at two high schools in one school district*. Unpublished doctoral dissertation, Stanford University, Stanford, CA.

Haughton, Claire Shaver. (1978). *Green immigrants.* New York: Harcourt Brace Jovanovich.

Heath, Shirley Brice. (1983). *Ways with words.* New York: Cambridge University Press.

Heidegger, Martin. (1962). *Being and time* (John Macquarrie & Edward Robinson, Trans.). New York: Harper & Row. (Original work published 1927)

Holmes Group. (1986). *Tomorrow's teachers.* East Lansing, MI: Author.

House, Ernest R. (1998). *Schools for sale: Why free markets won't improve America's schools and what will.* New York: Teachers College Press.

Hutchins, Robert M. (1964). *The university of utopia.* Chicago: University of Chicago Press.

Illich, Ivan. (1971). *Deschooling society.* New York: Harper & Row.

Jacoby, Susan. (2004). *Freethinkers.* New York: Metropolitan Books.

Journal of Aesthetic Education. (1987, Summer). Special issue: Discipline-based art education, *21*(2).

Jung, Carl G. (1973). *Answer to Job* (R. F. C. Hull, Trans.). Princeton, NJ: Princeton University Press.

Keller, Evelyn Fox. (1983). *A feeling for the organism: The life and work of Barbara McClintock.* New York: W. H. Freeman.

Keller, Evelyn Fox. (1985). *Reflections on gender and science.* New Haven, CT: Yale University Press.

Kierkegaard, Soren. (1959). *Either/Or* (Vol. 1). (David F. Swenson & Lillian M. Swenson, Trans.). Princeton, NJ: Princeton University Press.

Knowles, John. (1975). *A separate peace.* New York: Bantam Books.

Kohlberg, Lawrence. (1981). *The philosophy of moral development.* San Francisco: Harper & Row.

Kohn, Alfie. (2000). *The case against standardized testing.* Portsmouth, NH: Heinemann.

Kohn, Alfie. (2004, April). Test today, privatize tomorrow: Using accountability to "reform" public schools to death. *Phi Delta Kappan, 25*(8), 569–577.

Kozol, Jonathan. (1991). *Savage inequalities.* New York: Crown.

Levy, Leonard W. (1986). *The establishment clause: Religion and the first amendment.* New York: Macmillan.

Linn, Robert. (2003). Accountability: Responsibility and reasonable expectations. *Educational Researcher, 32*(7), 3–13.

Lounsbury, John H., & Vars, Gordon F. (1978). *A curriculum for the middle school years.* New York: Harper & Row.

MacIntyre, Alasdair. (1981). *After virtue.* Notre Dame, IN: University of Notre Dame Press.

Mager, Robert. (1962). *Preparing instructional objectives.* San Francisco: Fearon Press.

Martin, Jane Roland. (1984). Bringing women into educational thought. *Educational Theory, 34*(4), 341–354,

Martin, Jane Roland. (1985). *Reclaiming a conversation.* New Haven, CT: Yale University Press.

Miller, Jean Baker. (1976). *Towards a new psychology of women.* Boston: Beacon Press.

Montessori, Maria. (1966). *The secret of childhood* (M. Joseph Costelloe, S.J., Trans.). New York: Ballantine.

Murdoch, Iris. (1970). *The sovereignty of good.* London: Routledge & Kegan Paul.

Noddings, Nel. (1989). *Women and evil.* Berkeley: University of California Press.

Noddings, Nel. (1993). *Educating for intelligent belief or unbelief.* New York: Teachers College Press.

Noddings, Nel. (2002). *Starting at home: Caring and social policy.* Berkeley: University of California Press.

Noddings, Nel. (2003). *Caring: A feminine approach to ethics and moral education* (2nd ed.). Berkeley: University of California Press. (Original work published 1984)

Noddings, Nel. (In press). Caring as relation and virtue in teaching. In P. S. Ivanhoe & Rebecca Walker (Eds.), *Working virtue: Virtue ethics and contemporary moral problems.* Oxford, England: Oxford University Press.

Noddings, Nel, & Shore, Paul. (1998). *Awakening the inner eye: Intuition in education.* Troy, NY: Educator's International Press. (Original work published 1984)

Norton, David L. (1991). *Democracy and moral development.* Berkeley: University of California Press.

Phillips, John Anthony. (1984). *Eve: The history of an idea.* San Francisco: Harper & Row.

Powell, Arthur G., Farrar, Eleanor, & Cohen, David K. (1985). *Shopping mall high school: Winners and losers in the educational marketplace.* Boston: Houghton Mifflin.

Preskill, Stephen. (1989). Educating for democracy: Charles W. Eliot and the differentiated curriculum. *Educational Theory, 39*(4), 351–358.

Regan, Tom. (1983). *The case for animal rights.* Berkeley: University of California Press.

Rosenshine, Barak, & Stevens, Robert. (1986). Teaching functions. In Merlin C. Wittrock (Ed.), *Handbook of research on teaching* (pp. 376–391). New York: Macmillan.

Rossiter, Margaret W. (1982). *Women scientists in America: Struggles and strategies to 1940.* Baltimore, MD: Johns Hopkins University Press.

Ruddick, Sara. (1980). Maternal thinking. *Feminist Studies, 6*(2), 342–367.

Ruddick, Sara. (1989). *Maternal thinking: Towards a politics of peace.* Boston: Beacon Press.

Ruether, Rosemary Radford. (1983). The feminist critique in religious studies. In Elizabeth Langland & Walter Gove (Eds.), *A feminist perspective in the academy* (pp. 52–66). Chicago: University of Chicago Press.

Sagan, Eli. (1988). *Freud, women, and morality: The psychology of good and evil.* New York: Basic Books.

Sarason, Seymour B. (1990). *The predictable failure of educational reform.* San Francisco: Jossey-Bass.

Scheman, Naomi. (1989). Commentary on Sandra Harding's "The method question." *Newsletter on Feminism and Philosophy, 88*(3), 40–44. Newark, DE: American Philosophical Association.

Silber, John. (1989). *Straight shooting: What's wrong with America and how to fix it.* New York: Harper & Row.

Silberman, Charles E. (1970). *Crisis in the classroom: The remaking of American education.* New York: Random House.

Simon, Mark. (1990, June 20). Calculating how far a teacher has to go, and the hill to die on. *Peninsula Times Tribune,* p. B-1.

Singer, Peter. (1990). *Animal liberation* (2nd ed.) New York: New York Review Books.

Sizer, Theodore R. (1984). *Horace's compromise: The dilemma of the American high school.* Boston: Houghton Mifflin.

Sizer, Theodore R. (2004). *The red pencil.* New Haven, CT: Yale University Press.

Soder, Roger, Goodlad, John I., & McMannon, Timothy J. (Eds.). (2001). *Developing democratic character in the young.* San Francisco: Jossey-Bass.

Sommers, T., & Shields, L. (1987). *Women take care.* Gainesville, FL: Triad.

Spretnak, Charlene (Ed.). (1982). *The politics of women's spirituality.* Garden City, NY: Anchor Books.

Stone, Merlin. (1976). *When God was a woman.* New York: Dial Press.

Tillich, Paul. (1952). *The courage to be.* New Haven, CT: Yale University Press.

Troen, Vivian, & Boles, Katherine C. (2003). *Who's teaching your children?* New Haven, CT: Yale University Press.

Tyack, David, & Hansot, Elizabeth. (1982). *Managers of virtue: Public school leadership in America, 1920–1980.* New York: Basic Books.

Walker, Alice. (1983). *In search of our mothers' gardens.* San Diego, CA: Harcourt Brace Jovanovich.

Walzer, Michael. (1977). *Just and unjust wars.* New York: Basic Books.

Warner, Marina. (1976). *Alone of all her sex.* New York: Alfred A. Knopf.

Watson, Jean. (1985). *Nursing: Human science and human care.* Norwalk, CT: Appleton-Century-Crofts.

Weil, Simone. (1951). *Waiting for God.* New York: G. P. Putnam's Sons.

Index

About the Author

Nel Noddings is Lee L. Jacks Professor of Education, Emerita, at Stanford University. She is author of twelve books; the latest two are *Caring: A Feminine Approach to Ethics and Moral Education, Second Edition* (2003) and *Starting at Home: Caring and Social Policy* (2002). She is also editor of *Educating Citizens for Global Awareness* (2005, Teachers College Press).

Noddings spent 15 years as a teacher, administrator, and curriculum developer in public schools; she served as Director of the Laboratory Schools at the University of Chicago. At Stanford, she received the Award for Teaching Excellence three times, most recently in 1997. She is President of the National Academy of Education and a Laureate member or Kappa Delta Pi, and she holds two honorary degrees in addition to a number of awards, among them the Anne Rowe Award for contributions to the education of women (Harvard University), the Willystine Goodsell Award (AERA), a Lifetime Acheivement Award from AERA (Division B), and the Excellence in Education Award (Pi Lambda Theta).